LYING
EYES

LYING EYES

EYES

THE TRUTH BEHIND THE CORRUPTION AND BRUTALITY OF THE LAPD AND THE BEATING OF RODNEY KING

Tom Owens

WITH

Rod Browning

THUNDER'S MOUTH PRESS   NEW YORK

First edition
First printing, 1994

Published by
Thunder's Mouth Press
632 Broadway, 7th Floor
New York, NY 10012

Library of Congress Cataloging-in-Publication Data
Owens, Tom, 1948–
    Lying eyes : the truth behind the corruption and brutality of the
  L.A.P.D. and the beating of Rodney King / Tom Owens with Rod
  Browning.—1st ed.
       p. cm.
    Includes index.
    ISBN 1-56025-074-7 : $22.95
    1. Los Angeles (Calif.). Police Dept. 2. Police—California—Los
  Angeles—Complaints against. 3. Police corruption—California—Los
  Angeles. 4. King, Rodney. I. Browning, Rod. II. Title.
  HV8148.L55094 1994
  364.1'322'0979794—dc20   93-46101
                                                                        CIP

Printed in the United States of America

Distributed by
Publishers Group West
4065 Hollis Street
Emeryville, CA 94608
(800) 788-3123

Acknowledgments

I want to take this opportunity to acknowledge the following people and express my appreciation to them for their support, assistance and encouragement throughout the writing of this book. Most notably, Mike Madigan, my mentor, confidant, editor, cocreator, cheerleader, and mother of all worriers.

For months, Mike placed his family and business on hold while he created the foundation from which the opening chapters eventually evolved. Mike's book, *The Twisted Badge* served as the platform from which this book finally sprang. While I could never adequately express my gratitude to him, I want Mike to know I haven't forgotten his efforts.

Robyn Wingrove proved to be more than just a friend and supporter. Robyn's efforts on my behalf went far above and beyond his overt assistance, support, and encouragement. Without Robyn, I couldn't have devoted the time needed to complete this project.

The loyalty and friendship of many men and women serving on the Los Angeles Police Department provided inspiration during some of my darker moments of anger and frustration throughout this process. I will always be thankful to them. Most notably in this group are the officers and supervisors, who at some risk to their reputations, met with me as I stumbled along the path to the final days of the investigation. Blue Throat will never be publicly acknowledged by name for the valuable assistance given on Rodney King's behalf without which I couldn't have completed this task.

Odessa, Ron, Paul, and Angela King have all stuck by Rodney in spite of his occasional lapses of judgment or common sense. In a strange way, they too are victims.

Tim Fowler, Jim Brott, Julian Bailey, Harvey Goldhammer, Tom Beck, John Burton, Dave Linn, Sgt. Sedgewick, Bob Neubauer, Irv and Jeff Osser, Pete George, Lou King, Gabe Osorio, Mal Stone, Bill Anderson, Harry Johnson, Ray Wizard, and hundreds of others, too many to mention, all had some influence on the case and therefore, this book. I thank them all.

The first thing we do, let's kill all the lawyers.

WILLIAM SHAKESPEARE
Henry VI

Contents

Foreword

I began this book following the conclusion of the worst riots in the history of this country. With images of arson, vandalism, assaults, mobs, and even murders still fresh in my mind, I sat down to record my thoughts and feelings for my children and grandchildren. At that time, I'd been associated with this case for well over a year, and I believed I had a unique story to tell.

This is not the Rodney King story, nor is it intended to be. This is the story of my work on behalf of Rodney King and the changes I've undergone since becoming associated with this case. It's a story of deception, violence, and anger—my anger and the nation's. Manipulation by and of the media; local, state and national political influence and interference; and the proper uses and abuses of power at all levels of government are seen and recorded by one man who came closer to the eye of the hurricane than even he wanted to be.

My story examines the relationships of people drawn together or pushed apart by what many have called the most significant civil rights case and the second most significant legal case ever, behind only the Watergate break-in scandal which toppled a President and crippled a nation.

Everywhere I go, people ask me, "Why did you ever get involved in this mess with that criminal, Rodney King?" A legitimate question, considering my background as a cop with the LAPD for twelve years. My answer is quite simple really. Like the rest of the world, I was shocked beyond belief when I first watched George Holliday's video of King's beating. I couldn't imagine what King had done to justify the beating he'd taken that early morning in the Lake View Terrace section of Los Angeles.

So I can't be misquoted or misinterpreted later, let me say that I support the right of police officers to use appropriate levels of force when necessary under the law. I certainly know the pressures an officer feels when he or she decides to use force against another person. Unlike others who will undoubtedly write books about this subject in the future, I've walked that mile in the officer's moccasins. I know what it means when an arrestee tells an officer "You'll have to take me to jail." Unfortunately, in our society, some degree of force is necessary all too often.

Many police departments have a policy or procedure manual which dictates when and how much force can be applied in most circumstances. Generally, these policy statements have built-in discretionary actions and reactions by and for the officer using force. For the most part, problems with an officer's use of force occur when either the policy is unclear to the officer or when the policy is unenforced by the supervisors within the department. A poorly written use-of-force policy can get officers into trouble.

∎

While some have called Rodney King a role model and a person to be respected, others have called him a criminal, liar, and monster. After having spent two years with him, I believe Rodney King to be misunderstood, even by those closest to him. While I don't think of King as a hero or role model, I do think of him as a victim whose victimization continues to this day. I don't see myself as an apologist for King. Whatever baggage he had with him on March 2, 1991, he still has today. His abuse at the hands of Los Angeles police officers didn't change that. But since March 3, 1991, his life has changed, and those changes have affected those around him, including me.

Saying Rodney King is a victim, is a gross understatement. It's obvious from watching Holliday's video, King took the world's worst whoopin', but that is where his status as a victim merely begins. In the weeks and months that followed his instant rise to fame, I grew to know and even like this quiet, shy, hulking man who wants only to be left alone. While Rodney King is clearly a victim, he's not the only victim who was in Lake View Terrace.

Sergeant Stacey Koon and Officers Larry Powell, Tim Wind, and Ted Briseno are also victims in another way. These officers' lives have been drastically altered in much the same way as King's. Gone are the days when any one of these men could take his family out for a quiet night on the town, a dinner and a movie.

As much as King is recognized when in public, so are the involved officers. Well-wishers and ill-wishers alike fail to recognize the desires of these men to be able to sit quietly and privately, to enjoy an evening with family and friends. Gone are the days when they could take a neighborhood stroll with their wife or kids. Their notoriety keeps them close to home and, like their victim Rodney King, makes them public people.

■

With the prospect of a small fortune in his future, Rodney King has a network of newly found family and friends. Each with an agenda and concept of how to separate King from that fortune. People who three years ago wouldn't give King the time of day now stand in line to present him with their business cards or resumes. One of my assignments was to shield King from these vultures and leeches. In the end, it turned out they were better at their job than I was at mine.

As each day passes, I watch and listen to accounts of how far King has strayed from those who stuck by him in those early days of chaos and hype. His new friends and family protect King from his old family—his real family and friends. He is never left alone with any person who may tell him he's made some serious judgement errors, an indication of his continuing victimization.

■

If nothing else, the King Incident has not only shown the nation that some cops are capable of unbelievable violence, but once it's discovered, officers invoke a "Code of Silence" to aid their efforts in protecting those who administer street justice.

We must support our officers, pushing them everyday to the edge of the line marking the limits of appropriate actions and procedures. In some cases, we must give them some benefit-of-the-doubt discretion, but when officers clearly cross the line of reasonableness, the offending officers should be subjected to the fullest measures of discipline available under the law.

Admittedly, I haven't been totally successful at remaining

impartial in my recounting of the investigation. Writing this book has been painful at times. Remembrances of things that have occurred and words which were spoken still anger me. The system I once was a part of has taken a beating, and in so doing, people have forgotten why and how we got to where we're at.

Traitor, whore, scum, and turncoat are all names that I've been called by former partners. I've been asked to leave police facilities in which I once worked. There's no tolerance for anyone who breaks the Code. Yet, no one can answer my question, When did I quit being one of the good guys and become one of the bad guys? Was it when I resigned from the LAPD? Or when I became an investigator? Or when I started working for Rodney King? Maybe the answer isn't nearly as important as the question.

■

Throughout the text, I've attempted to identify my opinions as just that, my opinions. Where I've offered an hypothesis, I've provided factual information which led me to my conclusions. Facts are facts and I've formed my beliefs based on the facts I uncovered during the two years of this investigation. It's not my intent to convince anyone that my version of the King incident is the only version. This book may not change the opinion of a single reader. That's okay. I wish only to inform the reader that there is another side of the story that hasn't been told yet. That was my promise to Rodney King and the King family.

If we as a society don't hold those in authority to answer for their misconduct, then we really do deserve the kinds of police officers we get. . . .

Prelude

Date: March 3, 1991

Incident Number: 44
Dispatcher: 127
Console #:   D1
Card: 4
Determinant: B3

Units dispatched: Paramedics RA #98 and Engine #98.
Fire Department call taker:
Time: 0057

FD: Fire Department. 127.
PD: Hi 127, this is 795.
FD: 795, what might I do for you tonight. This morning.
PD: (3rd party conversation, laugh) busy, (laugh) we need you for ah . . .
FD: What's the joke?
PD: I'm just really swamped. Foothill and Osborne. In the Valley dude (FD dispatcher laughs) and like he got beat up.
FD: (laugh) wait (laugh)
PD: We are on scene.
FD: Hold. Hold on, give me the address again.
PD: Foothill and Osborne. He pissed us off, so I guess he needs an ambulance.
FD: Oh, Osborne. Little attitude adjustment?
PD: Yeah, we had to chase him.
FD: Okay!
PD: CHP and us, I think he kind of irritated us a little.
FD: Why would you want to do that for?
PD: (laugh) they should know better than to run. They're going to pay a price when they do that.
FD: What type of incident would you say this is?
PD: It's a . . . it's a . . . battery, he got beat up.
FD: Okay, by assailants unknown?
PD: Ah, well . . . sort of.
FD: Okay, any other information as to his injuries, anything at all?

PD: Nope.
FD: Okay.
PD: Are you kidding, that's asking too much.
FD: All righty.
PD: Thanks a lot.
FD: We'll send someone out there.
PD: Okay.
FD: Have a nice night.
PD: You too, bye, bye.

Fire Department Dispatcher:

Time: 0059
FD: Rescue 98, Engine 98: Assault. Intersection of Foothill and
        Osborne, that's Foothill Boulevard and Osborne Street. PD on
        scene. Your time of dispatch 1259. OCDS clear.

THE SHAPING OF ATTITUDES

The Rodney King incident began long before George Holliday cranked up his new Sony Betacam on March 3, 1991. King's beating was just another example of street justice in a long history of similar incidents. Street violence is not new. In 1969, Los Angeles police chief Daryl Gates formed the nation's first Special Weapons Attack Team (SWAT) and the Department evolved into a paramilitary organization. Force was met with greater force, violence with more violence. But there is a line between good, aggressive police work and abuse of power. Every time a cop steps over that line and is not disciplined for it, the line is moved.

Good street cops are a rare breed. They're overworked and grossly underpaid. Cops suffer the highest rate of work related burnout and account for the highest percentage of occupational-related suicides in the country. Why not? We give them guns, train them to use weapons of death, then we sit on our collective ass and criticize every move they make. Often, criminals are back on the streets before the ink is dry on their arrest reports. Citizens castigate the police, the police blame the courts, and the courts condemn the system. Little attention is placed on the fact that the citizens, the police, and the courts *are* the system.

We forget that every day, police officers must make life and death decisions in split seconds, while nine learned and honorable Supreme Court Justices can take months, even years, to decide some of the same critical issues. On those rare occasions when an officer steps over the line, we scream for his or her head. We, as a society, tend to react out of our anger or frustration. Sometimes we overreact. The plain and simple truth is that we get our police officers from within our own towns and communities. Accordingly, they bring with them the prejudice, dishonesty, hate, and aggression that trouble those communities. In other words, we get the police officers we deserve—no better, no worse.

How can I sound so philosophical about the attitudes and feelings of cops? It's easy, I've walked a mile in their moccasins. I understand the thought processes most police officers go through. I know the pride they have in their chosen vocation. For twelve years, I was a member of the Los Angeles Police Department and while I wasn't a model officer, I was a good street cop. Like most of my peer group, I joined the LAPD following military service. In the late sixties and early seventies police departments across the country filled their vacancies with returning Vietnam veterans. While Hollywood was depicting Nam vets as doped up psychos and baby killers, law enforcement agencies were benefiting from military-trained, experienced young men already tested and proven in battle, ideal types for modern police work. Most of my police academy classmates were veterans. I'd just recently finished six years on active duty in the U.S. Marine Corps, with nearly four years of that time spent in Vietnam.

I joined the Marines at seventeen, during my junior year in high school. I guess I was afraid that if I waited, the Vietnam War would be over and I would have missed it. Only after boot camp and two tours in Nam did I realize what a dumb shit I'd been. I wised up and looked around for an easier job than the infantry.

■

I applied for and was accepted to the Military Intelligence School in Baltimore, Maryland. After finishing there, I was given orders for my third Vietnam tour, this time as a military intelligence specialist. In Danang, I was assigned to a Vietnamese language course sponsored by the Vietnamese government. Ten weeks later, I was speaking pidgin Vietnamese. I thought I was pretty good and couldn't understand why the locals looked so puzzled when I tried to communicate with them.

I was an intelligence sergeant assigned to the regimental commander. This meant I spent less time in the bush, which was okay with me. By this time, President Nixon had implemented his Vietnamization program, whereby the locals took a greater part in their own war, and that was okay with me, too.

Between and during overseas tours, I completed high school and started college correspondence courses. Studying helped keep the horrors of the war in the back of my mind, out of my conscious thoughts. It provided good therapy and gave me a leg up when I started back to school after my discharge from the Corps.

Finally, after four tours of duty and a handful of Purple Hearts, I came home to a quiet welcome in Southern California. As I began out-processing from the Corps, many police departments were holding recruiting sessions at separation stations. I attended most of them held locally, and after considering the sky marshall program (there were frequent skyjackings during those months) and listening to the recruiters from the Washington, D.C., Police Department, I chose the LAPD and applied. As my final discharge date neared, I received the notice informing me I had been selected to begin police training in January, 1971. My discharge from the USMC preceded my start with LAPD by two days.

To more fully understand the principals and policy theories involved in the King incident, the training and supervising of police officers must first be understood. I believe some of my own experiences with the LAPD will help explain the attitudes of some of the officers involved in the King incident.

On that first day of training, I arrived at the academy an hour early, anxious and nervous. Big mistake. The training officers were already gathered in the gym and didn't waste any time welcoming me. "Stand there, on the little white dots!" the blue uniformed training officer shouted. "Come on, missy, I mean you."

For Christsake, I thought, I just left this bullshit day before yesterday. Many of the training officers at the LAPD Academy were U.S. Marines in their previous lives. If it walks like a duck, and talks like a duck. . . .

The Los Angeles Police Academy is universally recognized as one of the finest academies of its type in the world. Its stone and cinder block walls are covered with ivy and tradition. Behind the gymnasium, a path winds its way through the rock garden, beside a small stream running from the top of Elysian Park. In much the same tradition as at the military academies, rookie officers can't walk on that hallowed ground until they have earned the right by completing rookie school. Push-ups and hazing awaited those who violated the tradition. Well inside the academy grounds, across the road from the shooting range, stands a small set of classrooms built with monies donated by television actor and staunch LAPD supporter, Jack Webb. His *Dragnet* series ran many seasons and was influencial in forming the public's image of what a modern, effective police operation is supposed to be.

At the LAPD Academy, the emphasis was placed on physical training, academics, and ethics. Artificial stress was directed at rookie officers from the time they arrived on the grounds before sunup until they departed after dark. Instructors often said that if a rookie couldn't handle stress during training, he or she wouldn't be able to handle it out on the streets. I, too, subscribe to that theory. Good cops aren't born, they're trained, and the training at the Los Angeles Police Academy was and is the best.

In my time, basic police training took twenty weeks. The first four were orientation. During the second month, recruits spent one day each weekend in the field, working as an observer in a regular two-man car. This provided the first opportunity for rookies to wear their full uniform with a badge and a gun. In the third month, the rookie spent two weeks as the second man in a traffic car, writing tickets and watching his partner work accident investigations. The entire fourth month was spent in the field, experiencing the daily grind of real police work. The rookie spent the fifth month of training back at the academy honing the skills learned in both the classroom and the field.

In all, LAPD provided a well-rounded program. The rookie officer learned more criminal law and search-and-seizure rules than many lawyers do in their first years of practice. The history of law enforcement and the area within government from which police draw their authority were highlighted to give trainees an understanding of constitutional principals.

Self-defense, officer survival, and weapons training took up the remainder of the new officer's time. Every day, we were kept well beyond the scheduled end of training sessions for physical training instructors to work our asses off in unpaid overtime. If we complained we were reminded that we didn't HAVE to be there. For each applicant accepted by the academy, twenty-two were turned down. Those were the odds of getting the job, one in twenty-two. As each day of training began, I would look around to see who was missing, which classmates had dropped from the program. My class began with 122 smiling faces standing on those white dots painted on the gymnasium floor. On graduation day, fifty-five of us were still there.

Programmed attrition, as it was called, was a direct result of the artificial stresses applied during training. For twenty weeks, life was just one big "sit sim" (situation simulation). Typically, a block of instruction on a subject was presented in the classroom, followed by field sit sim, where the trainee put into practice what was learned. During these sit sims the recruit was forced by the training staff, acting the roles of suspects or victims, to use judgement and common sense to resolve whatever situations were encountered. Shouting and screaming were a constant.

Occasionally, the artificial stresses during a sit sim were so intense a trainee would literally piss in his pants. When this happened, the trainee was told to "report to the lieutenant's office and bring your hat and books." Gone, like a football player told to go see the Head Coach and take your play book. Programmed attrition.

Early in my training, I was seated in a classroom when a sergeant strode in unexpectedly. Standing there in front of all those impressionable minds, he announced, "Effective immediately, no member of this department will refer to a citizen as an 'asshole.' The public finds this term offensive. From now on, you will instead refer to them as 'rectal orifices' because they're too fucking stupid to understand the term." Laughter filled the classroom as the sergeant turned and walked out the door. The shaping of attitudes had begun. "Us versus them."

Physical training was a welcome relief after six hours in the classroom. Each session began with the customary exercises and long distance jog. Running up and down the hills of Elysian Park put the trainee in shape quick. By the end of the first month, a five-mile run was not uncommon. And woe to those who couldn't keep up. The instructors would make us turn around and pick up stragglers. This added miles to the runs, and additional pressures heaped on the unfit trainees by annoyed classmates. I recall thinking during some of the longer runs, why am I here? If the good Lord wanted us to run five miles chasing suspects, he wouldn't have given us radio cars and helicopters.

Self-defense techniques and combat wrestling followed the runs. During these periods of instruction, basic field survival skills were drummed into our heads—hours upon hours of baton training and control holds until they became second nature. Finally, as we neared exhaustion, we were pitted against each other in combat wrestling to test our will to win. Officers showing any timidity were quickly identified and just as quickly gone. This process gave us the confidence and skills necessary to carry us through the toughest of situations. But it also gave us a cockiness and sense of invincibility that formed the basis of aggression when the watchful eyes of the instructor were no longer on us.

Once in the field, an experienced partner would usually say, "Forget all that bullshit you learned in the academy. This is the real world out here. Theory doesn't apply," and "The only way to survive is kick ass first and worry about the paperwork later," and "If you ever fail to back me up, after I kick the asshole's ass, I'll kick yours. And while we're on the subject, what you see here, stays here. Never rat off a partner or you're history." A rookie's first exposure to the Code of Silence. It exists—don't let anybody tell you different. "Jump in, kick ass, and keep your mouth shut" was the attitude caught on George Holliday's home video of March 3, 1991 in Lake View Terrace.

■

My first assignment after graduating from the police academy was to Central Division, walking a skid row footbeat on East

Fifth Street, getting to know the people and problems of my beat by sight—real face-to-face cop stuff. Marion Hoover, my first training officer, was the real-life cop the television series *Joe Forrestor* was modeled after. Officer Hoover was a legend in his own time, with twenty-five years walking a beat. He was the best known and most highly respected of the old breed of beat cops. He had even been partners with Chief Ed Davis and other high ranking officers, and helped train many of the most respected detectives and command officers in the history of the department. When I met him, Hoover held two Medals of Valor, the highest award given for service above and beyond the call of duty.

Walking a beat with Hoover was one exciting experience after another. During those first weeks, he found every opportunity to initiate an altercation with a suspect so he could stand back and watch how I dealt with the situation, then laugh at me for getting my uniform torn or my knuckles bloodied.

The odors of stale urine and vomit filled the air on East Fifth. Kicking "short dogs" (empty wine bottles) out of the way became a way of life as I walked my beat. I earned my place in this subculture of man's inhumanity to man.

The original Hard Rock Cafe at the corner of Fifth and Wall Streets was an education in itself. Old hardwood flooring was cracked and worn. Stools lined the bar where men and women, looking twice their ages, sat for hours with nowhere else to go, sipping draft beer and listening to mournful country-western music played on a beatup old jukebox. Like the people, the music seemed stranded in this vast pit of desperation. I watched it all and listened to Hoover explain what I was sensing and feeling. The old guy knew, and I began to respect him, not for who he was, but for what he had learned.

He once told me, "You can't just go out there and have respect. You have to earn it by being the toughest yet fairest guy on the block. Once those assholes understand you can't be whipped, they'll leave you alone. When you take one of them to jail, they'll go without a fight, because you've already kicked the meanest ass on the street." He was right. Soon, the fights stopped and I got on with the business of learning what police work was really all about. It was much easier to laugh a guy into the cell than to drag him in kicking and screaming.

In hindsight, I learned that proper application of force was sometimes necessary, but force for the purpose of inflicting punishment was unacceptable and wrong. I hold to that principle to this day, though I admit there were times on the job when I forgot it. I tried to be fair. I wasn't always successful, but at least I tried. This ability to show fairness later proved to be an asset, particularly when I was assigned to the South Central area of Los Angeles known as Watts.

While working the streets at night, I attended college during the day, which gave me a chance to catch up on my sleep. I was required to take a course on the foundations of good police-community relations as a part of my major, but nobody said I had to stay awake. I felt my foundations in police-community relations were damn well formed after five years in the field, and I needed the shuteye more than the lectures.

■

I was well over my rookie attitudes by the time I was assigned to Watts. Like most of my peer group, I believed a career with the LAPD could not be complete without a tour of duty in South Central. Before my transfer, I really believed I was fully prepared to face any challenges associated with the area. Immediately after my arrival, I realized I didn't know shit about nothing. Walking a foot beat, daily face-to-face contacts with derelicts and the homeless, was nothing like what awaited me at Seventy-Seventh Street Division.

The fundamental skills of inquisitiveness, thoroughness, and an ability to pay close attention to detail, which I developed working with Hoover and other old salts in Central Division followed me to Watts, though my identification with those old guys carried a downside. I found I had little tolerance with my peers and was quick to point out their shortcomings. This created problems with partners; I quickly picked up the reputation of being difficult to work with. On more than one occasion, cops seeing their name next to mine on the daily assignment sheet went to the watch commander and asked for a change.

At my request, I was assigned to the mid-P.M. shift. My first few days in the division were devoted to learning my assigned sector and what problems I could expect in it. Unlike my foot beat in Central Division, I was stuck in a patrol car, handling forty-five to fifty service calls a night, which kept me so busy there was no time left for patrolling and crime prevention.

Any problems I may have experienced with interpersonal relationships took second position to making sound decisions and having just plain good luck in the field. The sergeant responsible for day-to-day supervision of my shift often said, "You may be a major pain in the ass, but you're the only guy I know who can step into a pile of shit and come out smelling like a rose."

One incident clearly illustrates his feelings. I was working a one-man car. My responsibility was nothing more than taking report calls on burglaries—stolen bicycles, stolen cars et cetera. Boring. About midway through my shift, I was stopped at an intersection in my black and white, just waiting for the light to turn green. I wasn't looking for traffic violators or chomping at the bit to assist another unit on a priority call or wanting to get involved in any action. I was just minding my own business.

All of a sudden, the light bar on top of my police vehicle exploded. At that same instant, I heard gunfire coming from my right. I looked across the street to see an employee of a Church's Fried Chicken restaurant exchanging gunfire with some clown, like a scene from a cheap western. I'd caught a stray bullet and my sense of security was shattered with my light bar.

I turned on my siren and grabbed my microphone to advise the dispatcher, "I'm under fire at . . ." Shit! I'd been daydreaming, not paying attention to my location. I had to stop broadcasting long enough to see where the hell I was. ". . . Vermont and Imperial Highway, a possible robbery in progress with shots being fired by numerous suspects. Officer needs help!" Instantly, I heard sirens being switched on from all directions as nearby units responded to my call.

I swerved across the intersection and into the parking lot of the fast food restaurant. I saw the suspect sprinting down an alley, chased by the employee, still blazing away.

Backup cars began to arrive. We set up a perimeter. It all happened so quickly, I knew we had the crook contained. He couldn't possibly get away. Within minutes, one of the responding units got me on the radio and said they had a guy in custody. As it turned out, the asshole had taken down a liquor store several miles away in Compton, then decided to hit one more place before he quit work for the day. I just happened to be in his way. No real skills there, just dumb luck.

My experience has been that working in a predominantly black or disadvantaged community carries with it some unique problems. Already hardened by the influences of basic police training and street experience, an officer assigned to a minority area too often undergoes a transformation in attitude. More often than not, the officer will choose a stricter interpretation and a tougher course of action than he would in a "better" neighborhood. Most African-Americans have known this for years. Everyone else saw it—perhaps for the first time—in the Holliday video.

I started to feel out of place at Seventy-Seventh Street. Daily, I saw things that made me uncomfortable. I began to wonder who were the bad guys here, the criminals on the streets or my own partners. We just hooked 'em and booked 'em. No understanding, no compassion, no tolerance. Take the high road and let the system weed out the losers. This isn't to say that every cop working a minority area is a racist or abuser. But if one is heavy-handed and is not disciplined or retrained, that's one too many. He crosses the line—and the line is moved.

My internal stresses began to show. My wife, Pat, sensed what was going on inside me but couldn't say or do anything to help. Our arguments increased in frequency and intensity. Despite dozens of commendations and two awards for valor, my mind just wasn't fully on my job, which compromised my partner's safety and my own. The streets and my feelings about the streets got worse.

■

After twelve years I resigned from the LAPD, deciding my marriage was more important than my job. I thought I could take my training and experience to a smaller city in another state where there was less crime and a cop job involved less stress. But small town America has its own set of problems. A small town cop isn't Andy Griffith in Mayberry. On the LAPD, I was so far down the political ladder, I was insignificant; just another street cop among seven thousand others. Ed Davis and later, Daryl Gates were involved in politics up to their necks—

in fact, Davis later became a Republican State Senator—but at the patrol officer level, we didn't feel it.

My dreams of working on a smaller police department bore no relationship to reality. I found the smaller the town, the more important the politics. In most small municipalities across America, everyone knows everyone else's business. Whether I wanted to or not, I learned who was sleeping with whom. When I was told not to write a traffic ticket, I knew the reasons. But before I could learn the political tricks of the trade, I found myself crosswise from the political power structure and just as quickly, unemployed.

I applied at other small departments in the area, but the word was out and so was I. Fortunately, when we arrived in the Midwest, Pat, my wife who had given me grief for years about my chosen profession, found a cop job herself. She quit being one of them, and became one of us. Within days of her graduation from the police academy, she was working the night shift.

■

I did the housekeeping while I searched for other work. One evening playing Mr. Mom, Pat called to tell me she had to work overtime. She'd arrested some guy for drunk driving at the end of her shift and had to do the paperwork and processing.

"What do you mean you have to work over? How come you have to book the guy? Why can't another officer on the grave-yard shift transport and book him? Don't you know better than to get involved in an end-of-shift caper?" I gave her hell for ten minutes. After fifteen years of marriage, I finally got to pay her back. Thank you, God.

I looked for a job outside law enforcement. My problems were compounded by the weak local economy. The larger industrial employers were laying off workers who had been with them for years. Many were postgraduates in engineering and computer science. As I stood in line at McDonald's for a job flipping burgers, the men and women in front of and behind me were Ph.D.'s applying for the same job.

To help make ends meet, I took a job as a hotel bellman that paid minimum wage and all the tips I could beg. I was embarrassed and ashamed of the position—a college graduate, decorated military veteran, experienced police supervisor with awards for valor from one of the most respected police departments in the country—bellboy at the Airport Hilton. I felt I had become one of life's practical jokes.

While working at the hotel, a friend referred me to an automobile dealership advertising for car salesmen. I was turned down the first time I applied; I had no experience selling anything, much less high-ticket items like cars. I drove away from the dealership, dejected. Then I thought, screw this! and turned my car around. Money could be made selling cars and I had a family to feed.

"You're right," I told Ray McManness, the sales manager when I arrived back at the showroom, "I don't have any experience selling cars. But did you ever talk a three-hundred-pound angry drunk into jail when he didn't want to go? Has a cop ever given you a traffic ticket and made you feel good about it? I've done both, and Mister, that takes some selling!" Ray McManness just sat there and looked at me. I could see his wheels turning. My appearance was neat. I was wearing a suit. I was educated, moderately well-spoken, and bold. Ray smiled, extended his hand and my career in car sales began.

It took two weeks before I finally closed my first sale. I sold more cars in the following month than any other salesman on the lot. My boss attributed my moderate success to "customer control"; I still thought like a cop, and when I told the customers they should buy a car from me, I guess they believed it. In two years, I sold enough cars that I was asked to present salesmanship seminars at other dealerships in the Midwest. During one of those seminars, I met a hot shot who needed someone to open a new dealership for him in Southern California. I jumped at the chance. I hated snow and wanted to go home.

Returning to Orange County was a dream come true. I assisted the guy in opening his new store in Tustin, but when sales didn't match his expectations, he did what all dealers do when sales are down—he blew out the sales manager. Me.

I spent the next year managing at several other dealerships and saving my money. I'd made big dough for others, I thought. With the same efforts in a field I knew, I should do pretty well for myself.

Selling cars was not without its lighter moments. The Midwest is frequently called the Bible Belt. The appropriateness became clear one day when I was trying to close a sale. A customer, feeling buyer's remorse, offered the excuse "Well, I'm going to have to go home and pray on this," meaning of course that the customer had run out of excuses for procrastinating and needed to say something to escape the pressure of the sale.

This excuse stopped me cold on more than one occasion. After all, how does one tell the customer not to consult God? Finally, in desperation, I came upon the one way to get the buyer to commit on the spot. After being told by a young professional woman, who I had been trying to sell for hours, that she needed to go home and pray on her buying decision, I placed my hand on her shoulder, knelt right in the middle of the showroom, and told the reluctant buyer that God was telling me she needed the car. Sold!

■

In 1988 I opened Owens & Associates, Investigations. For the first few months, I spent most of my time in the office seated at my desk, staring at the phone, hoping it would ring. Times were tough but Pat had landed a good job with 3M. Between her income and my savings, we managed to survive until the business caught on.

While most of my early business was examining accident claims for insurance companies, I did manage to get a few assignments from attorneys needing an investigator to work police misconduct and abuse cases. These assignments were fairly easy to land because many investigators are ex-cops who don't want to work against their brothers in blue. I didn't have that problem. It's even easier now, after my experiences with the Rodney King case.

Both the Orange County and the Los Angeles County Criminal Defense panels selected Owens & Associates to assist in capital crime work on behalf of defendants. I didn't especially like the work—helping murderers—but I met some good lawyers who began to ship me other types of cases. I found facts others had not. A few accused killers beat their raps based on materials my staff and I uncovered. I believed they were innocent and I helped get them off. I've caught some flack for it now and then, but that's show business.

By the summer of 1990, things were going well at Owens &

Associates. My marketing efforts directed at insurance companies were finally paying off. My client base had expanded to
include fourteen major insurance companies who were keeping
us busier than we sometimes wanted to be. Our bumpy start
seemed behind us. There was light at the end of our tunnel and
for once it wasn't an oncoming train.

For several years, Owens & Associates was the exclusive
vendor investigation company for the largest worker's compensation insurance carrier in California. That one company accounted for nearly a quarter million dollars in service in 1991
and provided full-time employment to five insurance fraud
investigators on my staff.

My work in the specialized field of police abuse and misconduct began quite by accident. Paul Klien, a personal injury
attorney in the San Fernando Valley contacted my offices and
asked if I could assist his associate counsel, Harvey Goldhammer, on a lawsuit against the Southern California Rapid Transit
District. He explained his case as difficult to prosecute because
his witnesses had disappeared in the years following the incident. I found that work done years before by investigators from
the LAPD was substandard at best and incomplete. As I looked
at the file materials, I saw instances where reports and evidence
were either overlooked or completely disregarded by investigators. The shooting was between black gang members, and I felt
the LAPD investigators just didn't give a damn. I'd seen it
before. An acronym sometimes appearing on police officers'
daily log sheets was NVNNHI, Nigger Versus Nigger—No Human Involved. No human, no crime.

This particular incident involved a shooting on a bus. Goldhammer needed help in all aspects of his trial preparation.
Despite his client's past gang affiliations, Goldhammer took the
case to trial and secured a verdict of nearly $800,000 against
the district. Goldhammer was direct, knew his case well, and
took full advantage of weaknesses in the defense testimony.

Members of the jury later commented to me during my jury
poll that Goldhammer's cross examination of defense witnesses
was masterful. His presentation to the jury helped him win the
case. Deep down, I knew it was my investigation Goldhammer
had used to prepare, and a small part of the jury's praise
belonged to me and my staff.

The results of that trial appeared in the *Daily Reporter*, a newspaper by and for the Los Angeles legal community. Attorney Joel Jacobs saw the story and asked if I could assist with a case involving excessive force by an officer. My successful investigation for Jacobs led to another assignment for yet another attorney. Soon, I was handling a dozen abuse and misconduct cases throughout Southern California.

And so it happened that on March 8, 1991, Joel Jacobs called and told me that Rodney King's attorney was looking for an ex-LAPD officer to assist him in the case of King versus the City of Los Angeles.

FIRST REVELATIONS

"Tom! Wake up! Wake up!" Pat stood at the side of the bed and gently shook my shoulder. "You've got to see this! Wake up!"

I'd been working a murder case until after midnight. I wasn't ready to get up. Grumbling, I buried my head in the pillow.

"Tom! Wake up," she said, sounding more like a mother than a wife.

"What . . . what time is it?"

"It's seven. Come look at this. Get up!"

The story on the Tuesday morning news struck me like ice water in the face. Cops were beating a defenseless black man. The sight of slashing batons brought back old memories. "Damn! Someone's in deep shit now," I said, lighting my first cigarette of the day. George Holliday's video reminded me of things I'd witnessed during my twelve years with the LAPD. Batons held like baseball bats. Keeping the peace by dispensing pain. Things hadn't changed much since I'd left.

■

I changed channels to see those violent scenes again and again. Taser wires clearly visible. Three cops pummeling a suspect. Déjà vu.

"Do you know any of those guys?" Pat asked as we watched the beating.

"Can't tell, haven't heard any names yet and I can't see their faces, but those guys're in serious trouble." Ashes from my cigarette fell to the floor, but Pat, as absorbed in on screen events as I, remained uncharacteristically silent. I had no idea what the black man had done, but I knew those officers were dispensing the kind of street justice I had known. Pat, a five-year veteran officer herself, understood the occasional need for some degree of force in making an arrest. But this was different. This was abusive, pure and simple.

For the next two days, we watched stories about the beating in the media. We saw reporters and photographers awaiting Rodney King's release from the jail ward of County USC Hospital. Later Rodney King would tell me the words of one of the deputies he had encountered, words many of the jailers might have spoken, when he whispered, "A hundred years ago, this wouldn't've been a big deal."

In that first press conference, held just prior to his release, King told the media that racism was not involved in the beating incident. This assertion, made while he was still in custody, was later to cause some concern to both Steve Lerman and me, when racial issues did surface several weeks into my investigation. At the time King made his comments, he was confined to a wheelchair and surrounded by deputies. He had to return to his jailers once the media and his attorneys left. He knew better than anyone that claiming racism while still in custody could cause him additional grief before they let him go.

Reporters pressed King. From his wheelchair he spoke, his words guarded because of his surroundings and difficult to understand because of his facial injuries. "They beat me and kicked me. I was scared for my life."

■

Two days after the beating, Mayor Tom Bradley, an ex-cop himself, issued an official statement at a hastily convened press conference. "Los Angeles will not tolerate rogue cops," he vowed.

Police Chief Daryl Gates, called the beating an "aberration." Ever confident, he boiled it all down to a simple explanation. "Possible PCP intoxication and King's size were factors in the beating, but the Sergeant in charge, Stacey Koon, was directly responsible."

.

At about ten on Wednesday morning, March 7, 1991 I got the call from my friend, Joel Jacobs, telling me that Beverly Hills attorney Steven Lerman had been retained by King and was looking for an investigator with LAPD experience to help him put the case together. I laughed to myself; if I'd stayed with the department, it might well have been me on that video. "Sounds like a big case. Should I call this guy Lerman?" I wondered aloud.

Pat, who had left her job at 3M once my offices were firmly established, liked things the way they were. "You don't have the time!" We both knew I'd make time. She then tried a different approach. "Lawyers always pay late. Do we need that aggravation?"

"What those cops did pisses me off!"

She knew the discussion was over. "Tom, do me a favor? Don't take it on contingency!"

I was already dialing the phone. Busy. The longer I sat redialing, the more impatient I became. I hate talking on the telephone but it is a necessary tool in my business.

"Law offices," the secretary finally answered, "May I help you?"

"Tom Owens. I'm an investigator returning Mr. Lerman's call." I fudged a little, hoping to avoid the normal screening questions.

"Can you hold please?" After a few minutes, Lerman came on the phone.

"Mr. Lerman," I said boldly. "I'm a former LAPD officer, now doing investigations. Joel Jacobs told me to call you, on the chance you haven't filled your investigator job in the King case yet."

"Do you have any experience in police misconduct or excessive force cases?" he asked.

"Sure. I've got several cases I'm working on now. I also commanded an Internal Affairs section of a small town police department," I replied.

"When can we meet?"

"Two hours." My answer seemed to surprise him. Two hours later, I was sitting in the cramped reception area of Attorney Steven A. Lerman & Associates on Wilshire Boulevard in Beverly Hills. The small waiting room was well appointed in soft colors. Several chairs and a plush sofa lined the walls. A small sliding glass window separated the waiting room from interior offices. I waited. I could hear the constant ringing of phones inside. Forty minutes later, I was about to take off when the young Latina receptionist appeared. Introducing herself as Carmen, and apologizing for the long wait, she led me through chaotic inner offices where frazzled secretaries and paralegals scurried about while phones rang off the hook.

I sensed a certain arrogance in Lerman, sitting across from the slender, fortyish, athletic-looking lawyer. He seemed to enjoy being the eye of the storm. Between telephone calls, he stretched, took a deep breath and said sideways, "If I give you the case, what would you do first?"

■

"I'd have lunch." The unexpected answer caught Lerman off guard. We walked across the street to Kate Mantilini's, an upscale nouvelle cuisine restaurant where the lunch rush had already ended. We exchanged small talk about our backgrounds and experiences as we waited for the waitress to take our order, a kind of feeling out process. We were hesitant to get down to the business at hand. Lerman was tired of interviewing investigators.

"This is a damn important case. It's got national implications," he said. "CNN shot that video everywhere there's a TV. I've got people calling me from places I didn't even know existed. Even the President of the United States has expressed his outrage. You've got no idea of the pressures I'm feeling here."

"Sure, the public profile's greater, but the issues involved are the same as every other police abuse case I've handled." I sensed Lerman would never admit it, but I was convinced he was overwhelmed. "You need someone to put distance between you and the media so you can get to work." I was thinking of a media consultant but Lerman had other ideas.

"Good, you got it! Now, how do you do your investigation?"

I hadn't thought media liaison would be part of the job.

Lerman and I began getting acquainted over pasta and salads. "We find out the officers' case and I try to prove it," I told him. "If I can, we've got problems. But, if I can't prove their version, neither can they."

"I like it! My cops versus their cops."

Steve Lerman wasn't shy. Recently divorced, he was sharing custody of his two young children with his ex-wife. His law practice consisted mostly of personal injury cases, but he had handled criminal defense and civil rights cases in the past. From some of the cases he cited, it sounded as if it had been a while since he'd done that type of work. I asked how he'd gotten the King case.

"I did some work for a friend of the King family several years ago. He referred them to my office when Rodney King was arrested. I can't describe the feeling of waking up one morning and getting the career case." He was stoked, on a high, and I was catching the same disease.

"When I first got to the hospital jail ward," he said, "and looked at King through the glass visiting window, I thought I'd be sick. Tom, he looked like he'd almost been beaten to death. I had no idea how bad the beating really had been till I saw that video on TV."

I asked for the bottom line.

"King was charged with driving under the influence, assaulting the arresting officers, and felony evading. I haven't even seen his arrest reports yet, so I don't know what they're specifically alleging. Hell, I don't even know how many officers were there or who they are. We need the reports. Can you get them?"

When lunch was finished, I had the job of investigator, and Lerman's liaison to the LAPD and the media. Before heading back to my office, I thought I'd stop in at Parker Center to see if I could get copies of the reports from R&I (Records & Identification).

The LAPD headquarters building, named in honor of former Chief William H. Parker, is in downtown Los Angeles. Across the street from City Hall, Parker Center houses many support sections of the LAPD. Arrest reports are kept by R&I on the second floor. In front of the building is a memorial dedicated to police officers who have fallen in the line of duty. There are nearly two hundred names inscribed on the memorial. Three of them are my former partners. Often, when I'm in the area, I stop there and reflect on the faces and smiles of my friends. I did that, then went upstairs.

We were entitled to copies of King's arrest reports for our investigation of the criminal charges against him and our civil rights lawsuit against the city. The clerk at R&I told me all reports related to the King incident were being held pending a release authorization. She couldn't tell me who needed to authorize the release, so I looked up an old friend who was still working in the building. My friend offered help in any way possible. King's beating had so embarrassed this person, that I was promised doors which would normally be closed to me would be opened. To protect the identity of this friend who is still on the department, I chose Blue Throat as a genderless name. Even Steve Lerman has never learned the identity of this very important ally.

When I left Parker Center, I had King's arrest reports, and a first insight into the official version of the incident according to the arresting officers, Laurence Powell and Timothy Wind. The reports also identified other officers present, including the Sergeant in charge, Stacey Koon, important information, considering the names of the involved officers were still being withheld.

I called Lerman from the car to inform him of my acquisition, the beginning of my cellular phone bill's spiral climb as I got more and more involved in the Rodney King case. I dictated the outline of my investigative plan driving back to my office and scheduled a staff meeting with my investigators for early the following morning.

My mind raced with possibilities and eventualities as I drove the thirty-five miles from downtown to my home in Orange County. I was struck by the enormity of the case I'd just been given by Lerman. The public reaction to the scenes on that video of King rolling around on the ground as cops pummeled

PAGE NO.	TYPE OF REPORT	BOOKING NO.	DR NO.
2/7	ARREST	2381162	—

ITEM NO.	QUAN.	ARTICLE	SERIAL NO.	BRAND	MODEL NO.	MISC. DESCRIPTION (EG. COLOR, SIZE, INSCRIPTIONS, CALIBER, REVOLVER, ETC.)	DOLLAR VAL.

USE OF F...

DEFT KING, RODNEY GLENN CHG 2800.2 VC FEL EVAD...

SOURCE OF ACTIVITY

ON 3-3-91 AT APPROX 0030 HRS OFCR T WIND #27745
AND I. L POWELL #25440, ASSIGNED 16A23 FTHL PAT.
WERE RESPONDING TO ASSIST CHP OFCRS M L SINGE.
#12403 AND T J SINGER #9301, UNIT 98-60 VERDUG.
HILLS OFFICE, WHO WERE IN A VEH PURSUIT OF
A RECKLESS DRIVER SB GLENOAKS BL FROM PAX...
BOTH POLICE VEHS WERE MKD BLK/WHT VEH'S WITH
EMERGENCY LIGHT BARS ON ROOFS. ALL OFCRS WERE IN
FULL UNIFORM.

OBSERVATIONS

OFCRS SINGER AND SINGER WERE WB I-210 FWY
APPROACHING SUNLAND BL WHEN THEY OBS DEFTS VE
APPROACHING THEM FROM THE REAR AT A HIGH RAT.
OF SPEED. DEFTS VEH PASSED THEIR PATROL CA
THEN SLOWED. OFCRS SINGER AND SINGER EXITED THE
FWY AT SUNLAND, THEN IMMEDIATELY RE-ENTERED IN AN
ATTEMPT TO PACE DEFT'S VEH. DEFT WAS DRIVING
A WHT 88 HYUNDAI EXCEL 2DR LIC "2KFM102". WHEN
THEY GOT BACK ON THE FWY THEY OBS DEFT'S VEH AGA
TRAVELLING AT A HIGH SPEED APPROACHING WHEATLAN.
AV. THEY WERE ABLE TO OVERTAKE DEFTS VEH AS IT
PASSED THE OSBORNE EXIT AND PACED THE SPEED
AT 110 TO 115 MPH USING THE #1, #2 AND #3 LANES
WHEN THEY WERE W OF OSBORNE, OFCR SINGER ACTIV.
THEIR VEH EMERGENCY LIGHTS AND SIREN. DEFTS VEH
SLOWED TO 80 MPH CONTINUING TO THE PAXTON ST
EXIT. DEFT FAILED TO STOP AT THE STOP SIGN AT
THE END OF THE OFFRAMP WHICH WAS APPROX S...
W FROM THE END OF A BLIND CURVE, ENDANGERING

CONTINUE ON REVERSE SIDE.

CONTINUATION SHEET

PAGE NO.	TYPE OF REPORT				BOOKING NO.	DR NO.
3/3	ARREST				2381162	—
ITEM CODE NO.	ARTICLE	SERIAL NO.	BRAND	MODEL NO.	MISC. DESCRIPTION (ICE. COLOR, SIZE INSCRIPTIONS, CALIBER REVOLVER ETC.)	DOL. AT.

OBSERVATIONS (CONT')

ANY TRF WB ON PAXTON WHO WOULD NOT HAVE
STOPPED IN TIME TO PREVENT A T/A. DEFT
DROVE WB PAXTON AT 45-50 MPH FAILING TO STOP
AT THE RED TRI-LIGHT AT FOOTHILL BL CAUSING
NB AND SB VEHS TO YIELD TO AVOID T/A's. DEFT
ACCELERATED TO APPROX. 80 MPH WB ON PAXTON'S
TO SB GLENOAKS BL. DEFT CONTINUED ~ [FFF
80 MPH IN 35 MPH ZONE PASSING OTHER VEHS. AND PEDS ON
THE SIDEWALKS, WHO WOULD BE INJURED IF DE
VEH HAD CAUSED A T/A. DEFT DROVE THROUGH
THE RED TRI-LIGHT AT GLENOAKS BL AND VAN NUYS
AT APPROX 35 MPH, CAUSING SEVERAL EB AND WB
VEHS TO SLAM ON THEIR BRAKES TO AVOID T/A
W'E CAUGHT UP TO THE CHP UNIT AND DEFTS VEH
THIS POINT, ACTIVATED OUR EMERGENCY LIGHTS
AND CONTINUED IN THE PURSUIT TO ASSIST THE CH
WE OBS DEFT AND 2 MORE PASSENGERS TURN AR
AND LOOK BACK TOWARD THE PURSUING UNITS SE-
TIMES. DEFT CONTINUED DRIVING EB AT APPRO.
65 MPH PASSING OTHER VEHS IN A 35 MPH MOSTL
RESIDENTIAL AREA. DEFT RAN THE RED TRI-L
AT VAN NUYS BL AND FOOTHILL BL CAUSING A SB
VEH TO SKID TO A STOP TO AVOID T/A WITH DEF
OR POLICE VEH'S. DEFT CONTINUED SB FOOTHILL AT
APPROX 60 MPH /55 MPH ZONE. DEFT DROVE THROUG
THE MID PHASE RED TRI-LIGHT AT TERRA BELLA A
APPROX 60 MPH. ANY VEHS EB ON TERRA BELLA W
VIEW OF THE INTERSECTION WAS LIMITED DUE TO 2
INGS ON N SIDE WOULD NOT HAVE BEEN ABLE
REACT AND STOP TO AVOID A T/A. DEFT STOP
SUDDENLY FOR RED TRI-LIGHT AT OSBORNE ST AND FOOTHIL
JUST BARELY AVOIDING A BROADSIDE T/A WITH AN E
VEH. DEFT THEN PROCEEDED SB #2 LN AND
STOPPED JUST SHORT OF HITTING A TRUCK TH
WAS YIELDING TO OUR LIGHTS AND SIRENS. OFF
T SINGER ORDERED ALL PERSONS OUT OF VEH USING

CONTINUE ON REVERSE SIDE.   **CONTINUATION SHEET**

PAGE NO.	TYPE OF REPORT					BOOKING NO.		DR NO.
4/7	ARREST					2381162		
ITEM NO.	QUAN.	ARTICLE	SERIAL NO.	BRAND	MODEL NO.	KIND, DESCRIPTION (SIZE, COLOR SIZE, INSCRIPTIONS, CALIBER, REVOLVER ETC.)		DOLLAR ...

USE OF FORCE

OBSERVATIONS (CONT.)

FELONY STOP PROCEDURES. BOTH PASSENGERS EXITED ON PASS SIDE OF DEFT'S VEH. COMPLIED WITH SINGER'S ORDERS AND WERE TAKEN INTO CUSTODY WITHOUT INCIDENT. DEFT HOWEVER DID NOT COMP WITH SINGER'S ORDERS. DEFT AT FIRST WOULD N EXIT VEH. AFTER SEVERAL MORE ORDERS OVER PA DEFT EXITED HIS VEH, THEN GOT BACK IN, AND THEN EXITED AGAIN. DEFT FAILED TO PUT HIS HANDS ON HIS HEAD INSTEAD PUTTING HIS LT HAND N PANTS POCKET AND PLACING HIS RT HAND ON THE ROOF OF HIS CAR. WE CONTINUED ORDERING DEFT TO PLACE HIS HANDS ON HIS HEAD AND LAY DOWN ON THE GROUND. DEFT FINALLY LAID DOWN ON THE GROUND AND I APPROACHED HIM TO HAND CUFF HIM. DEFT THEN STARTED TO RAISE UP AND I PLACED MY KNEE ON HIS BACK TO PREVE THIS MOVEMENT. DEFT CONTINUED TO TRY AND RISE UP CAUSING ME TO LOSE MY BALANCE AN FALL OFF. DEFT STARTED TO TURN AND CHARGE TOWARDS ME. I BACKED AWAY AND SGT KEE #3667 FIRED A TASER AT DEFT STRIKING H IN THE BACK AND TEMPORARILY HALTING DEFT'S ATTACK. DEFT RECOVERED ALMOST IMMEDIATELY AND RESUMED HIS HOSTILE CHARGE IN OUR DIREC. OFCR WINO AND I DREW OUR BATONS TO DEFEND AGAINST DEFT'S ATTACK AND STRUCK HIM SEVERAL TIMES IN THE ARM AND LEG AREAS TO INCAPACITATE HIM. DEFT CONTINUE RESISTING KICKING AND SWINGING HIS ARMS AT US. WE FINALLY KNOCKED DEFT DOWN HE WAS SUBDUED BY SEVERAL OFCRS USING TH SWARM TECHNIQUE. DEFT CONTINUED STRUGGLING WHILE ON THE GROUND AND THEN STARTED LAUGH AND MAKING INCOHERENT STATEMENTS. DEFT CONTINUED STRUGGLING AND WAS SPITTING AT OFCRS AND PARAMEDICS EVEN AFTER BEING TOLD TO:

PAGE NO. 5 / 7	TYPE OF REPORT ARREST			BOOKING NO. 2381162	DR NO.
ITEM NO.	QUAN.	ARTICLE	SERIAL NO.	BRAND	MODEL NO.	MISC. DESCRIPTION (EG. COLOR, SIZE, INSCRIPTIONS, CALIBER, REVOLVER, ETC)	DOLLAR

OBSERVATIONS (CONT)

DEFT WAS TRANSP TO PACIFICA HOSP FOR INITIAL MT THEN TO LACO USC MC JAIL WARD FOR BOOK. WE DETECTED A FAINT ODOR OF ALCOHOL AND A [...] ODOR ON DEFTS BREATH. DEFT WAS UNABLE TO ANSW. QUESTIONS ABOUT WHAT HAPPENED AND HIS HOSTIL [...] AGITATED DEMEANOR CONTINUED FOR APPROX AN [...] DEFTS SPEECH WAS HURRIED AND USUALLY INCOHER. AND HIS MUSCLES WERE EXTREMLY RIGID. DEFT WAS POSSIBLY UNDER THE INFLUENCE OF A [...] DRUG, PROBABLY PCP, BUT DUE TO HIS INJURIES WE WERE UNABLE TO EVALUATE [...] AFTER ABOUT 1 HR, DEFT WAS SEMI-CO-OPERATIVE AND STATED HE THEN REMEMBERED FIGHTING WITH O[...]

ARREST

DEFT WAS ARRESTED 2800.2VC FELONY EVADING.

BOOKING

DEFT WAS BKD 2800.2VC AT LACO USC MC JAIL WAR. BKG WAS APPROVED BY SGT TROUTT #15392 UTO L

MT

DEFT WAS MT'D FOR ABRASIONS AND CONTUSIONS ON HIS FACE, ARMS, LEGS AND TORSO AREAS.

ADDITIONAL

DEFTS LICENSE STATUS WAS SUSPENDED. DEFT WAS ON PAROLE FOR 211 PC   CDC #E4835[...] AND A PAROLE HOLD WAS PLACED ON HIM.

CONTINUE ON REVERSE SIDE.   **CONTINUATION SHEET** him signaled that this wouldn't be simply another case of alleged police misconduct. The case had already taken on a steam rollerlike momentum which had propelled it to the forefront of every local and national news broadcast. With the Gulf War recently won and America feeling pretty good about itself, the Holliday video jolted us back to real world issues at home.

Comments by former Presidential candidate Jesse Jackson, Congresswoman and Black activist Maxine Waters, and many other national African-American leaders only seemed to heighten the feelings of outrage in minority communities. A single wrong comment by the right person could blow the lid off the city. The thought of LA exploding into another Wattslike riot frightened the hell out of me.

Between moments of genuine concern for the safety of the city, and thoughts directed at the tasks ahead, I was also feeling a great deal of satisfaction. I'd gone to Lerman's office hoping to get a small piece of the case, in what I'd thought would be a massive investigative team effort, and left with the whole enchilada. I recalled the old warning, "Be careful what you wish for—you might just get it."

■

In establishing the investigative staff at Owens & Associates, I had devoted considerable time and effort to the selection and hiring of experienced ex-cops, men and women who needed little or no training before taking on a caseload.

Former Boise, Idaho, police sergeant Don White had been with me for over a year when the King case came in. Six feet four, 240 pounds before cancer got him, he wasted no time developing sources within the district attorney's office and other law enforcement agencies in order to collect background data on trends and patterns of police abuse, and litigation arising from police misconduct across the country. This information would later be used in court to establish that the policies and practices of the LAPD were out of line with other metropolitan police departments. Throat cancer claimed Don White's life in the winter of 1991. He hid his illness from everyone until the day he was hospitalized.

Former La Palma police officer Bill Anderson made it known

very quickly that he didn't relish the idea of working against other cops. He was a good insurance fraud investigator, one of the best, loyal and dependable. At age fifty, he wanted to take life a little easier. The King case just didn't fit into that agenda.

Harry Johnson had been with the company for several months. He really threw himself into the job, but his commitment got him into trouble at home. His wife warned him that he had better pay more attention to her and less attention to his job. When told of the King assignment, Harry smiled and nodded his head. He knew that as the rookie of the team, he'd get the grunt work, but that was okay with him. He just wanted in. His wife wanted out. Six months later, she left him.

No company is complete without its token intellectual. John Huelsman filled that position at Owens & Associates. A certified paralegal, John was also an ordained minister at a local church. As a retired cop, he had the experience and ability to handle assignments with minimal supervision. Allowing him to do so later proved to be one of my bigger mistakes. John placed a much higher priority on his church work than on the King case and it soon became apparent I would have to find an investigator to replace him.

I called my old friend and ex-partner Jack White. The timing was perfect. Jack had been working at a car dealership that had gone out of business. Jack needed a job and I needed his help. For all his enthusiasm, Jack never gave the 110 percent I expected of him. Another mistake. So much for old friends.

Soon after receiving the King case, I hired Malcolm Stone. An African-American in his mid-forties, Stone had recently retired from the Los Angeles Unified School District (LAUSD) Police Department. I felt confident that this intelligent, soft-spoken man with a degree in journalism from USC would more than earn his keep. As the investigation expanded, additional professionals were added to the staff as needed.

■

I got home late that first night and told Pat about the King assignment. She accepted the news with mixed emotions. I understood. I had the same feelings. We had just gotten into bed after watching *Nightline* when the phone rang. It was Steve Lerman, the first of his midnight calls. "Sorry to call you so late, but I was just thinking, have you given any thought to the personal security requirements for Rodney? I'm not only worried that some nut case might try to take him out, but he's going into the hospital in a few days to get his face put back together and I don't want the media to have access to him while he's there."

The investigative plan I'd dictated allowed for the immediate deployment of members of my staff to act as security for King and Lerman. I hadn't planned on a twenty-four-hour-a-day security requirement but Lerman was right. The media was already camped out at King's home in Altadena, as well as at his mother's, his aunt's, and even his sister's home in Sacramento. I figured it was likely that for a few bucks, some hospital employee might drop a dime and announce King's stay to a hungry reporter. "I'll detail three of my guys to stay around the clock at the hospital while he's there," I assured Lerman, "But have you considered just how much money it'll cost you to have twenty-four-hour security for two to three weeks?"

"Just work me a deal, and make it happen," Lerman replied, "But no one gets to the client without going through your guys first."

"How do you want me to deal with the medical staff?"

"Hell, you're the expert. Just make sure no unauthorized people get in to the client."

By the time Lerman and Rodney King arrived at Westside Hospital four days later, I had coordinated with the hospital's director of security and set my staff's schedule for around-the-clock shifts. I'd spoken to various medical personnel who would come into contact with King and had activated a visitor sign-in and sign-out system. The hospital personnel were cooperative and tolerant of the tight security requirements imposed on them by my staff. They understood that in this particular case, the good guys were possibly the bad guys.

THE FUNKY CHICKEN

The early days of the investigation were filled with one revelation after another. While Steve Lerman was barraged with questions at press conferences, my staff and I worked behind the scenes. Lerman was spending a considerable portion of his time meeting with members of the media, hungry for King-related stories. It soon became apparent the media posed the biggest hindrance to my investigation. It seemed that every time I arrived at a location to seek out a witness or examine a document, there were the reporters, the cameras, the confusion. They quickly grew to be a major pain in the ass.

The investigative plan I'd promised Lerman was approved and in the works before week's end. Multi-tasking was the key. It allowed for the timely gathering of information from witnesses, whose backgrounds were then checked to avoid surprises down the road. Some members of the team were assigned to hang out at police watering holes while others got less glamorous gigs.

The staff meeting I'd called on the day following my first meeting with Steve Lerman lasted several hours. I sought input and suggestions from each assistant investigator. I wanted each man and woman to know just how important I felt the case was. I wanted them to feel they each had experience or individual abilities to contribute. This first meeting set the tone for my staff eventually becoming known as the King Team.

■

Hospital security assignments were made with little discussion. All knew they would be spending nights away from home with Rodney King. The assignment eliciting the biggest negative reaction was the "dumpster detail."

Trash dumpsters outside the Los Angeles Police Protective League (LAPPL), LAPD's Foothill Station, and the offices of attorneys hired to defend the four officers had to be searched for documents, notes, anything related to the King case. The CHP's Verdugo Hills substation was scouted, but proved too risky to be "trashed." Their dumpsters were located in a well-lighted area and could be seen from everywhere in the rear parking lot. We reluctantly decided to let them keep their secrets.

For all the professionalism of my staff, life in the office was no bed of roses. There was dissention in the ranks at being a support team for Rodney King. Germs of attitudes responsible for his beating still survived in some of my ex-cop associates. During one staff meeting at which I was assigning hospital shifts and dumpster duty, one man erupted.

"I'm not climbing in and out of trash dumpsters," he groused. "Besides, maybe King got what he deserved."

"Let's talk privately," I said, not wanting a confrontation in front of the others. My man had always spoken his piece, but I didn't like his tone. I called a break. As the others left the room for coffee and doughnuts, we had our first of many discussions about his sentiments on the King investigation.

"Look Tom, you and I both know what it's like to chase some asshole loaded on dope at high speeds."

"Well, I can't speak for you," I said, "but in my case, once the guy was down, it was over. I didn't beat the dog shit out of him just because I was pissed."

"I'll work the hospital detail because I don't have to have

contact with King, but I won't climb into no fucking trash bin,"
he said flatly.

"Okay, you win," I said reluctantly, "No dumpsters. But
you'll have to take a larger insurance caseload, so I can free up
a couple of the others to hit the bins." He smiled at his minor
victory.

If I knew anything at all about the LAPD, I knew the places
where off-duty cops went to drink and bullshit. In days past,
this was done over the hood of someone's car with a couple of
six packs and was called "choir practice." Cops tend to stick
together when they socialize for a very good reason. Too often,
some drunk at a party starts to complain about this chickenshit
cop or that dumb son-of-a-bitch CHP officer who wrote him an
undeserved ticket, until you've finally had enough and apologize for all the bad cops who ever lived, just to get away from
the guy.

Or, you're out on a date and see something you shouldn't
and get caught between being an average guy or a police officer.
Too many people try to test the officer's values or ethical
systems and will, for example, light a joint, daring the off-duty
officer to do something about it. That's why cops tend to isolate
themselves from civilians when they're kicking back. That way,
they don't have to worry about what they might see or say.

Malcolm Stone joined me on one occasion at a country-
western bar in Foothill Division. Our objective was to engage
off-duty cops in mindless conversation, then bring up the beating. But this particular bar was located about a mile from the
KKK's Valley headquarters and Malcolm's color closed a lot of
mouths that evening. It was a healthy dose of reality.

The honky-tonk detail began to pay off the following night
when Harry Johnson and former Phoenix police officer Barbara
Lavarias, a new member of my staff, overheard officers identifying by name, other LAPD personnel at the scene of the
beating. Harry and Barbara spent suspicious amounts of time
in the restrooms, scribbling names on paper towels and drink
napkins. No one suspected this young couple was gathering
information. They looked liked they belonged. They walked the
walk and talked the talk, just like their unsuspecting buddies.

I took a shift on the dumpster detail and hit it big. In the
trash bin outside the Police Protective League, I found a memo
summarizing the content of a meeting that took place a few

days after the airing of the Holliday video. This memo identified by name, the four defense attorneys and the administrative representatives who would defend the officers. As a result of my crumpled, coffee-stained discovery, Lerman knew the hierarchy of the entire defense team several months in advance of public disclosure. This was important because I could now complete background investigations on all of them. Advantage Lerman.

It also allowed us the same advantages the other side was enjoying. It seemed every time someone on our side became publicly known, confidential information about that person's background surfaced. Within two days of appearing at a press conference, a doctor who had initially scheduled various specialists to work with King became the target of a minor scandal. Confidential information about an alleged past problem of the doctor's—an overbilling to an insurance company—was leaked to the media "from an informed source." As quickly as the smear was out, the doctor resigned from the team. It was a cheap shot. The doctor had merely scheduled medical consultations for King. He was never a primary medical provider.

The next target of the smear merchants was Bob Rentzer, King's criminal defense attorney, originally hired by the family to work with Lerman while King was still in custody. Like the doctor, he apparently had a skeleton in his closet. Once his participation on the team was known, the bones were publicly rattled.

■

In every criminal case where a blood alcohol level is used to prove intoxication, the defendant has the right to retest blood and urine samples using his own expert to evaluate the result. There are many variables in this process, such as when and how the sample was taken. At the time of his arrest following the beating, King was charged with drunk driving. Lerman would need tests for his defense expert.

One of the first things I did was contact the toxicology department of the Los Angeles County USC Medical Center. The lab said there wasn't enough blood or urine left, and even if there were, to release it would require an authorization from the D.A.'s office.

District Attorney Ira Reiner had assigned Terry White, a

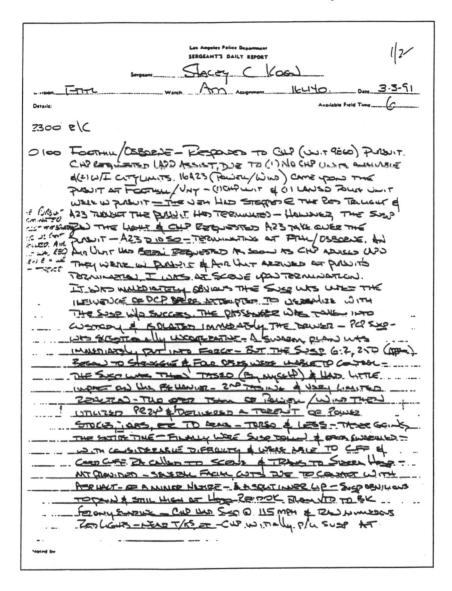

Los Angeles Police Department
SERGEANT'S DAILY REPORT

Sergeant....... Stacey C Koon

Division ...FTHL... Watch... Am Assignment... 16140. Date... 3-3-91

Available Field Time ... 6

Details:

2300 E\C

0100 FOOTHILL/OSBORNE – RESPONDED TO CHP (UNIT 9860) PURSUIT.
CHP REQUESTED LAPD ASSIST, DUE TO (1) NO CHP UNITS AVAILABLE
&(2) W/I CITY LIMITS. 16A23 (POWELL/WIND) CAME UPON THE
PURSUIT AT FOOTHILL/VAN — (1)CHP W/UT & (1) LAUSD POLICE UNIT
WERE IN PURSUIT — THE VEH HAD STOPPED @ THE RED T/LIGHT &
A23 THOUGHT THE PURSUIT HAD TERMINATED — HOWEVER, THE SUSP
RAN THE LIGHT & CHP REQUESTED A23 TAKE OVER THE
PURSUIT — A23 DID SO — TERMINATING AT FTHL/OSBORNE. AN
AIR UNIT HAD BEEN REQUESTED A SOON AS CHP ADVISED LAPD
THEY WERE IN PURSUIT & AIR UNIT ARRIVED AT PURSUITS
TERMINATION. I WAS AT SCENE UPON TERMINATION.
IT WAS IMMEDIATELY OBVIOUS THE SUSP WAS UNDER THE
INFLUENCE OF DCP &/OR ATTEMPTED TO VERBALIZE WITH
THE SUSP W/O SUCCESS. THE PASSENGER WAS TAKEN INTO
CUSTODY & ISOLATED IMMEDIATELY. THE DRIVER — PCP SUSP—
WAS EXCEPTIONALLY UNCOOPERATIVE. A SWARM PLAN WAS
IMMEDIATELY PUT INTO FORCE — BUT THE SUSP 6:2, 250 (APX)
BEGAN TO STRUGGLE & FOUR OFFRS WERE UNABLE TO CONTROL—
THE SUSP WAS THEN TASED (BY MYSELF) & HAD LITTLE
IMPACT ON HIS BEHAVIOR — 2ND TASING & VERY LIMITED
REACTION — TWO OFFR TEAM OF POWELL/WIND THEN
UTILIZED PR24 & DELIVERED A TORRENT OF POWER
STROKES, JABS, ETC TO ARMS — TORSO & LEGS — TASER GOING
THE ENTIRE TIME — FINALLY WERE SUSP DOWN & OFFRS SWARMED—
WITH CONSIDERABLE DIFFICULTY & WERE ABLE TO CFF &
CORD CUFF. RA CALLED TO SCENE & TRANS TO SIERRA HOSP. —
MT PROVIDED — SEVERAL FACIAL CUTS DUE TO CONTACT WITH
ASPHALT — OF A MINOR NATURE — & A SPLIT INNER LIP — SUSP OBVIOUS
TO PAIN & STILL HIGH AT HOSP RE-BOOK. ASSOC/VID TO BK.
FELONY EVADING — CHP HAD SUSP @ 115 MPH & RAN NUMEROUS
RED LIGHTS — NEAR T/KS ETC. — CHP INITIALLY P/U SUSP AT

Noted by

Los Angeles Police Department
SERGEANT'S DAILY REPORT

2/2

Sergeant _____ Stacey C Koon _____

Division ___ Ftr ___   Watch ___ Am ___   Assignment ___ 16L140 ___   Date ___ 3-3? ___

Details: _____   • Available Field Time ___ 6 ___

PAXTON/ETHL — SUSP BKD AT LAC·USC DUE TO RCP STATE
By A23.

AT SCENE, I DISCUSSED HOW CHP WANTED THE
INCIDENT HANDLED — & DUE TO RCP STATE OF SUSP &
LIMITED CHP RESCURCES AVAILABLE & DUE TO THE
FACT LAPD WAS PRIMARY WIT @ TERMINATION &
SOLELY INVOLVED IN USE OF FORCE — IT WAS DECIDED
WE'D HANDLE BOOK—MI & ARREST & CHP HANDLED
IMPOUND & SPERS SECURED AS WITS.

USE OF FORCE & PURSUIT WILL BE COMPLETED BY
SGT DISTEFANO. UPON COMPLETION OF ZEPTS BY
POWELL & WIND

Q. IMPORTANT NOTE FOR EC TRAINING — ALWAYS HAVE
A B/U PLAN WITH A USE OF FORCE — IT DOESN'T
ALWAYS WORK THE WAY YOU'RE TRAINED — TASER
DOESN'T ALWAYS IMMOBILIZE — PR24 DOESN'T ALWAYS
CRIPLE, OR IF YOU DON'T HAVE A FRAME OF
REFERENCE — PPOS TEND TO PANIC — WHEN THINGS
DON'T WORK THE WAY THEY'RE SUPPOSE TO — A B/U
PLAN PREVENTS PANIC — & IT DON'T HURT TO HAVE
A B/U — ESPECIALLY WITH PCP SUSPS —

HAVE
SGT KOON
DISCUSS
AT EC.

0745 EOW

Noted by
Watch Commander _____   Signature _____ Stacey C Koon 21:??

black deputy D.A., to head up the prosecution of the case. I couldn't get through to White, but a female assistant agreed to tell the lab I was authorized to order the tests on behalf of Lerman. In late March when I followed up with the lab, they told me the leftover specimens had been destroyed. Advantage LAPD.

My second bit of luck came within days. I was scrounging for documents tying any officer directly to the beating, when I came upon the daily supervisor's log, completed by Stacey Koon following the beating—Blue Throat came through again. In his log, Koon is critical of Powell's baton techniques but maintains the force used against King was totally within policy and acceptable. He recommends additional roll call training (given to officers each day before they go into the field) on controlling violent suspects. Most important, Koon acknowledges minor injuries inflicted during the incident but fails to detail either the severity or locations of wounds suffered by King. As it later turned out, King's injuries were much more serious than depicted in either Koon's log or Powell's arrest report. This failure to include specific information relating to King's injuries later led to charges of falsifying the arrest reports. They were later acquitted in Simi Valley.

By March 10, 1991, only a week after the beating, we began to compile the names of officers present at the scene. Gates's public relations media mouths initially put only twelve officers at the location. We already knew that was a lie.

Reporters, eager to trade information for a comment from Lerman or King, were referred to my offices. Soon, a steady stream of messengers were delivering envelopes full of tidbits. I was amazed. The kind of background information they brought would have taken weeks of hard investigative efforts to gather. Within days, my desk was piled high with records of prior civil cases filed against the involved officers and stories about police brutality, including use of the notorious choke hold.

I had used the choke hold many times while I was a cop. It was legal then, and my preferred method of controlling an unruly suspect. The choke hold was designed to cut off both the blood and air to a suspect's brain. The arrestee usually passed out and in the process of regaining consciousness, his or her body would twitch involuntarily. Sometimes they would lose control of their bodily functions. Officers dubbed these convulsions "the funky chicken." In the black humor of copdom, many officers rated performances of the funky chicken on a scale of one to ten for their entertainment value. Shitters always got a ten.

In 1983, the choke hold was outlawed; several arrestees had died following its use during their arrests. One of the cases cited in the decision involved the death of Thomas Mincie following an altercation with Officer Robert Simpach who, ironically, we identified early on as a bystanding officer at the King arrest. Officers protested that the restriction reduced the number of options available to them when force was necessary. I told Lerman we could expect to see the issue raised later in King's criminal defense hearing or in his civil lawsuit. However, when this issue surfaced in the officers' criminal trial in Simi Valley, I was quite surprised.

Nearly every national magazine and major newspaper ran extensive coverage of the case. The *Los Angeles Times* jumped to the forefront with its daily profiles on every person known to be associated to the King incident. For a number of months, *Times* reporter Richard Serrano was assigned to work the King story exclusively. He gained access to the inner circles of the King Team and the defense, even talking off the record to King himself.

As I became more fully involved in the case, I began to understand what Lerman was referring to during our first meeting in the restaurant when he told me I had no idea of media interest in the King case. I read articles about an issue I hadn't yet considered: growing tensions between African-American residents and Korean shop owners of South Central Los Angeles.

The King beating occurred in the wake of an emotionally charged shooting involving the alleged murder of a black teenage girl, Latasha Harlens, by a female Korean grocery store owner, Soon Ja Du. In that case, the store's video camera filmed the girl arguing with the shop owner, Ms. Du. As the teenager turned to leave the store, the woman pulled a gun from under the counter and shot her in the back of her head.

Latasha died at the scene. Soon Ja Du was charged with murder but a jury later found her guilty of manslaughter. When Judge Joyce Carlin sentenced her to probation without jail time, the black community was outraged. Picketers outside Judge Carlin's Compton courthouse, and her home, demanded her removal. Tensions mounted as rhetoric spread from both camps.

Savvy local and national politicians and activists, each with an agenda, were quick to tie the two incidents together, alleging unfairness or inequity in the justice system. Among the most vocal in her condemnation of the LAPD in the King beating and the judicial system in the Harlens shooting was Congresswoman Maxine Waters. Then and now, these crusaders proved troublesome.

In the first weeks after the Holliday video aired, Lerman and I gave considerable thought to every public statement or reaction coming from the King team. We felt the community could erupt into violence if the wrong thing was said or inferred. While many responsible people like L.A.'s Urban League President John Mack and chairman of the Brotherhood Crusade Danny Bakewell called for community calm and rational thinking, others like Waters appeared to try to evoke outrage at gut level within the community, thereby threatening to undermine our best peace efforts. Privately, I wished the crusaders would leave the situation alone, quit looking for a headline, and simply shut up.

Repeated airings of the Holliday video during newscasts seemed to threaten the already uneasy peace in Los Angeles following the Harlens shooting. Many highly respected journalists chuckle and shake their heads in disbelief that LA station KTLA-TV was presented a Peabody Journalism Award for its handling of the Holliday tape. The facts are, KTLA opted not to air the tape on the day they got it. The following evening, when they did air the video, it was given little prominence: They essentially buried it in the second section of the broadcast. KTLA, like George Holliday, seriously misjudged the value of what they had obtained but was rewarded nonetheless.

■

My daughter, Jamie, a typical fourteen-year-old ninth grader in an Orange County high school, was proud that her dad's company had been assigned the investigation on behalf of King. Against my advice, she wrote a current affairs report for her

English teacher on the King beating. In her report, she commented during the last paragraph that her dad was the investigator for King. The teacher's comments, written at the bottom of her report in red pencil, showed an incredible insensitivity for her feelings of pride when he wrote, "Don't brag about your dad. . . . King probably got what he deserved." After that, Jamie did the best she could to avoid any public association with her dad's business.

■

It was a bit easier for my middle son, Sean. At nineteen, he'd already graduated from high school and was working part time for me as a computer data input clerk. His friends were inquisitive about what was really going on in the case, compared to what the media was broadcasting, but were generally supportive of him.

My eldest son, Steve, was making plans to get married when I got the assignment. At age twenty-one, he'd been working for the same employer, a medical supply company, since he'd graduated from high school. He was earning fairly good money as was his fiancée, Joanne. Like his brother, Sean, Steve kept his feelings about the King beating to himself when outside the house, but he commented to me many times about conversations he overheard at work.

Several coworkers spoke frequently of their feelings about the beating, about racism, and about how we must support the police, even in the face of possible misconduct. Somehow, through this process, my elder son changed his mind about becoming a police officer. I felt relieved, but also disappointed. I had looked forward to his wearing the uniform that had meant so much to me. I was concerned that this case was carrying over into the lives of my kids.

■

Before meeting King, I spoke with most of his relatives. The King family are Jehovah's Witnesses and refused to grant interviews with the media. They feared any public statements by them would only serve to heighten the growing public outrage. They hoped that when the jury heard Rodney King's story, the world would learn the truth. But I was concerned. No positive comments were coming from the victim's side to counter the LAPD press blitz.

I was madder than hell by what Paul King, Rodney's older brother, told me. Freddie G and Pooh, the passengers in Rodney King's car during the chase, called Paul right after the beating. He entered the Foothill Division of the Los Angeles Police Department as Sunday's dawn was breaking. A bored uniformed officer sat behind the counter in the empty lobby.

"Help you?"

"I want to talk to the person in charge."

After a while the watch commander appeared. Paul spoke first. "Some friends told me my brother, Rodney King, was arrested. They said he was beaten. I want to find out what happened and file a complaint."

The white sergeant escorted Paul, who is shorter and much less muscular than his brother, to an interview room. "You ever been in trouble?" he asked.

"I'm here about my brother." Paul, who had never been arrested, expected this kind of treatment.

The Sergeant told him Rodney was "in big trouble" for driving more than one hundred miles an hour and endangering the lives of police officers who had pursued and arrested him. Then he left Paul alone.

A half-hour later, when the officer had not returned, Paul knew he was wasting his time. Police hurry to catch a crook, but are slow to accept criticism, especially from a black man.

Freddie G and Pooh had told Paul they'd seen a man with a video camera at the scene. He wondered if that might make a difference and went looking for the Sergeant. He told him about the videotape. Still no interest. As Paul left in disgust, the Sergeant wrote in his daily log that the complaint required no further action.

A few days later, I cleared my schedule for my first meeting with Rodney King himself. Lerman had moved him to the Beverly Hills Ramada Inn where his privacy and safety could better be controlled than at home. This temporary residence was closer to King's doctors and seemed like a good place to hide him from the media.

Early on Saturday morning, I called the hotel and asked for

King's room by number. A strained and shaky man's voice answered the phone.

"Mr. Johnson, please," I said, using King's code name.

"I'm Johnson," came the quiet reply.

"I'll be by in a few hours so we can talk."

"See you then." The conversation ended that quickly. We never knew if one of the desk clerks at the hotel might be listening, so the security plan called for only essentials to be discussed on the phone.

I hung up and leaned back in my chair. Coming face to face with the man whose beating set off a firestorm that continues to this day made me nervous. I was excited, yet hesitant. Here I was, a former police officer in Watts, representing a black convicted felon against my former brothers in blue. I loaded up my car and headed for the Ramada Inn.

The one-hour drive to Beverly Hills felt like forever. As I knocked on the hotel room door, I knew reporters would kill for the opportunity to hear this interview. My ego soared. But . . . what if King and I didn't like each other? What if a white ex-cop was the last person in the world Rodney King wanted to sit and chat with? Suddenly, the word compromise took on a whole new meaning. Crystal, King's wife, opened the door.

"Hi, I'm Tom Owens, I'm here to . . ."

"Sure, come on in. Glen's just finishing a shower."

"Excuse me, but I'm here to see Rodney King."

"Yes, I know. We call him Glen. That's how he likes to be called." Crystal smiled and offered me a cold soda once I was inside the room. So far so good. When she went into another room, I stopped worrying about making conversation and looked around. On a wall was a bad copy of an oriental painting. My thoughts drifted to my days in the Far East, so many years ago. Then the bedroom door opened. Dressed in a dark blue jogging outfit, Glen entered the room on crutches. It was clearly painful for him to move. I was immediately struck by the sight of his face. With all my experiences in Vietnam, I should have been prepared for anything, but that was a different time, an alien place. This shit wasn't supposed to happen in America. Brother officers had done this. It saddened and disgusted me.

King needed help sitting down. With his jaw swollen shut, it was tough for him to talk. He continually rubbed the right side of his face, numb from nerve damage. His right cheek was dotted with bright red broken blood vessels. His right eye was bloodshot and swollen. We appraised each other. Neither of us spoke. Neither knew what to say. Finally, I took a deep breath. "Glen, I'm your investigator. It's my job to get the facts and help Steve Lerman prepare your case for trial. I'm not a cop now, but I used to be. I hope that doesn't bother you, but in this case there's some advantage to my knowledge of their mindset. I need to get your account of what happened out there the other night. I'm in no hurry, so please relax, take your time. If you need to take a break, just let me know."

King took a deep breath. I had no idea what to expect. "Why did they beat me like this?"

"I don't know. That's what I hope to find out."

King managed a slight smile, but he was clearly in pain.

"Would you rather I come back in a few days?"

"No, let's do this now."

I fumbled as I turned on my tape recorder, uncomfortable just looking at his injuries. King's forehead had been stitched up, as well as the interior of his mouth. I saw familiar baton shaped bruising on his neck and wrists. These parallel black and blue lines appear within seconds of a baton strike on the skin. Most notable was the redness in his right eye caused, I believed then and believe now, by a baton blow to his cheek.

In short sentences, King described what happened, word after painful word. It bothered me to ask him to repeat words I couldn't understand. I tried to ease the tension by getting him to smile. Several times, Crystal called from the adjoining bedroom, asking if I wanted something to drink. It was like they could sense my nervousness.

Soon Glen was smiling, but wincing at the pain it caused. Slowly, we began to trust each other. King didn't know it, but some of the questions I asked him during our first meeting were specifically designed to test his credibility. I needed to know early on if I could trust him. I'd already decided if I caught him in a lie, I'd withdraw from the case.

King remembered CHP Officer Melanie Singer. On the morning of March 3, 1991, Singer and her husband, Officer Tim Singer were the two CHP officers who began the chase of the Hyundai King was driving. It was Melanie Singer who estimated his speed in excess of 110 miles per hour on the freeway.

"She told me to open the door up with my left hand, put both of my hands on the window where she could see them, both of my hands. I was pushing the door open. At the same time she said 'Okay, I want you to get out of the car and lay face down on the . . .' I got out of the car, lay face down in the street. Uh . . . they came over."

"Who were they?"

"Uh, well, I know the officer, whoever it was, came over and I felt . . . immediately after they grabbed me and had my hands behind my head . . . I felt this shock in towards my shoulder . . . a shock go in my shoulder and right after that I felt a hit on top of the head, then the sidewalk—boom!—with billy clubs and again another shock in the other shoulder."

"Did you see any of the officers?"

"I didn't even look. I didn't even bother to look. The only thing I was worried about and looking at was what she was telling me to do. I was looking at the spot where I was going to lay down at and making sure she had contact—eye contact with my eye contact—and my hand contact to make sure that they knew that I was . . . they all had guns on me."

"Do you know who beat you?"

"I know it was a him, I could tell by the feet. I could see a woman don't have feet like that."

King talked about the taser: "Then after that I felt that . . . I could feel the currents going through my body. It was like I was paying more attention. I was paying attention to the currents. You know, the feeling that was going through me." He paused, struggling to remember. "Then after that, it just went blank. I'm blank after that . . . I can't . . . after that, I woke up. I was being lifted up by the handcuffs in a hogtie, put in the back of a police car. . . ."

I figured King meant ambulance, but as the interview continued, I wasn't so sure.

"Yeah . . . I was taken for a ride to the police station and then one of the officers got out. One of them was in the back seat with me and I was telling him, you know, you didn't have to do this to me, you didn't have to do this to me. I was telling him, you know, you can let me go right now. I'll get out. I'm scared and I'll get out and just leave right now. I will leave right now and I won't say nothing. I'll leave. And he was just looking at me, you know, real sad, with a big sad face . . . and he didn't say a word." I checked my tape recorder. This statement was important. His description of this officer (who turned out to be Powell) was important. I asked King if he remembered where he was kicked.

"All over . . . all over."

"Tell me about the hospital."

"I wanted some kind of proof, you know? I said, Something's gotta be done about this. I was thinking to myself, Damn, here's another case that's gonna go . . . it's just gonna go to waste. They're just gonna get away with this. So I was trying to hold on to the pants . . . when the police came in. First the janitor threw my pants away, then I asked him 'Did you throw those pants away?' And the guy said he did, and he said 'Oh yeah' then he went back and got them for me. And the next day, one of the policemen came in . . ."

"From where, one of the police from where?"

"From the county. From the hospital ward."

"One of the sheriffs?"

"Uh-huh . . . and threw the pants away. He threw my pants away."

"Did you tell him not to throw the pants away?"

"Yeah, I asked him. He was a white officer, he said, 'I'll put them with your personals.' "

"Did he do that?"

"No, he didn't. He didn't put them with my . . . When I got ready to leave, I asked him, 'Can I have my clothes?' He said, 'You don't have any clothes.' "

I hesitated to ask about racial epithets King might have heard during the beating which were already being reported in the media by some of the witnesses. None had been mentioned by King, so I decided to leave it alone. For the moment.

Almost three hours after I arrived at the hotel, I finished taking the statement of Rodney King. He went right through my setup questions without batting an eye. While parts of his memory were still sketchy, I was convinced he wasn't lying. King passed his first tests with me. I felt confident I'd passed my first test with him.

It was late in the afternoon by now. We'd worked right through lunch. I was hungry and asked Glen and Crystal to dinner. He chose a nearby Sizzler's. King ordered a steak, but when our food arrived, he couldn't eat it. He'd forgotten that all the fillings had been knocked out of his teeth during the beating. I felt the need to apologize but ordered him jello instead. While we sat in the restaurant talking over dinner, lookie-loos, and well-wishers who recognized his face from the television broadcast of his press conference at the jail ward, stopped by the table to offer Glen a handshake and a smile of encouragement.

I took Glen and Crystal back to their hotel, then drove out to the location of the beating. I wanted to get a feel for the scene I'd read about in Powell's report.

■

As I stood on the spot where King had been beaten nearly to death, I couldn't help feeling sorry for everyone involved. No matter how it ended, there would be no winners—not Rodney King, not the officers, not the department, not the city. Maybe just Lerman and me. We'd get career boosts and pockets full of cash. Later events would prove me wrong there, too. We were all losers.

I had a clear view of the balcony where George Holliday stood to shoot his home video. Someone else must have seen the beating, I figured. Decks and patios of the middle class, racially mixed Mountainback Apartments overlooked the scene. All shared an unobstructed view of the road in front of the boarded-up Tastee Freeze where King had been beaten six nights prior.

Holliday wasn't home so I canvassed the area for other witnesses. No one would talk to me. I realized that looking like a cop at this place, at this time, was a disadvantage. An hour of denials and refusals and I gave up, knowing I'd be back.

■

I hadn't even kicked off my shoes after driving home from this fourteen hour day when Lerman's call came in. "How'd it go with Glen? What did you think of him?"

For the next hour, I recounted my interview with King. Lerman's questions were never ending, or so it seemed. I told about my trip to the scene of the beating and suggested he consider calling in an associate who was black. I felt a backup to Malcolm Stone would speed up information gathering from the Hispanics and African-Americans at the Mountainback Apartments. Some kids out at the complex told me the LAPD, other detectives, and the ever-present media were still around, looking for witnesses to the incident. I wanted to get to them before the authorities did.

Lerman okayed my request to bring in an African-American investigator and told me to get statements from King's passengers. He'd already set up interview appointments for the following day. A Sunday.

Sunday morning. Sleeping in. Quiet time. Hot coffee. But not this Sunday. The two young men in King's Hyundai, Freddie G. Helms and Bryant Allen, known as Pooh, had retained Steve Lerman for companion lawsuits. Instead of relaxing on this Sunday morning, I drove to Altadena, where they were literally hiding out. I figured Sunday was a good day because the media might not be working. I was right.

Following narrow streets past the local high school and Baptist Church, I found Freddie G's house amid a row of older homes crying out for paint and new roofing. The racially mixed neighborhood seemed unusually quiet. The old chain link fence bordering the front yard was in desperate need of repair.

Pooh was waiting for me at the front door of the faded gold stucco home. I found Freddie G waiting inside, head bandaged from the injury he'd suffered during the incident. A week after the event, fresh blood still oozed through the gauze. A quick greeting with Freddie G's family, and I followed my two unlikely clients into the kitchen where we sat at the table and got down to business.

■

Freddie G and Pooh were as different from each other as they were from Glen—or Rodney, as they called him. Slight of build, Freddie G. Helms, twenty years old, walked with a crutch. He'd had a serious auto accident several years earlier that permanently injured his left leg. He spoke fast, eager to tell his story, though he seemed dazed and disoriented. I struggled to understand and finally had to slow him down. Freddie G had a criminal record. He'd been arrested for fighting at John Muir High School, the same school King had attended. He'd also been arrested for commercial burglary and had some previous contact with the Bloods, one of LA's dominant street gangs. He told me he slept through the pursuit and woke up only after King pulled over in Lake View Terrace. He thought I was joking when I asked him if the Hyundai could have been going more than 100 miles per hour on the 210.

Freddie G said he got out of the car and lay down on the ground. I glanced at my tape recorder. "Then what?"

"Then I just heard Rodney start screaming. Rodney started screaming."

"Okay. Were you on crutches that night?"

"Yes, I was."

The rhythm and pronunciation of Freddie's words reminded me of my days on a beat in Watts, and I talked the talk. "Where were the crutches at?"

"In the backseat."

"Did you tell the cops that you were on crutches?"

"They didn't give me a chance to say nothin' to them. They had some guns pointed all at me. I was just doin' what they told me to do."

"Okay, and then what? You heard Rodney screaming?"

"Yes, I did."

"Did you ever try to turn your head to look at what was going on over there?"

"Yeah, I tried once."

"What happened when you did?"

"One of the officers hit me in the head," Freddie G said. Within hours of his release he sought treatment in the emergency room of Mercy Hospital in Altadena. I was fascinated by Freddie G. It was not hard to like this small, crippled, black youth with a smile so big it never ended.

"All I heard was them just tell him to lay on the ground and he didn't say . . . he really didn't get to speak too much. I heard them asking him to do something, but I wasn't really too sure what I heard them ask. But I know that . . . as well as I know his voice . . . that he didn't say nothin'. I know that he did what they asked him to do."

I asked Freddie G if he knew Holliday was taping the incident from his balcony across the street.

"When the cops released us, we was walking over by where

some people were watching, I saw a guy standing in the group with a video camera, but I don't know if that was the guy."

"You saw a guy standing in a group with a camera?" I asked, startled by this revelation. Could there be a second video? My mind raced with the possibilities.

"Yeah, he was next to some girls, out by a fence in front of the apartments."

"What did he look like? Did you get a good look at him?"

"Black . . . he was a black man but I couldn't see his face, he had the camera in the way."

Holy shit! There's another video, I thought. Now, I needed to hurry through Allen's statement and get back out to the location. I wanted that second video.

■

Bryant Allen, known as Pooh, is a large, twenty-five-year-old black man. He too attended John Muir High School, where he also ran with the Pasadena Bloods. He was arrested for assault and battery in his junior year and didn't graduate. He completed his high school education at an L.A. County juvenile camp. I'd expected him to be tougher than he was. It was as though the pressures from the media and the authorities were wearing on him. He was much less expressive than Freddie G and seemed uneasy with my presence.

Pooh told me he'd been arrested once as an adult. He had burglarized a car in 1989 and was still on probation. I was suddenly struck by the problems black men seem to have with cars. They get pulled over when officers suspect a fancy car they're driving might be stolen, or they often get stopped simply because they're black. Pooh seem puzzled by my silence. Embarrassed by my thoughts, I asked about the night King was beaten.

"We were on the freeway for awhile, you know, listening to music, relaxing . . . and all of a sudden, I seen lights flashing."

"And then what happened?"

"He kept driving and I got kind of worried why he wasn't pulling over, so I told him, 'Rodney, pull over.' I think it was a little blackout moment, that's how I feel. He was like . . . he was like ignoring me. I don't know if the radio was too loud or what."

Bryant Allen talked about what he saw after they pulled over at the boarded up Tastee Freeze. "They told him to lay flat down. He laid flat down and they ordered Freddie G . . . they ordered me to get out of the car.

"All of a sudden I heard a loud scream. I tried to look and that's when they said, 'Don't look!' you know, 'Don't move.' And then he bust up my head . . . the hand in my face and just kept it like that."

"On the ground?" I asked.

"On the ground. So I couldn't look, you know? I couldn't see Freddie G. I just heard a lot of whacking and . . . like . . . whooping sounds."

Pooh was handcuffed and left lying on the ground. Someone stomped on his back and kicked him in the lower neck. He and Freddie G were not arrested. After they were released, he called his sister for a ride home. The Hyundai had been impounded by the police. Pooh showed me the area of his back where the unknown officer stomped him. Unlike Freddie G, he hadn't seen anyone video taping during or after the incident, but he did remember the small group of people assembled near the fence in front of the apartments.

■

Like everyone else in America, I'd only seen the same twenty seconds of the Holliday video played and replayed on every newscast for over a week. My efforts at meeting George Holliday had been a bust and frankly, I was aggravated. I wanted that video. After getting the statements of Freddie G and Pooh, I drove back out to the Mountainback Apartments.

Lake View Terrace is a section of Los Angeles, much the same as Hollywood or Watts, a city within a city located in the Northeast corner of the San Fernando Valley, a quiet residential community with a scattering of minor industry and small businesses. One of the poorer sections of the Valley, Lake View Terrace affords low- and middle-income wage earners a comfortable and scenic place to live and work. I busted my ass getting there. I wondered if anyone else even knew of the second tape.

I listened passively to the radio talk shows as I drove north along the 210 freeway, past the gently rolling hills and open land, my mind on another drive along this same freeway.

A high speed freeway chase is one of the most dangerous situations an officer can face. While the officer is highly trained to handle the road and his own car in high speed pursuits, he can't control the actions of other drivers. "Black and white fever" can set in when a motorist sees a police car approaching. Instantly, brake lights blink on as motorists check their speed. A cop car's emergency lights act as a shit magnet, attracting frightened motorists toward the pursuing officer. They don't remember the rule that when they see the red lights and hear the siren, they should pull to the right. Instead, they are likely to skid into a panic stop and it's pileup time.

A lot is going on inside the patrol car too. Windows must be rolled up to muffle the siren so the officer can use the radio. Then, the officer must watch for other traffic and road conditions along the pursuit route. Cross traffic, school zones, driveways, pedestrians, parked cars, even other police cars joining the chase pose potential danger. Responsibility for safety rests with the pursuing officer. Under the law, if the risks to others are too extreme, the pursuit must be terminated.

I was the driver-officer on one chase that covered over forty-three miles of city streets and freeways, cutting through three LAPD divisions, parts of LA county, and two smaller cities. The chase lasted twenty-five minutes, and when it was finally over I just sat in the car and shook. I was scared to death—mentally and physically exhausted. The robbery suspect I was chasing nearly broadsided several other cars during the chase. This really pissed me off.

Partly because of near misses and partly because of the officer's adrenaline surge, too many pursuits end in an altercation. This phenomena is known as "post-pursuit syndrome." I've had firsthand experience with the condition, both as pursuing officer and as a backup officer to another's pursuit. The LAPD is aware of post-pursuit syndrome, and requires a sergeant to respond at the termination point to ensure rules and policies of the department are followed by pursuing officers. Many people question the need for so many, sometimes dozens, of police cars in a pursuit. The answer is simple: cops want to get in on the action that concludes many pursuits, to show the scumbag not to run from the police. In the case of Rodney King, he took his lickin' and kept on tickin'.

■

I was more persistent this time with some of the apartment residents than I had been on my previous visit to Lake View Terrace. Again, Holliday didn't answer his door, but I did set several appointments for the following Wednesday with some of his neighbors and talked to some kids playing in the courtyard near the swimming pool. I had learned as a young cop, that if kids think they have a secret, they can't wait to tell anyone who'll listen. The children told me the second video was shot by the night manager. They didn't know his name or which apartment he lived in but said he worked weeknights at the complex. I had made minor progress. I now had a second source telling me there was in fact, a second video of the King incident.

The following day, I started looking for a black investigator to help me get to the reluctant eyewitnesses at the Mountainback Apartments. The California Association of Licensed Investigators (CALI) referred me to African-American investigator George Rhodes, one of their past presidents. With an office in the predominantly black city of Compton, Rhodes and his staff were able to obtain statements from some of the witnesses who had refused to talk to me. They spent time with these crucial witnesses and recorded their chilling observations.

Dorothy Gibson, who lived in the apartment beneath Holliday, said she stepped onto her patio and saw LAPD Sergeant Stacey Koon, carrying a taser electronic stun weapon, take control of the situation. As King, who was already lying on the ground tried to stand, Sergeant Koon shot the taser into his back. She saw Powell and Wind wield their batons. Dorothy Gibson wept as she described how Officer Powell swung his baton at King's head as hard as he could. All police officers know LAPD policy clearly states, no headshots under any circumstances. Gibson reported she stood paralyzed with horror as other officers moved in on King.

Elois Camp, Gibson's neighbor, watched King try in vain to avoid dozens of baton blows to his head, back, and legs. She heard the crackle of the taser and saw King quiver and fall to the ground. Mrs. Camp saw four officers surround King. Powell and Wind braced themselves as they swung—harder and harder—like they were chopping logs. White men in blue uniforms kicking and beating a downed and defenseless black man. She saw Sergeant Koon point and shout, "Get his knees! Get his knees!" More blows. Too many to count.

Carol Frazier, Valerie Gray, and Ned Camp stood in the chilly night air bearing witness to the bedlam that had invaded Lake View Terrace. Thirty, forty, fifty baton blows. Two cops stood around like referees at a wrestling match while others formed an audience. Civilian witnesses heard King scream in pain from as far away as 150 feet as police batons broke his leg bones.

Ned Camp, Elois's husband, said he saw blood glistening all over King's face. He saw Officer Briseno stomp on King's bleeding head, grinding his shattered face into the gravelly surface.

Dawn Davis watched King try to roll onto his back. One cop kicked him in the head while another pounded his baton into King's left side. Then both cops swung their batons like baseball bats.

These eyewitnesses watched a group of LAPD officers, carefully avoiding taser wires, force King to the ground. When he tried to sit up, they saw Officer Powell smash a baton to the right side of his head. They watched Sergeant Koon shoot a second taser into King's back, moving wires out of the way so his officers would have more room.

When George Rhodes's investigators reported in, they told me George Holliday's neighbors, Hioberto and Josie Morales, were not answering their telephone or their doorbell, so I decided to drive to their apartment at lunchtime with no idea what I'd say. I just wanted to try one more time.

Gently knocking on their door, I kept my fingers crossed. When I heard movement from inside the apartment, I spoke through the closed door. "Mr. and Mrs. Morales, my name is Tom Owens. I'm Rodney King's investigator."

Josie Morales opened the door a crack. "I've told them everything."

"Please, no one will tell me what you said. Did they tell you not to talk to me?"

"Not exactly. But they're coming back today."

I knew it had to be now. "Mrs. Morales, I don't know what you saw. Your neighbors said it was horrible."

"My neighbors? What did they say?"

"I have their statements and I'd like to ask you just two questions."

She opened the door. Hioberto, her husband, standing behind her, accepted my outstretched hand. Josie motioned me in. She was curious. "What are the two questions?"

I was ready. "What did you see? What did you hear?"

Josie leaned against her husband. The ice was broken. Suddenly, she was near tears. "I thought he was dead."

They were awakened by the sirens and helicopter. They stepped out onto their balcony, next to George Holliday's, just as the pursuit ended. They watched in horror as King exited his car, lay on the ground, and the beating commenced. It was easy to see Mr. and Mrs. Morales were shaken by the retelling. Josie recalled, "After . . . I made notes. I wanted to remember." She told me this incident had to be reported and she wanted to be a good witness. She said she added comments to her notes for three days following the beating.

I could hardly control myself. Notes—an investigator's dream. "May I see your notes?"

"The man said not to show them to anyone else."

"What man?"

"From the district attorney. He's coming today to pick them up."

My heart sank. "He can't tell you that! Do you have his name? I'll call him so you can show me what you wrote down." I could tell she wanted me to see the notes. She gave me the name and I was on the phone to some assistant D.A. "This is Tom Owens, Rodney King's investigator. I'm with Josie Morales, who just told me you instructed her not to show her notes to anyone else. She's willing to cooperate in this investigation. I want a copy of her notes and I want to know what right you have to tell her that."

"That's not exactly what I said." The assistant D.A. was unprepared for my onslaught.

I went for the jugular. "She's here with me. I want you to tell her I'm entitled to see her notes."

"I can't tell her that."

I knew he was stalling. "Listen, you know I'm entitled to see those damn notes."

Covering the phone, the D.A. spoke with someone else, then came back on the line. "Put her on the phone." He told her she could show me the notes, but that they couldn't leave her possession.

Hioberto accompanied me to a nearby office supply store to make copies of the seven descriptive pages. Several days later, when Josie Morales told the Los Angeles County Grand Jury what she'd seen, she read the details from her notes.

■

George Holliday was a hard man to chase down. His video was the single most important piece of evidence in the King case to date and I hoped there might be more to learn from the parts not aired. Finally, I caught up to him at the Van Nuys plumbing company he manages. When I got there, Holliday was awaiting officers from the LAPD Internal Affairs Division. He wanted me gone before they arrived, which was no problem for me; I could argue with the D.A., but Internal Affairs was different, *very* different. Cops investigating cops. Scary stuff.

A word about Internal Affairs: LAPD detectives assigned to that division conduct investigations of officers accused of misconduct. The division is commanded by a senior captain and all investigators are supervisors within the definition of the department. It's said that if a supervisor wants to get promoted, the quickest way up is through IAD. It's a stepping-stone to the higher ranks. You get there by stepping on the field officers. When I worked Internal Affairs on the small town force, I made sure no officer could say that of me.

Trying my best to look friendly and trustworthy, I crossed my fingers. Holliday handed me a copy of the video, promised to spend more time with me later, and I was gone, my heart beating like a snare drum. From the car, I called Pat to meet me at home to view the entire video.

We played and replayed the tape, glued to our chairs. In focus, out of focus, jerky, these images of raw violence burned into our minds. I remembered the times I'd watched cops cross that angry line when force becomes excessive. I remembered crossing it myself. And the line kept moving. I knew the city would someday have to pay bigtime for letting it move. Someday might just be now.

The first ten times I watched the video, I just sat in amazement with my mouth open. In all my years on the department, I hadn't seen that kind of officer-inflicted violence. Watching King roll around on the ground, I got a fresh perspective on how minorities view police officers. Christ, I was angry too. As I began taking notes on what I was watching, a whole new picture emerged.

The LAPD had announced the beating lasted eighty-one seconds and the officers delivered fifty-four baton blows. I did my own computation. From the first frame of the video, where King is seen lying in a prone position fully under control and compliant, to the last frame after he had been hogtied and dragged face down across the pavement, the incident took just under three minutes, nearly double the time stated by the department. Kicks, blows with a baton, punches, and stomps account for ninety-one separate strikes against Rodney King, again almost double what the LAPD was reporting. If this incident was well within policy, as they were claiming, I wondered why they were minimizing what could be seen and counted so easily. Lying eyes?

Two seconds after the start of the video, King is seen to push up on his hands and knees, then stand, while turning to his right. He takes two steps in a diagonal direction, splitting the distance between the Hyundai and Officer Powell as Powell, already in a Casey-at-the-bat stance, makes two shuffle steps forward and slightly to his right, putting him directly in King's path, and delivers a home run swing to the right side of King's face.

LAPD spokesmen announced King was beaten because the officers suspected he was under the influence of PCP and felt no pain during the beating. On my copy of the video, King is clearly heard screaming from the pain of continued baton strikes throughout the entire incident. At one point, his leg is broken by a baton blow. That sound too is heard on the video, followed by another scream of pain from King.

Defenders of the officers claimed Ted Briseno tried to *help* King by pushing Officer Larry Powell away during the early frames of the tape. From the first, I believed it more likely that Briseno was trying to warn Powell away from Sergeant Koon's taser wires, fearing the metal baton Powell was using on King would act as a conduit for the electricity from the taser and shock the officer. Twenty-seven seconds later, as King is lying face down again, putting his hands behind his back, Briseno stomps him on the back of his head. King's movement in response to Briseno's stomp prompts Powell and Wind to rain another torrent of blows upon the downed man.

To add more drama, an LAPD helicopter circles overhead, its engines helping to cover King's screams of pain, while its light stays fixed on the action. Two officers from the Los Angeles Unified School District—with no reason to be there in the first place—have left their siren on, its wail a maddening intrusion.

A minute into the beating, a gray Ford Probe drives slowly across the screen from left to right. The car's driver was closer to the beating than any other civilian and could prove to be an important witness if I could find him. At the conclusion of the beating, Holliday's camera reveals a band bus which, like the Probe, had gotten caught in the stopped traffic when the chase ended. After I'd watched the video twenty to thirty times, I took it to a photo shop and ordered stills copied from the tape.

■

A more relaxed George Holliday met me as promised at his apartment. I gazed through the sliding glass door leading out onto the balcony overlooking Foothill Boulevard. What if the battery on his video camera had been weak? What if the door had stuck? What if . . . ?

Lost in thoughts of his newfound and unwanted fame, Holliday stood by quietly as I looked across to the opposite side of the street. Best described as soft spoken, even timid, Holliday told me of threats against himself and his family from crackpots and would-be terrorists. Still, he drove to work each day in the same car, wearing the same work clothes. He was so overwhelmed by media attention that his supervisors asked him to leave his fame at home. Holliday said he watched his video for the first time the next morning. Its violence startled him. He was surprised he hadn't noticed it while it was happening. He mentioned the tape to family and friends at a Sunday barbecue. Some felt he should give it to the police, others thought a television station might buy it. Holliday decided to contact the police; he felt it was the right thing to do.

Holliday was unprepared for what happened when he called Foothill Division to offer his witness statement and the video. The officer who took the call told him, "Mind your own fucking business and don't interfere with a police investigation."

Holliday stiffened as he repeated the words of the officer. "Mind your own fucking business!" This statement was singularly responsible for Holliday's decision to offer the video to Los Angeles TV station KTLA. They paid him $500 and first aired it on the 10 P.M. Monday night news. Then everything changed.

■

On his first trip to the apartments, George Rhodes, the black investigator I had recently retained, contacted night manager, Clifford Bernard. Mr. Bernard provided us with the video he had shot the night of the beating. While the tape doesn't have any scenes of the beating, it does provide insight and documentation of other important evidence.

As the video rolls, witnesses discuss their observations of the incident. Three young women are heard talking about the types and locations of the officers' baton blows. Most importantly, the video captures a conversation between Freddie G and Pooh as they walk toward the group assembled near the fence. Freddie G tells Pooh that he too was beaten and hit on his head. The importance of this conversation was later seen in Simi Valley, where this tape was not shown to the jury. During a post-trial talk show the female jury foreman announced that she found the officers innocent because they didn't hurt the passengers in King's car. She couldn't accept that the officers were sharks in a feeding frenzy when only one person in the car was beaten.

Something still bothered me. Why had Koon tased King in the first place? Later that night, I called an old friend, retired FBI Agent Jack Jansen, a Ph.D. in criminology. Since leaving the FBI, Dr. Jansen earned his living as a consultant in security matters, and as an expert in law enforcement related litigation. I knew Jansen was fair because his past efforts had helped both plaintiffs and defendants. I hoped Jack would have materials about patterns and practices of most larger police departments. I needed the information to show a jury how out of step the LAPD had become compared to other law enforcement agencies.

"Jack, Tom here. How's things among the peasants?"

"Same old. You got a real job yet?"

"Hell, I'd have been an FBI guy like you, if they hadn't found out my parents were married when I was born." I always gave Jack a bad time for being a Fed.

"OK smartass, what do you want?"

"Jack, I got the King case assignment from King's attorney."

"Have you lost your mind?" Jansen shouted over the phone, "I thought I taught you better than that."

"Down to business . . . do you have anything in your comic book collection related to use of the taser?"

"Absolutely. I'm sure you read that paper in the *Forensic Sciences Journal*, by the L.A. County Coroner, Dr. Kornbloom."

"I missed it, Jack. What'd he say?"

"Nothing important, except he contends that use of the taser constitutes application of deadly force. He cited case histories of thirty-four deaths resulting from tasing suspects. Good stuff. I'll fax it to you."

Within minutes, I was reading the pages as they were cut away from the fax machine. The stuff was better than good. It was great. The report highlighted the case studies Jansen had mentioned. In effect, it cautioned law enforcement agencies that the taser should not be used unless deadly force is the only other alternative.

■

I knew the report was right on. While working a Central Division footbeat twenty years ago, I was present when officers from the elite LAPD Metropolitan Division used a taser on a man threatening to jump from the roof of the Atani Hotel in downtown Los Angeles. When the officers failed to convince the jumper to step away from the edge of the roof, they shot him with the taser, hoping to disable him. He reacted by convulsing backwards and fell 280 feet to his death. I wondered then if the jumper would really have gone off the edge. The taser left no room for speculation; the man was dead.

I thought, if the taser was considered deadly force by LAPD, it would fall into the same classification as the so-called choke holds. In this scenario, if King were aggressive enough to tase, then he would be aggressive enough to choke, and the beating would then be unnecessary.

SKELETONS IN THE CLOSET

As Rodney King recuperated from his injuries, Lerman and I dealt with enormous amounts of information. Mayor Bradley held another press conference and promised a full investigation. Police Chief Daryl Gates announced, "The actions of these officers were inconsistent with the policies and procedures of the Los Angeles Police Department."

What a crock. The only policy they violated was they got caught. But Gates's statement went right to the heart of the legal issues in the King case. In order for King to successfully sue the city for damages, his attorney would have to convince a jury that the involved officers were poorly trained, poorly supervised, and that the established policies and procedures of the LAPD were responsible for the incident. Mean, nasty, out-of-control cops are great for headlines, but rogue officers would only help serve the city's interests. Discipline those cops and the problem is solved: bad cops aren't necessarily indicative of a bad system.

King and I became very close as we spent more time together. There were moments when this closeness made me feel ashamed of the way my partners and I had treated people on those rare occasions when we got bored. I came to realize Rodney King is not a violent man. King must have sensed a change in my attitude. One night, when we were in his apartment, King shared his single most frightening memory with me. "He told me I'd better run, cause he was gonna kill me."

I was shocked. King's comment came from out of nowhere. "Who? Who told you that?"

"The officer. The one with the taser."

"You mean Sergeant Koon?"

King waited for a moment. "I didn't want to tell you before. He said something like 'You better run now, nigger, cause we're gonna kill you!' That's when I tried to get up . . . tried to run away."

I reached for the phone to call Lerman but King grabbed my hand. "Please . . . don't tell Steve. Not yet. I'm afraid for my family. They know where we live."

"He'll have to know. I told you, I don't keep secrets from Steve," I reminded him. "That's an important piece of information. I've asked why you got up and you always said you couldn't remember. When did you recall this?"

"A couple of days ago. I was kicking back and thinking about the whole thing, you know, wondering why they didn't stop beating on me."

The whole world wanted to know the answer to that question. Why indeed? Officers own the streets and if someone needs an occasional reminder, it's their pleasure. The issues involved in the King incident go far beyond disciplining officers. Steve Lerman and I set out to prove that problems within the LAPD leading up to the beating were the real targets in King's civil suit. The fact that King ran from the officers, or that he may have resisted arrest, or even his parole status, had little to do with what the civil rights jury should consider.

King's attorney would have to convince that jury that conditions in the LAPD led up to the beating and that those conditions are systemic in nature: If a part is flawed, the whole is also flawed. Officer Laurence Powell best illustrates this theory.

Powell had been on the force for two-and-a-half years, with a rank of Training Officer. As such, he was charged with overseeing rookie officers. From my years of training police personnel, I've formed the opinion that until a cop has at least four years' experience, he is not knowledgeable enough himself to train a younger officer. Powell's partner, Timothy Wind, had *seven* years of previous police experience in Kansas. A fair question to ask then is, why was so inexperienced an officer training a more experienced recruit?

Powell is typical of the training-officer pool available. Street policing is not considered a choice assignment. Getting off the streets becomes a priority for cops with four to five years service. Assignments like vice or dope are sought after, leaving the streets to younger, less experienced officers. The more seniority and experience an officer acquires, the more likely he'll find an "inside" job and kiss the streets good-bye.

Another big problem for the LAPD has existed for decades. After the Watts riots in 1965, a commission was formed to look into the causes and recommend solutions to conditions contributing to unrest. The McCone Commission found racism throughout Los Angeles. I said it before—a city gets the police force it deserves. The McCone Commission report highlighted those areas where the LAPD could implement policies and procedures that would lessen community tensions. Remarkably enough, the Christopher Commission made many of the same recommendations some twenty-five years later.

Complaints from minority communities concerning excessive force or misconduct by LAPD officers increase every year, as does the number of judgements, settlements, and jury awards arising from litigation against the department. The city auditor's office in March 1991 specifically spoke to this issue. They reported that settlements awarded for police abuse and misconduct during the twelve months preceding March 1991 came to over eleven million dollars. The 1991 total was greater than all monies awarded in 1989 and 1990 combined. The figures for 1992 are expected to exceed 1991's by fifteen percent.

Of the 153 police abuse litigations examined by city auditors for their March 1991 report, only three officers were fired as a result of complaint investigations. One additional officer was removed after publication of the report for an act of misconduct that occurred during the review period. Only forty-four cases resulted in investigations and most of those involved officers that had previous personnel complaints against them. Assuming the data is accurate, the LAPD's enforcement policy is not cost-effective. We pay officers to do their jobs, then we pay citizens upon whom those officers did their jobs. Systemic.

In addition, over the years, increasing violence has made Los Angeles into a war zone. Police officers became soldiers, covering each others' backs. Former Department of Treasury agent George Wright, now a Professor of Criminal Justice at Santa Ana College, recently stated, "The primary goal of any paramilitary organization is to protect its leadership, and the LAPD is no different. Force was necessary to maintain control and respect for the badge, and the level of force used has increased."

I was still on the department when, in the eighties, tanklike battering rams were introduced. They slammed into crack houses, bashing down steel doors, behind which evidence was being flushed down toilets. Drug traffickers began using children with beepers to deliver their goods. Law enforcement reacted by stepping up their efforts to fight crime. As the criminals became more inventive, police became more violent in a war that could not be won, and the residents of South Central Los Angeles lost big. As L.A. goes, so goes the country.

The four officers accused in the Rodney King beating have families and plans for the future. They have hopes and dreams. They aren't monsters, but what they did in Lake View Terrace was monstrous and cannot be undone. Like many people charged with crimes, they were caught in the act, yet maintain their innocence. During the weeks that followed the beating, Owens & Associates obtained extensive background information on the four officers.

Timothy Wind was removed from the LAPD after the indictment. *Removed* is LAPD-talk for *fired*. At the time of the beating, Wind had been out of the police academy for only three months and was still on probation. He'd been working with Laurence Powell for less than a week.

Wind, a rookie on the LAPD, was in fact a veteran police officer. He received his basic police training from the University of Kansas Law Enforcement Training Academy in Hutchinson. After completing training, he worked for the Shawnee, Kansas, police department as a patrol officer.

Wind was known as "Timmy" to his fellow officers, who told me that he "always wanted to fit in." Shawnee police officers described him as a follower, not a leader, who wanted to be accepted by the more senior officers on the department. Timmy was liked by some, disliked by others. He always attended church on Sunday with his family, and was a "good husband and father."

But Timmy had a dark side. Officers with whom he had worked in Kansas told me of an incident they felt was indicative of his temperament. Wind and a partner were assigned to work a traffic accident in which a motorist was killed on the highway near Shawnee. After the field investigation was concluded, Wind and his partner went to the station to complete their reports on the accident. The widow of the driver had to be notified of her husband's death. Wind wanted to do it.

When he attempted to convince his partner, the senior officer, that he should call on the widow, they got into an argument. Wind allegedly threw a D-cell battery into his partner's face, injuring him. Fellow officers weren't surprised at his involvement in the King beating, and told me why: "Wind liked making those death notices. He got off on watching the grief of the next of kin."

Wind and his partner were disciplined after the altercation and shortly thereafter, Wind resigned from Shawnee because he "wanted to get to where the action was." He went to work for the Kansas City, Kansas, police department, then left in search of even more action. He found it on Foothill Boulevard in Lake View Terrace.

It later turned out that at least one of my sources was speaking out of both sides of his face. While in Kansas City conducting Wind's background investigation, I had difficulty in reaching an officer who had worked with Wind. I believed this witness was important because I'd read his comments in a local Kansas City newspaper. He finally returned my telephone call just a few days before I returned to L.A. He refused to meet with me in person but consented to talk to me on the phone, off the record, while he was taking a bath.

"So, let me get this straight," he said. "You're a former cop, now an investigator working for the lawyer representing Rodney King, and you're here doing a background investigation on Timmy?" His voice revealed his annoyance.

"Yeah, I just wanted to spend a few minutes with you before I headed back to L.A.," I replied.

"Well, I'll save you some time," he said. "I really like Tim

Wind, no matter what the papers said." We talked on for forty minutes while he lathered up and rinsed off. When the conversation was finished, he wasn't quite as strong in his support of Wind as he had first indicated to me.

Less than a week after my return to Los Angeles, I got a call from FBI agent, Dave Harris. "We hear you were in Kansas City last week." He was being his usual cryptic self.

"I needed to complete Wind's background. Why? What did you hear?"

"We got a call yesterday from our Kansas City office. Someone you talked to there called and complained about you. The complainant alleges you represented yourself as a police officer working on the King case, and wanted an official interview."

"Who's the complainant?" I asked, knowing the answer in advance.

"Sorry, I can't tell you that. You know our policy about releasing information."

"Well, what else did he say?" I wanted to know.

"Something about you harassing him while he was trying to take a shower or bath . . . wouldn't leave him alone."

"Dave, when he made his complaint to your Kansas City offices, was his mouth moving?"

"I suppose, why?"

"If his mouth was moving, he was lying," I replied, a little ticked. I told Harris the entire story, beginning with the officer's comments in the newspaper.

"I just wanted you to know we're getting calls on you," Harris stated. "For whatever it's worth."

I think in his own quiet way, Agent Harris was warning me about stirring the pot. Seems I'd touched a nerve, going to Kansas City, Tim Wind's home territory.

■

Laurence Powell comes from a family steeped in law enforcement tradition. Raised in the Los Angeles metropolitan area, he worked as a civilian court services officer and a reserve police officer before being accepted as a regular with LAPD. His father, a recently retired lieutenant with the marshall's office, served in many areas of Los Angeles County. The senior Powell and his wife have been lauded for their efforts in foster parenting of minority children.

Yet early in the investigation, a black female deputy marshall contacted me, telling me she had worked with Lieutenant Powell before he retired. She alleged she saw him wearing a ring similar to those worn by a racial hate group operating in the Lynwood section of Los Angeles County. According to the *Los Angeles Times*, this group of L.A. deputy sheriffs, called the Vikings, has been under investigation for several years. I could never confirm this information from a second source, but the deputy was very convincing. She showed me a caricature Lieutenant Powell had presented to her as a Christmas present. In it, she is depicted as an African tribal woman with a bone through her hair. The deputy said Lieutenant Powell laughed and thought it funny. Other female and minority workers under Lieutenant Powell's supervision were given similar Christmas gifts. While this doesn't make his son a racist, it speaks loudly to the mindset that may have been ingrained in Larry Powell's head years before George Holliday's camera lens came into focus on March 3, 1991.

Powell's encounter with Rodney King was not his first experience with allegations of excessive force. In 1989, while responding to a call for service, Officer Powell confronted Salvadore Castaneda on the street in midtown Wilshire Division. During the ensuing altercation, he broke the man's arm. Powell's actions resulted in a $70,000 settlement paid by the city, and an admission that Powell had used excessive force against Castaneda.

In his deposition regarding the incident, Castaneda's attorney asked Powell standard questions about his background and prior excessive force complaints. Powell, who was represented by Deputy City Attorney and retired LAPD Captain Don Vincent, displayed his attitude toward litigation when he replied, "That's none of your business. You've got no right to know that information."

Much to Attorney Vincent's credit, after Powell displayed this poor judgment towards Castaneda's attorney, Mr. Vincent took him out of the room for a short conference. When they returned, Powell appeared to have had an attitude adjustment. His answers were still short and vague, but his overt hostility ceased.

Powell's background is a major issue in the King case. If it can be shown that the City of Los Angeles and/or the Los Angeles Police Department had knowledge of a history of excessive force complaints against Powell and did nothing to interdict similar episodes, they are guilty of negligent retention (keeping an officer in place knowing he has a history of violence). This creates a direct link in liability to the city and reaches deep into the pockets of its taxpayers.

A third lawsuit, by a young Hispanic, alleging excessive force by Powell, is still unresolved as 9of this writing. I have also spoken with Mario Duran, the fourth person to allege excessive force by Powell. With public attention focused on Powell's actions in the King beating, a runaway verdict against the city in the case where Powell is named as a defendant could result.

None of this background information about Wind and Powell was known to the jurors in Simi Valley, though they were aware that Rodney King was an ex-con on parole. Advantage LAPD.

Could a more thorough background investigation by department recruiters have found any of what is reported here? The City will argue that the costs of such a background investigation for all applicants would be prohibitive, and they will be very convincing.

Sometimes, it is difficult to remember that policemen are people, too. They are hired to do a job that we know from past experience will burn them out. We work them overtime until they're exhausted, then we scrutinize their every move and are guilty of Monday morning quarterbacking. We cry with their families when an officer is injured or killed in the line of duty and think to ourselves, we don't pay them enough. Police officers, however, are and should be held to a higher standard. Citizens have the right to expect they will act within the law. Do we expect too much? The answer must be no.

■

Sergeant Stacey Koon is a fifteen year veteran street officer and supervisor. He holds two master's degrees and has served in some of the rougher areas of the city. In early 1991, Sergeant Koon, recently assigned to the Foothill Area of Los Angeles, supervised the mid-P.M. shift. It's well known in the department that this is where the rowdies are assigned. Mid-P.M. is by far the hardest working of all the shifts. The officers assigned to mid-P.M.s normally work the most overtime and spend the most time testifying in court. The busiest of the shifts, mid-P.M.s also account for a large number of personnel complaints.

I know all about the mid-P.M. watch. I had worked it many times as an officer in Central Division and in Watts. Somewhat rowdy myself, I spent a lot of time in court and received my share of personnel complaints.

Married, with five children, Koon's life has undergone a tremendous change since the beating. Most outspoken of the accused officers, he has steadfastly maintained Chief Daryl Gates let his officers down by not defending them more strongly. He has often called for the chief's resignation.

While on suspension without pay awaiting the criminal trials, Koon was employed to perform swimming pool maintenance and wrote a book, originally entitled *The Ides of March* that defines his unique perception of the King beating. In his manuscript, a copy of which I acquired, Koon accepts full responsibility for the actions of his officers at the scene. He writes with absolute conviction that he followed LAPD procedures to the letter. The most chilling aspect is that, according to Koon, departmental guidelines allowed for the amount of force used in the King arrest.

Koon describes Internal Affairs investigators as henchmen and writes very candidly about their desire to make him a scapegoat. On one hand, he accepts responsibility, but on the other, no way. Like every good soldier, Koon followed orders. Like every good soldier, Koon covered for his men. But when the time came for him to fall on his sword for the LAPD, Koon started writing his side of the story. When his book was released in October of 1992, the name had been changed to *Presumed Guilty*. The title, which had first been used in the sixties on a book about John Kennedy's assassination, was also used in 1991 by Ohio investigative reporter Martin Yant. In one of the many ironic twists of this case the *Los Angeles Times* referred to Yant's book in articles about the King beating.

Koon's original manuscript refers to George Holliday as "George of the Jungle" and Rodney King as a "Mandingo warrior." Those references do not appear in the published book.

■

Ted Briseno and violence are not strangers. I located his former wife, Cindy, now remarried and living in another state, who described Ted as violent since they were sweethearts in high school. They married after he graduated from Mattoon High School in Mattoon, Illinois. Shortly thereafter she became pregnant with their first child, Angie.

Cindy told me life was not easy for them. Ted began to drink. He'd stay out till all hours of the night and when he returned home, would fight with her. She described one argument they had in which Briseno hit her on the left side of her face, rupturing her left ear drum. The injury still plagues her to this day; she has only partial hearing in that ear.

Despite their arguments, Cindy became pregnant a second time. Ted decided they should move to California to be near his brother Mike, who was then a Santa Ana Police Officer. Cindy and Ted lived near the Orange County airport and continued to fight while Ted worked at Hunt-Wesson Foods in Buena Park, near Knott's Berry Farm. Then came the incident that was to cause the breakup of their marriage.

Cindy began to weep as she told me of the fear and violence that had filled their home. While Ted and his brother, Mike, watched a program on television, Angie and one of Mike's young children were playing. They began to fight over a toy and after several minutes, Ted snatched his daughter by the scruff of her collar and flung her against the living room wall. On that day, Cindy left Ted.

Some months later, while the divorce was pending, Cindy was in bed late at night when Briseno kicked in her front door without warning and came crashing into her bedroom, waving a gun. She later learned that he had been hired by the LAPD and that the gun he threatened her with was a city-issued service revolver. He pointed it at her ear and told her that if he had caught her with a man in her bed, he would have shot them both.

Then began a custody battle for the kids. Ted alleged that Cindy was unfit, while Cindy claimed he was violent and that she didn't trust him with the children. A report on Ted Briseno, completed by the Orange County Probation Department, was ordered sealed by the Court. Custody of the children was awarded to Cindy. After the divorce, she moved her family out of California to protect them from her ex-husband.

Through Cindy, I was able to interview her daughter Angie, also living in another state and a mother herself. She recalled the incident in the family living room. She spoke of her father in the past tense, saying she feels he no longer cares about her, as evidenced by this failure to attempt any communication with her or her brother.

"My dad has lied to me so many times that I don't believe a word he says anymore. He says that he will send some Christmas presents for my daughter [his grandchild] but then he doesn't send a thing. It's like it was when I was a kid. He'll say anything to make you happy, but then he lets you down. He's a liar."

She described an incident that occurred when she and her brother were living in Los Angeles for the summer with their father. The two siblings had been arguing and were sent to their rooms as punishment. When they said they were thirsty, Briseno told them they could not have a drink of water. They drank from the toilet. Angie was clearly upset and angry as she told me this type of treatment continued until they returned to their mother at the end of the summer. She told me her father appears to treat the children from his second marriage differently; he seems to be more caring and giving with them.

Cindy is still attempting to collect more than $25,000 in back child support from Ted Briseno but is getting little assistance from the LA County District Attorney's Deadbeat Dad unit. Cindy raised Ted's kids without him and without any support. When he was working for LAPD, Cindy tried to garnish 25% of his pay on her court judgment, but the D.A.'s Office was unable to collect because by that time Briseno had been suspended without pay.

In a December 1991 telephone conversation over child support, Briseno told Cindy, "If you knew this guy King like the rest of us, you would know why he deserved that beating." There is no indication Ted Briseno ever met King prior to the night of the incident at Lake View Terrace. His comment to Cindy also indicates he feels no remorse.

Like Powell, Briseno has a history of personnel complaints. In 1987, he was suspended for sixty-six days without pay after he beat and kicked an arrestee. The average suspension runs

Name, Address and Telephone Number of Attorney(s)

CHARLES GARRITY
MARIANNE C. PALMER
Attorneys at Law
611 West 17th Street
Santa Ana, CA 92706

Attorney(s) for _____ Petitioner

Space Below for Use of Court Clerk Only

FILED

JAN 11 1979

_____ County Clerk

_____ Deputy

SUPERIOR COURT OF CALIFORNIA, COUNTY OF _____ ORANGE

In re the marriage of

Petitioner: CYNTHIA S. BRISENO
and
Respondent: THEODORE J. BRISENO

CASE NUMBER D 15-36-85

ORDER TO SHOW CAUSE (MARRIAGE)*
CHILD SUPPORT, ATTORNEY'S FEES,
COSTS, INJUNCTIVE ORDERS,
OTHER ORDERS.

_____ BLANKS HEREWITH SERVED UPON YOU
MUST BE COMPLETED AND FILED AT THE HEARING

TO: _____ Respondent THEODORE J. BRISENO
_____
(PETITIONER/RESPONDENT/OTHER [Specify] AND NAME)

You are ordered to appear in this court,

located at 700 Civic Center Drive West, Santa Ana, California
(STREET ADDRESS AND CITY)

on 1-25-79 at 1:45 M., Department 36 to give any legal reason why certain
(DATE)   (TIME)

orders requested by Petitioner, CYNTHIA S. BRISENO should not be made
(PETITIONER/RESPONDENT AND NAME)

by this court as set forth in the attached REQUEST FOR ORDER AND DECLARATION, to which is attached:

Financial Declaration

Pending a hearing in this matter, the court further orders: No known opposing counsel.

Respondent is restrained and enjoined from:

1. Harassing, annoying, molesting, harming or otherwise bothering
petitioner in any manner whatsoever;

2. Transferring, selling, hypothecating, encumbering or in any way
disposing of any of the community, quasi-community or separate property
of the parties, except in the ordinary course of business or for
necessities of life; or from taking or removing the 1975 Chevrolet Monte
Carlo motor vehicle from the possession of petitioner.

Dated _____ 1/11/79

_____
_____ Judge of the Superior Court

* Indicate nature of orders requested and, if modification, so indicate by inserting "RE MODIFICATION."

Form Adopted by Rule 1285.10 of
Judicial Council of California
Effective January 1, 1972

ORDER TO SHOW CAUSE (MARRIAGE)

© 0142-235.2

In addition to the ex parte orders requested herein, petitioner requests
that she be awarded exclusive use of the 1975 Chevrolet Monte Carlo
motor vehicle;

At the time of the hearing, petitioner requests that respondent show
cause if any he has why he should not be ordered to vacate the family
rental residence at _____ West Baker St., Costa Mesa, California, and
why petitioner should not be awarded exclusive occupancy of said
residence;

Petitioner is a competent person to be awarded the care, custody and
control of the minor children, but she is without sufficient funds to
properly care for and support said children, or to pay attorney's fees
and costs, and she requests that respondent be ordered to pay reasonable
child support, attorney's fees and court costs herein,

Petitioner requests of this court an order restraining respondent from
removing the minor children of the parties from the 7 southern counties
of the State of California.

DECLARATION

I am the petitioner herein, and I am fearful that unless restrained,
respondent will harrass, annoy, molest, harm and bother me, and will
dispose of community property of the parties, to the detriment of the
community.

On Friday, January 5, 1979, respondent grabbed my arm and slammed me into
a motor vehicle, badly bruising my right elbow and used verbal abuse and
profanity in the presence of our minor children. In the past, respondent
has broken my ear drum, bruised my face and choked me and threatened to
kill me.

Since coming to California last summer, I have been employed at ITT Cannon
and the 1975 Chevrolet Monte Carlo motor vehicle is my sole means of
transportation to and from my employment, to and from the childrens' baby
sitter, the grocery store and laundromat, etc. Respondent is employed at
Hunt Wesson Foods and he is in a car pool each day with his sister-in-law.
When she does not go to work, he takes her car. On January 5, 1979,
respondent removed said motor vehicle, but has now returned it to me, and
I am fearful that unless restrained, when he is served with these moving
papers, he will again take the car from me, preventing me from going to work.

I declare under penalty of perjury that the foregoing, including any attachments, is true and correct and that this
declaration was executed on _____ JANUARY 10, 1979 _____ at _____ Santa Ana _____ California.

_____ Cynthia S. Briseno
(Signature)

CYNTHIA S. BRISENO
(Type/print name)

ATTACH (OR INSERT ABOVE) REQUIRED SUPPORTING INFORMATION.

A declaration under penalty of perjury must be executed within California. An affidavit is required if executed outside California.

ten to twenty-two days, e.g. two weeks to a month. Briseno's three-month suspension well exceeds the norm. This incident was widely reported after the King story broke. Another allegation arising from the same complaint but less widely reported provides additional background. An article in the *Daily Journal*, a Los Angeles legal community newspaper, stated Briseno was also charged with attempting to have his rookie partner lie for him in an effort to cover up his misconduct. Briseno's past violence was kept from the Simi Valley jury.

On August 28, 1992, Briseno appeared on Larry King's talk show on CNN. He answered several questions from viewers and described how difficult life had become for him since the beating. He told the nationwide audience of his home life and that his new wife and seventy-three-year-old mother-in-law must now work to support him. Millions of viewers listened intently and undoubtedly felt genuine sympathy for him.

His first wife Cindy and the children he forgot saw him tell his story. They, like the unflinching Holliday video, have judged him on his actions. On October 1, 1992, *Inside Edition* aired a short interview with Cindy and Briseno's daughter, Angie. They described Ted as a deadbeat dad who had forgotten them, and they presented documentation to back up their claim. Briseno's new attorney, Harlan Braun, refused to allow *Inside Edition* to interview Ted, but when Cindy was in Los Angeles for the interview, she called Ted while he was on a radio talk show. She confronted him on the air with his forgotten obligations. Attorney Braun immediately demanded the phone call be taken off the air and the conversation ended.

Now comes the big question: How is it that *I* was able to acquire this background information in a short time and with limited resources, though it was apparently unknown to the LAPD when they hired Ted Briseno? If it *was* known to the department, why was he hired? Information like this must be discovered and considered if the department hopes to decrease incidents of excessive force in the future.

Some question remains as to the number of officers present at the scene of King's beating. We've counted thirty-one at the location at various times during the incident. In addition to the four defendant officers, the following officers were present. LAPD: Officers David O. Avila, Timothy E. Blake, Susan J. Clemmer, Paul R. Gebhardt, Christopher J. Hajduk, Glen King,

Ingrid Larson, David A. Love, Joseph Napolitano, Paul Nelson, Kenneth A. Phillippe, Danny Shry, Robert J. Simpach, Rolando Solano, Louis Turriaga, Russell Graybill, and Danny Gonzales. Los Angeles Unified School District: Paul Beauregard and Mark Diamond. California Highway Patrol: Tim Singer, Melanie Singer, Gabriel Aid, and Frank Schultz.

All the above officers are named as defendants in the civil case of King vs. the City of Los Angeles, et al. Several have had previous involvement in similar incidents. The most widely known involved Robert Simpach. In the early 1980s, Simpach was working in the Foothill area of Los Angeles when he became involved in a confrontation with a Thomas Mincie, Jr., who lived in the area. Officer Simpach tried to arrest Mincie and an altercation ensued. After his arrest, Mincie was taken to Foothill Station and booked. He died at the station shortly thereafter. An autopsy determined he had been choked during the altercation and his trachea was crushed. No criminal charges were ever filed against Simpach but the Mincie family filed a civil suit against the City of Los Angeles, which was later settled out of court for $900,000. Simpach, still on the job, watched Rodney King get beaten.

I reviewed case after case involving excessive force. L.A. is not alone. In every major city in the country, citizens are seriously injured and killed by law enforcement officers sworn to protect.

■

Like the defendant officers, Rodney King came to the party that night with his own baggage. Fairness dictates I examine King's background also.

The accused officers and the media made many references to King's soiled background. It's widely known King was on parole for robbery when the beating occurred. This very situation caused Lerman and me many concerns in the wake of the incident. Our biggest fear was that the California Department of Corrections would violate King's parole and order him back into custody. A question which many people still ask is, why didn't he get sent back to the slammer?

The fact is that King was never charged for any crimes arising from his actions on the night of the beating. That's not

```
 1  STEVEN A. LERMAN & ASSOCIATES
    9100 Wilshire Blvd, Suite 250 West
 2  Beverly Hills, California 90212
    Tel: (███) ███-████
 3
    Attorneys for Plaintiff,
 4  RODNEY GLENN KING
 5
 6              UNITED STATES DISTRICT COURT
 7            CENTRAL DISTRICT OF CALIFORNIA
 8
    RODNEY GLENN KING,            )  Case No: 91 2497(JGD)(TX)
 9                                )
              Plaintiff,          )  FIRST AMENDED COMPLAINT
10                                )  FOR VIOLATION OF CIVIL
                                  )  RIGHTS UNDER COLOR OF
11                                )  STATE LAW (42 U.S.C.
    v.                            )  SECTIONS 1981, 1983,
12                                )  1985); DEMAND FOR
    THE CITY OF LOS ANGELES and THE LOS )  JURY TRIAL
13  ANGELES POLICE DEPARTMENT; THE LOS )
    ANGELES UNIFIED SCHOOL DISTRICT; )
14  MAYOR TOM BRADLEY; CHIEF OF POLICE )
    DARYL F. GATES; ASSISTANT CHIEF OF )
15  POLICE ROBERT VERNON; LOS ANGELES )
    POLICE OFFICERS CAPTAIN JOHN MUTZ, )
16  LIEUTENANT P.J. CONMAY, SERGEANT )
    JOHN DOE FLORES, SERGEANT STACY KOON, )
17  SERGEANT ROBERT TROUTT, DAVID O. )
    AVILA, TIMOTHY E. BLAKE, THEODORE )
18  BRISENO, SUSAN J. CLEMMER, PAUL R. )
    GEBHARDT, CHRISTOPHER J. HADJI, )
19  GLEN KING, INGRID LARSON, DAVID A. )
    LOVE, JOSEPH NAPOLITANO, PAUL NELSON, )
20  KENNETH A. PHILLIPPE, LAURENCE M. )
    POWELL, DANNY SHRY, ROBERT J. SIMPACH, )
21  ROLANDO SOLANO, LOUIS M. TURRIAGA )
    and TIMOTHY WIND; CALIFORNIA HIGHWAY )
22  PATROL OFFICERS CAPTAIN DENNIS TRUMAN, )
    LIEUTENANT JOHN KIELBASA, SERGEANT )
23  ROMAN VONDRISKA, GABRIEL AID, FRANK )
    SCHULTZ, MELANIE SINGER and TIMOTHY )
24  SINGER; LOS ANGELES UNIFIED SCHOOL )
    DISTRICT OFFICERS PAUL BEAUREGARD and )
25  MARK DIAMOND; and DOES 1 through 200, )
              Defendants.          )
26  _____)
27
28
```

to say there wasn't merit in charging King. After all, he did flee
the police and, as he later admitted in his testimony during the
federal trial in downtown Los Angeles was probably driving
under the influence. Indeed, after several conversations with
King's parole officers, we learned that only on rare occasions is
a parolee violated for low-grade misdemeanor offenses. In Los
Angeles, as in too many other cities across the nation, King
could have plea-bargained his offenses down to lesser charges
for which he need not have served any additional days beyond
his stay at the hospital jail ward. In that respect, King is no
different from any other person arrested.

Another issue arising from King's arrest is, how could the
state prosecute a victim, once his victimization was so widely
known? In this scenario, officers charged with beating King
would have to take the stand to testify against him. A jury could
infer malice in the officers' testimony because of the arrest, and
the charges pending against them.

Lastly, in considering whether or not to charge King for
offenses committed during the incident, it's important to recall
that once King is charged, he is entitled to every report completed by the arresting officers in preparing his defense. Could
the district attorney or the city attorney have any reasons for
not wanting King to have access to all reports related to his
arrest, reports which could later be used in his civil case against
the very officers who arrested him? Getting those reports
months to years in advance of his civil case would give bonus
time to prepare his litigation, and could have put the City at a
distinct disadvantage. Even with all the materials I've already
collected on behalf of King, I believe that there are still possibly
thousands of pages written by investigators and attorneys that
I don't yet have.

That issue aside, the robbery for which King actually served
time merits some discussion. The incident occurred in the fall
of 1989, at a small stop-and-rob in Monterey Park, California.
In his complaint to the police, the Korean store owner alleged
King assaulted him when he refused to allow King to pay for
cigarettes and a soda with food stamps. He told the police King
got angry, threw the food stamps down on the counter, opened
the cash register and removed money. While King was attempting to flee, the store owner tried to stop him by grabbing a tire
iron from under the counter. He says King pushed him down,

ran from the store, and got into his car, the same Hyundai he was driving on the night of the beating. King then drove away, but was arrested days later. The store owner had gotten the license number of the Hyundai and gave it to the police.

Following his arraignment, King pled guilty to a lesser charge on advice of the public defender and was sentenced to two years at a conservation work camp fighting brush fires. King eventually spent one year in custody and was released on parole in November 1990.

Prior to that arrest, King had had several encounters with police and sheriffs but was not arrested for any felonies. King's arrest record, though serious following his plea in the robbery case, is not the arrest history painted by the defendant officers. What it does show is King's consistent lack of good sense and sound judgment.

■

I believe it's also fair to look at my disciplinary background while I was an officer. During my early years on the department, I received several complaints for excessive force or official misconduct. On one occasion, I was given four days of unpaid duty (a form of unofficial suspension) for stepping on the hand of an arrestee as he lay on the ground following my use of the infamous choke hold. I didn't want to take the guy to jail, so I didn't cuff the guy once I choked him out. As he awakened, he began to hit my ankle with his fist, so to stop him, I stepped on his wrist, pinning it to the ground. I thought it ironic at the time, that if I'd defended myself by striking the suspect with my baton for hitting me, I'd have gotten only a warning for not cuffing the suspect. But because I chose instead to handle it less aggressively, I was disciplined. Oh, well . . . Guilty! Book 'em Danno, murder one!

Did I ever hit someone who didn't deserve it? Yes. Did I ever make an arrest where lesser actions could have worked just as well? Yes. Did I ever kick down a door without a warrant? Yes. Do I regret any of those incidents? Some. Have I learned anything from those incidents? Maybe, but I never, nor did any of the old salts who trained me, beat a suspect once he or she was controlled, like what we saw on the Holliday video in Lake View Terrace.

Mea culpa!

THE STEALTH HYUNDAI

A week after the beating, I heard about a California Highway Patrol audio tape of radio broadcasts by Officers Tim and Melanie Singer during their chase after King's Hyundai. A media source gave me a dubbed copy of the tape in exchange for a story on Lerman's reaction to it. With that trade-off, media manipulation became a two way street. The CHP pursuit tape provided the first specific information about King's route during the chase and the time sequences needed to calculate his speed throughout the pursuit.

Once we had the tape, Lerman told me to fire off letters to the CHP and LAPD requesting copies of the tape for our use. We used deceptions like this to keep the cops and their attorneys off guard and disinformed of the specifics of what we had and how we got it. I followed up the letters with telephone calls to the CHP in Sacramento and to Commander Rick Dinse, Chief Gates's point man in the King incident. My calls to Commander Dinse failed to get any action, though he had a tough time explaining why the media had the pursuit tapes for publication and we couldn't get them to assist in our investigative efforts.

Blue Throat let me know my calls generated many exchanges between Dinse and Linda Lefkowitz, his liaison in the City Attorney's office. Our strategy kept them on their toes and made me a real pain to the LAPD brass hats. That gave me great pleasure—I cannot tell a lie.

By knowing the locations Tim Singer broadcast during the chase and the precise time it took King to drive between those locations, I computed King's aggregate speed. With the Singer's tape in hand, I drove out to Lake View Terrace where the 210 freeway crosses the Paxton off-ramp and adjusted the speed of my car to match the locations Tim Singer called out on the audio tape. I drove the route, measuring the exact distances between locations mentioned on the tape. I made three passes through the circuit. Each time, results were the same. King's average speed during the "high speed chase" on surface streets was less than 45 MPH, allowing for stops and turns as broadcast by Tim Singer.

A message transmitted by the CHP dispatch center a few minutes after King was in custody provides a clue to what I believe is vital neglected information. The message reports, "All units. For information only. A citizen reports a 23152 (drunk driver) left six (minutes) ago, eastbound on the 118 (Simi Valley Freeway) from Paxton. Suspect vehicle is described as a white Pontiac TransAm with no headlights on, driving in all traffic lanes. All units . . . for information only . . ."

I drove to the spot where Melanie Singer said she had stopped her patrol car to write a traffic citation. I proceeded a half-mile along the 210 freeway to the Sunland Avenue exit, which she said she used to "ramp" the Hyundai. *Ramping* is a CHP term meaning exiting an off-ramp, then immediately reentering the on-ramp to get behind a motorist. This allows the officers to pace the violator's speed from behind, a requirement in most traffic tickets written for excessive or unsafe speed.

CHP Officer Melanie Singer initially said and later testified in Simi Valley that after writing the ticket, as she was pulling back into the traffic lanes of the 210 freeway, she looked in her rearview mirror and saw, "A light-colored vehicle with bright headlights approaching from the rear at speeds estimated to be in excess of 110 MPH. Wanting to get behind the violator, I exited the freeway at Sunland, then reentered and saw the light-colored vehicle quite a distance ahead. I could see the taillights as I began to chase the vehicle. My speedometer showed 115 MPH and the car ahead of me appeared to be pulling away."

Using her description, I too exited the freeway at Sunland and within yards, lost sight of the freeway traffic passing above on my left. There it was! The pursuing CHP officers *lost sight* of the speeding "light-colored vehicle with bright headlights" during their entire ramping process. I continued to the stop-light at the base of the off-ramp. The freeway was twenty feet above. Turning left, I drove 250 feet, where I turned right onto the on-ramp. I couldn't see any traffic on the freeway until I had driven another 250 feet up the ramp. Then, the first thing I saw was the sign indicating the Wheatland Avenue off-ramp, exactly one mile ahead.

A car driving 110 miles per hour travels just under two miles in one minute. For at least forty-seven seconds, Officers Singer and Singer lost sight of the suspect car while they transitioned through the off- and on-ramps. This time lapse could allow the speeding car to travel far enough to exit at Wheatland, sit under the freeway waiting for the officers to pass overhead, then reenter and take the 118 freeway at the Paxton interchange, turning headlights off to help remain undetected, or because the intoxicated driver had cut the lights under the freeway and simply forgot to turn them back on. Certainly, a Pontiac TransAm is capable of 110 MPH.

D.A. Terry White and his investigator, Mike Gillum scoffed when I told them my theory. Regardless, a good case could be made that the CHP officers were chasing the wrong car and everything that followed was unnecessary.

My wife, Pat, found another problem with Melanie Singer's statement. The officer said she saw a "light-colored vehicle with bright headlights" in her rearview mirror. As any person who has driven at night knows, it's impossible to see the color of a car behind its "bright headlights." When I tried looking into bright lights through my rearview mirror at night, I couldn't tell if a car was light or dark.

On March 11, 1991, just eight days after the beating, a Los Angeles County Grand Jury was convened. During four days of closed-door testimony, twenty-two private citizens heard evidence that LAPD Sergeant Stacey Koon and Officers Laurence Powell, Theodore Briseno, and Timothy Wind had used excessive force during the arrest of Rodney Glen King, then tried to

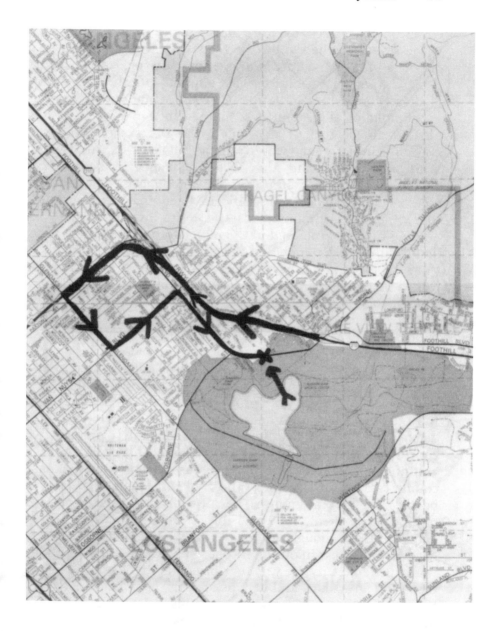

cover up the attack by filing false police reports. Fourteen witnesses were called to testify. Consistent with all grand jury hearings, no defense to the allegations was presented by the defendants and no spectators were allowed in the hearing room. Media reported that indictments would come within days of the completion of the hearings. Time seemed to drag on. Everyone sat and waited. It was solely the D.A.'s show, and the expected indictments would signal District Attorney Terry White and his associate, Alan Yochelson had performed well.

Literally within hours after the announcement of indictments against the defendant officers, I acquired a transcript of the witnesses' testimony. This was quite a coup considering nothing would be released to the public for ten days. It was our first documentary evidence of the official version of the incident from the bystander officers' point-of-view. Most important, it locked in their testimony. Any changes after the Grand Jury would be too hard to explain.

The officers should have begun their testimony with, "Once upon a time." As I read through the pages, I highlighted areas where I knew witnesses were fudging or incorrect. I would address those issues in the following weeks and months.

Once the indictments were handed down, our civil case of Rodney King v. the City of Los Angeles was put on hold pending the outcome of a criminal trial against the officers. Their defense rightfully argued they couldn't adequately prepare two concurrent defenses at the same time. While I agreed with them and understood their assertions, I was disappointed our case couldn't go forward. Besides, the civil case wasn't expected to be filed for several months because of legal considerations beyond our control. We knew the criminal indictments were helpful to us, though guilty verdicts were not necessarily needed for success in our civil case. Of course, George Holliday was called to testify. He was very brief and to the point. He told the grand jurors how and why he shot the video and confirmed his sale of the tape to television stations in Los Angeles. When he was finished, his video tape of the beating was admitted into evidence.

Officer Melanie Singer had quite a bit to say. She stuck with her story that the speed of the Hyundai exceeded 110 MPH. I kept reading the transcript, waiting for Terry White to challenge her on the speed issue, but he never did. I found this strange, considering Hyundai manufacturers were already denying publicly that their car was capable of such speeds.

Singer testified that after exiting the freeway, the Hyundai stopped at Foothill and Paxton, then drove on to Glenoaks where they were joined by the two school cops, who stayed with them until they finally stopped at the pursuit termination point in front of Holliday's apartment. Melanie Singer said at that time she didn't feel King posed a threat. When the pursuit stopped, she saw cops everywhere. As King placed his hands on the roof of the car, the helicopter was already there. She said King looked up and smiled at the helicopter and began to wave and move around on his feet, like he was dancing. She said he was laughing "like a smirk, smirking." King then went partially down on his hands and knees but wouldn't go down all the way.

In fact, every civilian witness said exactly the opposite. King did as he was told. He complied with the officers' commands until they started to beat him. My thoughts flashed for a second to the Holliday video where from the opening shots King is seen lying in a full prone position surrounded on three sides by ten to fifteen officers. Singer failed to mention this fact to the grand jurors. Considering her other statements about the evening's events, this was certainly no surprise. I thought her inconsistencies would eventually have a negative effect on her overall value as a witness.

I noted she made no mention of a three-page memo she had completed after returning to her station following the incident, which differs greatly from her grand jury testimony. I had gotten the memo from a media source and reread a few sentences to compare it to her testimony: "The Sergeant then fired one more stun gun cartridge into the body of the subject. The subject then dropped to his knees. It was then that Officer Powell struck the subject *in the face and head several times* as the subject fell to the ground."

Rodney King had told me that his seat belt yanked him back into the car as he started to get out, but no mention was made of that.

I knew from my own past experiences how officers might tense up when a suspect made any kind of jerky movements in an already stressful situation. That may explain the fear displayed by the officers immediately after King stopped and

State of California

Business, Transportation and Housing Agen

Memorandum

To *VERDUGO HILLS*

Date : 3-4-91

File No.:

Subject : *PURSUIT*
TURN OVER TO L.A.P.D.

From : Department of California Highway Patrol

VERDUGO HILLS

ON MARCH 3, 1991 @ 0040 HRS. MY PARTNER T.J. SINGER #9301 AND MYSELF ENCOUNTERED A HIGH SPEED VEHICLE W/B I-210 BTWN SUNLAND AND SR-118 WITH SPEEDS UP TO 115 MPH.

AFTER THE EMERGENCY LIGHTS WERE ACTIVATED ON THE SUBJ. VEHICLE (S/V) @ W/B I-210 JUST E. OF SR-118 THE S/V SLOWED YET FAILED TO RESPOND OR YIELD TO OUR PATROL VEHICLE EMERGENCY LIGHTS AND SIREN.

THE S/V EXITED THE FWY @ PAXTON ST. AND CONTINUED S/B STILL NOT RESPONDING TO OUR LIGHTS OR SIREN. THE S/V THEN CONTINUED S/B ON PAXTON ST. RUNNING LIGHTS @ FOOTHILL, GLENOAKS, VAN NUYS AND ONCE MORE @ FOOTHILL BLVD, AS THE S/V MADE AN ATTEMPT TO EVADE US ON THE SURFACE STREETS.

DUE TO NO AVAILABLE C.H.P UNITS BEING AVAILABLE FOR BACK UP. ASSISTANCE WAS REQUESTED FOR AN ADDITIONAL UNI FROM L.A.P.D.

IT WAS @ GLENOAKS BLVD AND VAN NUYS THAT "1" L.A.P.D WAS OBSERVED TO BE IN THE FAILURE TO YIELD - PURSUIT AND BEHIND OUR PATROL UNIT.

THE S/V THEN CONTINUED N/B ON VAN NUYS TO FOOTHILL BLVD., MADE A RT (E/B) AND CONTINUED TO OSBORNE ST.

CHP 81 (REV. 3-81)

State of California—Business, Transportation and Housing Agency   **GEORGE DEUKMEJIAN, Governor**

DEPARTMENT OF CALIFORNIA HIGHWAY PATROL

Pg. 2 of 1

WHERE THE S/U RAN THE RED LIGHT AND THEN SLOWED AND PULLED TO THE SHOULDER OF FOOTHILL BLVD. JUST S/O OSBORNE. IT WAS THEN THAT I OBSERVED 6 L.A.P.D UNITS. ATTEMPTS TO GET THE DRIVER OUT WITH FELONY PROCEDURES WERE UNEVENTFUL AS THE DRIVER EXITED AS ADVISED BUT WOULD NOT COMPLY WITH THE ORDERS DIRECTED TOWARDS HIM.

AS THE SUBJ. EXITED, THE SUBJ. APPEARED RATHER JOVIAL AND HAPPY, AS HE WAVED TO THE HELICOPTER AND SMILED TO THE OFFICERS THAT WERE DIRECTING HIM TO LIE FACE DOWN ON THE GROUND. IT WASN'T UNTIL SEVERAL MINUTES LATER THAT THE SUBJ. COMPLIED, STILL SMILING AND LAUGHING. I WAS PREPARING TO ADVANCE TOWARDS THE DRIVER WHEN L.A.P.D SGT. KOON ADVISED ME THAT THEY WOULD HANDLE. OFFICER POWELL OF L.A.P.D FOOTHILL DIVISION MADE AN ATTEMPT TO PLACE HANDCUFFS ON THE SUBJ. IN THIS PRONE POSITION AND AS HE DID SO, THE SUBJ BECAME RESISTANT AND BEGAN TO SWING HIS ARMS AND KICK HIS LEGS. OFFICER POWELL, BACKED AWAY AS SGT. KOON ADVISED THE SUBJ. TO HALT OR HE WOULD USE THE "STUNGUN", THE SUBJ. DID NOT COMPLY, BUT KEPT KICKING THE OTHER OFFICERS (UNKNOWN) AND PUNCHING THOSE THAT GOT CLOSE TO PUT CONTROL HOLDS ON THE SUBJEct. THE SGT. FROM L.A.P.D. THEN ORDERED THE SUBJ. TO COMPLY, BUT THE SUBJ. REFUSED. THE SGT. THEN ADVISED HIS OFFICERS TO BACK AWAY. THE SGT. THEN F₁ THE "STUN GUN" @ THE SUBJ. STRIKING THE SUBJ. ON HIS BACK. THE SUBJ. THEN BECAME ALMOST VIOLENT NOT FALTERING @ ALL IN HIS STEPS, BUT CONTINUED TO TAKE SWINGS @ THE OFFICERS. THE SGT. THEN FIRED ONE MORE "STUN GUN" CARTRIDGE INTO THE

State of California—Business, Transportation and Housing Agency   **GEORGE DEUKMEJIAN, Governor**

DEPARTMENT OF CALIFORNIA HIGHWAY PATROL

PG. 3 OF 1.

BODY OF THE SUBJ. THE SUBJ. THEN DROPPED, TO HIS
KNEES. IT WAS THEN THAT OFFICER POWELL STRUCK
THE SUBJ. IN THE FACE AND HEAD WITH HIS BATON
SEVERAL TIMES AS THE SUBJ. FELL TO THE GROUND.
THE SUBJ. WAS THEN PLACED UNDER ARREST. THE
PASSENGERS (FREDDIE HELMS RT. FRONT)(BRYANT ALLEN RT. REAR)
COMPLIED WITH THE FELONY PROCEDURES AND WERE TAKEN
OUT OF THE S/U ON THE RT SIDE WITHOUT ANY INCIDENT.
THEY WERE LATER RELEASED, WHEN THEY PRODUCED
PROPER I.D AND WHEN IT WAS KNOWN THAT THE
VEHICLE WAS NOT STOLEN.
L.A.P.D THEN REQUESTED AN AMBULANCE FOR THE
DRIVER WHO SUSTAINED INJURY DURING HIS RESISTANT
ALTERCATION. HE WAS THEN TRANSPORTED TO PACIFICA
HOSPITAL WHERE SGT. KOON OF L.A.P.D. FOOTHILL DIVISION
ADVISED ME THAT DUE TO THE SUBJ.'S INJURIES THAT
HIS DEPT. WOULD HANDLE TO ITS CONCLUSION.
THE OFFICERS THAT I WAS ABLE TO OBTAIN NAMES WERE:
L.A.P.D OFFICER SOLANO # 27647
         OFFICER POWELL # 25440
         OFFICER WIND # 27745
         OFFICER CLEMMER # 26950
         OFFICER HAJDUK # 27600
       -OFFICER SHRY # 26001
THERE WERE ALSO 2 L.A. UNIFIED SCHOOL DISTRICT POLICE
OFFICERS PRESENT, OFFICER PAUL J, BEAUREGARD AND MARK
DIAMOND. DR. MANCIA TREATED THE DRIVER IN RM # 2 OF
THE EMERGENCY RM. FOR HIS INJURIES.

MELANIE C. SINGER STATE TRAFFIC OFFICER #12/03

Melanie A. Singer STO 12/03

could have contributed to the initial levels of force Powell and Wind displayed when they started the beating.

In her memo, Officer Singer wrote that King punched officers who tried to get close to him, while to the Grand Jury she said King was mostly compliant. It occurred to me that differences between her testimony and the memo existed because at the time she wrote the memo, she didn't know there was a video camera trained on the incident, and her allegations were made only to protect her fellow officers. When confronted by the video she became fearful of a perjury allegation and changed her view of what had happened. I still can't fully account for White's decision not to use the Singer memo in Simi Valley except that it would have shown the inconsistency and that would make her entire testimony useless. White needed Melanie Singer's statement that Powell hit King in the face with his baton to win convictions against the officers. I also believe her testimony alleging 110 MPH on the Hyundai made her not believable to the jury. Terry White should have put more trust in that jury to see the truth.

Her memo also gave us the names of three additional officers present at the incident which we had not known before. I now understand there is at least one additional memo by Melanie Singer which I still haven't seen, and it contradicts the first memo. Go figure.

The Singers were working under the supervision of CHP Sergeant Roman Vondriska on the morning of March 3, 1991. (Remember the name, it will appear again later.) A few minutes after the incident concluded, Tim Singer talked to Sergeant Vondriska over their car radios. The CHP pursuit audio tape gave me a clue into this conversation. When Singer told him there had been an altercation during the arrest of King, Vondriska advised Singer to call him on the phone at Burbank Police Department, where he was transporting an arrestee. Singer arrived at Pacifica Hospital and called Sergeant Vondriska. I believe it was during this phone conversation that the PCP story was hatched.

Why PCP? It's simple really.

The beating of Rodney King was so egregious even to the hardened eyes of veteran police officers that some kind of justification for the violence had to be found. It's fair to say the public as a whole has little sympathy for drug users or dealers.

Add to that, PCP is reputed to make people impervious to pain while heightening anger and agitation. In my opinion, problems with the officers' PCP intoxication theory are numerous, beginning with the fact that not one officer at the scene was qualified to render a lawful opinion on the probability of King's PCP ingestion. Moreover, the chemical tests run on King's blood and urine at the hospital jail ward showed no evidence of PCP in his system.

My efforts in getting a split sample of King's blood and urine failed because *after* I called them, the hospital lab destroyed the small remaining amounts of specimen. Our tests were needed to provide King a defense for the criminal charges he was still facing from his arrest following the beating. My theory is further validated by listening to the video itself. Clearly, King screams from the pain he feels during the beating, which directly contradicts the PCP intoxication allegations by the involved officers. PCP was a bad idea for the defense as I'm sure we'll see in future hearings on this incident.

Josie Morales, George Holliday's neighbor, appeared before the Grand Jury with her notes of the incident. As I read her testimony, I looked for differences between what she had told me and what she told the Grand Jury. There weren't any. She testified from her notes:

> . . . What happened next was I heard a muffled sound, like a command maybe, come out of . . . I don't know if it was an officer yelling. And then I saw the driver's door open and a man emerged from the car. He got out of his car and put his hands on the roof. Then he laid down.
>
> He was knocked to his knees by a blow to his face, the first time he stood up. He was hit mostly in the face and head at this point. When he went back down on his stomach, the officer who instigated the beating delivered fierce blows with his night stick to his back.
>
> The poor guy was getting hit mostly in the back . . . so he turned over and sit down and got hit by other officers as well. At this point when he was sitting up, there was a clear gunshot sound, which coincidentally, almost matched the sound of something like glass striking pavement and possibly what I thought to be something being thrown down to the left of his head. It could have been a shot from a stun gun instead. There was a few seconds' pause, and an officer put what appeared to

be a device around King's neck. [She was referring to the taser wires.]

The officers continued to deliver blows and again, that officer who instigated it, hit King with all his might, the blows landing in the back, rear, and legs. The rest is on video and everyone can see the degree of violence which took place.

Page after page, she recalled the horrors she watched inflicted on the man who, minutes before, was lying on the ground, complying with the officers' instructions.

Mrs. Morales's recounting of her feelings in front of a jury would devastate the defense. Who could have guessed that a year later, she would *not* be called as a witness against the officers in Simi Valley.

■

Lawrence Davis told the Grand Jury he was the charge nurse on duty in the emergency room at Pacifica Hospital when King was brought in. He was with King for about an hour and a half. During that time, he didn't smell any alcohol on King's breath. King told him he worked at Dodger Stadium. Then Officer Powell said to King, "Do you know who we were playing ball with tonight, Rodney?" and talked about hitting a home run. Davis testified King was not combative and lay on the treatment table without movement. As many as five officers, including Tim and Melanie Singer, were in the treatment room with King at different times throughout the medical examination, during which King was cooperative with the officers and medical staff.

The two Unified School District officers, Paul Beauregard and Mark Diamond, were called to testify. They told the Grand Jurors they first saw the CHP chasing King at the intersection of Glenoaks and Van Nuys Boulevard. They followed, something they were not allowed to do and had been disciplined for doing before, and parked behind the Hyundai when it finally stopped on Foothill near Osborne. Beauregard told them he concentrated on the passengers on the opposite side of the car from King and didn't see anything related directly to the beating. He said King looked "glassy-eyed" when he got out of the car.

From my own experience I know being "glassy-eyed" has

nothing to do with PCP. "Dusters," persons under the influence of PCP, do have one symptom, nystagmus, that affects the eyes. This condition causes an involuntary fluttering of the eyes at the most extreme left and right corners of the eye socket. This is not a condition easily seen at night from a distance of twenty feet. Even if that symptom had been present in King, no expert could render an opinion of PCP intoxication without questioning him about past head or eye injuries that could result in a similar condition. In 1977, I was recognized as an expert on PCP intoxication. This came after I had made dozens of arrests of persons under the influence and taken down some of the biggest PCP labs in the city.

In the mid- to late seventies, I was working the area where PCP use originated in the gang environment. I confronted people every day who were dusted and I *never* had to resort to the level of violence seen on Holliday's video. Many of us officers assigned to South Central Los Angeles were part of a team testing implements we hoped could help in the control of violent PCP suspects. In the days before Stacey Koon, the most senior officer at the beating scene, came on the job, we tested "leg grabbers," a device resembling a twelve foot long pair of pliers; "nets," much like giant fish nets, and even the infamous taser. All these implements had potential for use in the field, but all carried some risks in their use. I left LAPD before the final evaluation reports were in on the test equipment, but not before knowing that they all shared one thing in common, reduced likelihood of injury to suspects or officers during an arrest.

■

The district attorney called retired Los Angeles Sheriff's Lieutenant Joe Callahan as an expert witness in the use of force. He'd been a lieutenant with the department for twenty-two years and had commanded the SWAT team for three of them before he retired. Presently, he trains departments and individual officers in the proper uses of force, force policy and procedures, and testifies *for* accused cops. Appearing for the prosecution must have been a new experience for him.

His testimony was lengthy because he went to great effort to acquaint the grand jurors with use of force principals before addressing specific allegations against the individual officers. To best illustrate his points he introduced a use-of-force chart with which he explained the theory of escalation and deescalation of force. His chart clearly demonstrated various levels of force available to police officers. Once the grand jurors understood the basic concepts, he went on to evaluate the accused officers' individual application of force by commenting on their actions and reactions as seen on the Holliday video.

When Callahan finished his testimony, the fate of the accused officers seemed obvious. He told the members of the Grand Jury that the accused officers had indeed used excessive force on Rodney King when they struck him on his head with their PR-24 Side Handled batons.

I finished reading Callahan's testimony, sat back and took a deep breath. As I slowly exhaled, I smiled knowing the deed was done. Like Josie Morales, Callahan's testimony to a jury would be dynamite. But like Josie, Callahan wasn't called as a witness against the defendants in Simi Valley. No force experts were called by White or Yochelson. They had all refused to testify.

Sergeant Freddie Nichols, an instructor at the LAPD academy was called by White as a use-of-force rebuttal witness in the closing days of the trial, but he never testified in front of the jury either. He was excused by Judge Weisburg following a hearing where he testified that he faced reprisals from his peers and superiors at the academy for his public statements in support of the indictments of the defendant officers. Nichols used medical reasons, stress, for his cop out.

Glenda Tosti, a civilian employee of the LAPD, is a supervisor in the Communications Division. She explained to the grand jury that Mobile Digital Terminals (MDTs) are small computers installed in all LAPD patrol cars. All typed messages transmitted to and from patrol units, or between patrol units, are stored in the computer at Communications Division and may be retrieved only by authorized personnel.

Tosti identified the MDT messages sent prior to and immediately following the arrest of Rodney King. She showed the Grand Jury a printout of the messages sent by Stacey Koon to Foothill Division, as well as previously undisclosed exchanges between Powell and Officer Corina Smith in which Powell uses

<u>USE OF FORCE MODEL</u>

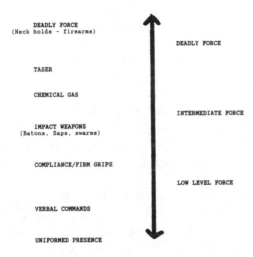

DEADLY FORCE
(Neck holds - firearms)

TASER

CHEMICAL GAS

IMPACT WEAPONS
(Batons, Saps, swarms)

COMPLIANCE/FIRM GRIPS

VERBAL COMMANDS

UNIFORMED PRESENCE

DEADLY FORCE

INTERMEDIATE FORCE

LOW LEVEL FORCE

UNIFORMED PRESENCE

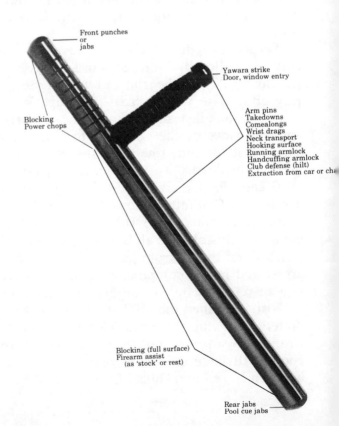

Front punches
or
jabs

Yawara strike
Door, window entry

Arm pins
Takedowns
Comealongs
Wrist drags
Neck transport
Hooking surface
Running armlock
Handcuffing armlock
Club defense (hilt)
Extraction from car or ch‹

Blocking
Power chops

Blocking (full surface)
Firearm assist
(as 'stock' or rest)

Rear jabs
Pool cue jabs

the phrase "gorillas in the mist" a few hours prior to the King beating.

LAPD Officer Corina Smith had been Powell's partner when they worked together at Rampart Division. The two had also lived together, which she never mentioned during her testimony, nor was she asked about the nature of the relationship by District Attorney White.

Smith said she had no idea what Powell meant by the reference to gorillas in the mist. She confirmed that in an exchange following the incident, when Powell said he "hadn't beaten anyone this bad in a long time," she responded, "Why for you do that? I thought you agreed to chill out for a while." She said she was referring to an arrest six months earlier when she and Powell responded to a call involving a black family. An altercation occurred which required her use of a baton. She testified Powell didn't use his baton at all. When the D.A. asked her what other use-of-force incidents Powell had been involved in, she said she didn't recall.

As a part of my preliminary background investigation of Powell, I had talked to another female officer, who requested I keep her identity confidential. The officer told me once Powell broke it off with Smith, Smith had threatened suicide and was immediately reassigned to station duty where she could be watched. Her gun was taken away and she worked Community Relations until she returned to field duty several months later.

Internal Affairs Detective Taky Tzimeas testified he went to Foothill Division on March 4, 1991, less than two hours after the Holliday video aired on KTLA-TV, to investigate an allegation of misconduct by the officers involved in the arrest of Rodney King. According to LAPD policy, he said, a supervisor must file a personnel complaint whenever he has reasonable cause to believe misconduct has occurred. No personnel complaint was filed by Sergeant Stacey Koon.

Tzimeas didn't mention Paul King's attempt to file a complaint at Foothill Division. He was on and off the stand in less than five minutes.

The remainder of the fourteen witnesses' testimonies ran fairly consistent with what these witnesses said, with minor variations. It fell to D.A Terry White to sum up his case to the grand jurors. His summation took fourteen pages to record and parts of it were quite well presented. He recounted each officer's

participation in the incident and the resulting allegations arising from their individual misconduct and unlawful actions. He
presented a strong case on several of the allegations, while
others seemed slight.

On March 14, 1991 indictments were returned against Officers Powell, Wind, Briseno and the cops' cop, Stacey Koon.

The grand jury reconvened the following week to consider
additional allegations against some of the bystander-officers
but no more indictments were forthcoming.

THE HOLLYWOOD DRAG QUEEN
CAPER

After the grand jury indictments, the four defendant police officers found themselves on the receiving end of the system of justice they once represented. Because they were charged with criminal acts, the city attorney declared a conflict of interest and would not defend them. The Los Angeles Police Protective League immediately agreed to pay defense costs for their brother officers. High-priced attorneys were brought in to oversee defense efforts within two days of the video's first airing. The memo we found in the trash dumpster recorded that first meeting of the accused officers and their lawyers.

Citizens have few options when officers use excessive force. If they can find a lawyer to take their case, they begin a slow uphill climb in the legal system. If they are ultimately successful in collecting a settlement, it comes out of the taxpayers' pockets. The accused officer, on the other hand, will be defended by the city attorney or, as in the King case, by lawyers hired by their protective league free of charge. In most cases the officers will lose neither pay nor sleep in the process.

This case was different. This time there was an eye witness

who was unbiased and wouldn't suffer from fear of reprisals. George Holliday's video wasn't blinded by the shine of the officers' badges and would not honor the Code of Silence.

In the days following his March 5, 1991, release from jail, King started recalling bits and pieces of the beating. Considering the damage done to his head, it surprised me that he remembered anything at all. Two weeks after the beating, King entered a small West Los Angeles hospital for surgery to repair some of the facial bone damage done by police batons. On the eve of this surgery, Pat and I went to the hospital to review the entire Holliday video with King, who had only seen the excerpts on television but not the full nine minutes. I looked forward to recording King's first impressions of the video. By this time, King was feeling more comfortable with me and we began talking about things other than the beating. He was having nightmares when he slept, so he fought off sleeping. He was exhausted and still suffered from considerable pain in his face, head, and broken leg.

I set up the equipment, and we began watching the video frame by frame as King lay in his hospital bed. His wife Crystal and his Aunt Angela left the room; they didn't want to be there to see his reactions to his own beating. We watched the opening frames where Powell hit him in the face. Glen took a deep breath and stiffened from head to toe. He winced at each additional blow to his body. His first words sent chills down my back. "You know, I didn't feel anything after the first time I was hit in the face, except the electric shock. It was like my brain just turned off. I knew I was still being hit and kicked. I know it was hurting like hell, but I don't remember the pain. I went numb all over."

I stopped the VCR and just looked at him. I couldn't speak for what felt like minutes. It was an eerie feeling, being with King while he watched his own beating. The air in the room seemed unusually still. I wanted to get up and open the door, but I couldn't. Finally, Pat swung the door open; she was feeling it too. King just lay there, lost in his own thoughts, his eyes still focused on the screen. "I prayed someone would step in and stop it," he said, ending the deafening silence. "I remembered that Tastee Freeze from when I was a kid, going fishing at the dam with my dad. I really hoped someone would be there, you know, a crowd. I knew I'd be safe if there was a crowd." I advanced the video forward a few seconds and stopped it. The air in the room was circulating again.

"What's happening here?"

"I don't know . . . I don't know why they're still beating me. I haven't done nothing. I can't remember why I ran . . . can't remember." Pat sat across from Glen, taking notes.

For the next two hours, I'd play a few frames, then stop and get King's explanation for what he thought was going on. Most of his answers were the same, "I don't remember."

About two minutes into the video, Officer Briseno is seen leaning in toward King. He appeared to be shouting something, but the poor quality of the equipment in the hospital room made it unclear. Noise from the helicopter all but drowned out other sounds. Suddenly, King sat straight up and shouted, "I know what he's saying! He called me a nigger!"

Pat and I were startled. "He called you a nigger?"

"I know you can't hear it, but this is where he called me a nigger and told me to lay down or something like that."

My initial impressions were right. This was an LAPD "let's teach this nigger a lesson" beating.

It had been an exhausting session. When I turned off the VCR, we all felt drained. King was alseep within minutes. Pat and I gathered up our equipment and quietly left the hospital.

■

Constant use and age finally caused my old television set to give up the ghost. I'd wanted a big screen for years; I just needed an excuse for the purchase. My search for a new one took me to a Good Guys store in the city of Orange where the new RCA ProScan televisions were on display. It could do just about everything in video: freeze-frame function and the sound quality was like nothing I'd ever heard. Great for football—all the bells and whistles. Eager to show off this state-of-the-art equipment, the salesman slid a demo tape into the VCR. Seeing the quality and capabilities of the equipment gave me an idea; I went out to my car and got the Holliday video. I hadn't taken it out of the trunk since the night before, when I'd shown it to King at the hospital. Returning, I gave it to the salesman who was happy to play it on the ProScan.

A crowd gathered as sounds of the video filled the store. The clarity was amazing. As the growing crowd watched, Officer Ted Briseno leaned over King, pointed toward him, and could be heard shouting, "Nigger, put your hands behind your back!" The date and time stamp on the bottom of the screen read March 3, 1991 A.M. 00:53:04. The salesman switched the audio to the speaker bank and rewound the tape. "Nigger, put your hands behind your back!" Three, four, five times, I replayed the video and each time, the sound seemed more intense. I ran to my car and called Lerman. "Damn! I knew it! Bring the tape up."

An hour later, the equipment at Lerman's office, though not as clear, played Briseno's words. I could have gotten there quicker but I took time to take the names and phone numbers of all the people in the video store first.

Early the next morning, Lerman told District Attorney Terry White about the statements. White said he had listened to the tape many times and heard no racial comments. Later that day, I returned to the video store and purchased the ProScan for use in the King investigation. I hadn't even gotten it out of the box when Lerman phoned.

"I've talked to Internal Affairs. I want you to call Detective Tzimeas and tell him how you discovered the racial stuff." When I called later, Detective Tzimeas asked me to bring my copy of the tape to IAD headquarters.

I figured Tzimeas was suspicious and wanted to compare my tape to the sound track of his copy. Tzimeas, a small, cold-eyed Greek-American, was waiting for me at the fifth floor offices of the Internal Affairs Division in Parker Center. After a less than cordial greeting, he told me not to bother trying to pronounce his name. "Everybody calls me TZ."

I was on my guard and prepared for anything. I knew I was the hen in the fox house. I'd had several previous experiences with IAD investigators while on the department, none of which were enjoyable, and I felt this experience would be no different. As I walked past the small, cramped offices on the fifth floor, I recalled my first experience at IAD. I'd been out of the academy for only a few weeks when we were deployed to a downtown hotel to handle a small riot between the Jewish Defense League and members of the local Nazi Party.

Once these two groups confronted each other in front of the Embassy Hotel, fights broke out and we were sent in to quell the disturbance. That night, all the local news broadcasts filled the airwaves with scenes of uniformed police officers dragging little old ladies to awaiting paddy wagons. Within days, a personnel complaint was filed alleging excessive force against many of the officers present. Oddly, this was one complaint I escaped. I was called to IAD and asked to offer a statement against several other officers present. I recall sitting in one of the tiny interview rooms, waiting for over two hours before an investigator came into the room. A favorite tactic—let the subject of the interview sweat for awhile. Mind games. No, nothing had changed, except the faces.

"I brought along a list of the people who were with me at the video store, in case you need witnesses," I said to Tzimeas.

TZ wasn't impressed. We went to a small room where a TV and VCR were ready and waiting. Without further discussion, he inserted my copy of the Holliday video and pressed the play button. Expressionless, emotionless, TZ replayed it five or six times. "I do hear someone, possibly in the background crowd, saying, 'Ger, put your hands behind your back.' "

I did a double take. "All you hear is 'ger'?"

"Yeah, just ger. And how do we know it was Briseno? It could be anyone out there that night, even someone in the crowd at the apartments."

I felt my blood pressure rising. "Bullshit! Briseno's lips are moving. It's his voice. You're just refusing to accept it. What do you think he's saying, 'Tiger, put your hands behind your back'?" I knew the second I said it, the meeting was over. I'd penetrated TZ's cold facade and found his hot button. As I left IAD and stepped into the fifth floor elevator, I recalled my days as a blue suiter. I remembered how intimidated I'd been by the mere mention of IAD. Cops with no guidelines. Cops investigating cops. Cops who don't want respect and don't get it. I was proud of myself. I'd stood up to this robotic putz and refused to back off. I knew the department was in for some heat on this one. I pictured TZ on the phone to the chief after I'd left. I envisioned Gates sitting at his oversized desk on the sixth floor hearing about the racial slurs. For the first time in many, many years, I left Parker Center with a smile on my face.

A few days later, I was contacted by PBS television station KCET-TV in Los Angeles, which was doing a special on the King incident and wanted to include information on racial

George Papcun, Ph.D.
1081 Buckman Road
Santa Fe, NM 37501
May 5, 1991

Jeffrey Kaye
KCET Television
Los Angeles, California

Dear Mr. Kaye:

I have received from you via Federal Express a video cassette tape recording labeled "M/C PB SPCL 'Rodney King' 4-24-91" followed by what appear to be the initials "R.S." In accordance with your request, I have enhanced the acoustic part of the recording by attenuating ambient noise which appears to be the noise of a helicopter) that interferes with the intelligibility of the recording, and attempted to discern what was being said in the recording.

I have listened to the recording with appropriate equipment that transduces the full range of audio frequencies relevant to understanding the speech in this recording. I have also listened to the recording under various conditions of parametric filtering. Consequently, I can report to you the following words shouted by men in the distance:

12:53:04
Voice 1: "Nigger, hands behind your back!"

12:53:09
Voice 2: "Hands behind your back!"

12:53:15
(Voice2:) "Behind your back!"

Page 2
Jeffrey Kaye
May 5, 1991

I am prepared to explain in detail the technical characteristics of the playback and filtering methods I used, and to testify under oath as to the conclusions I have reached.

Enclosed you will find a copy of the video cassette recording with the soundtrack enhanced under three of the filtering conditions I used in my assessment of the recording.

I make the representations contained in this letter solely as a private citizen, and not as a representative of the United States Government or the University of California.

Under separate cover I will send a curriculum vita listing my technical qualifications in this area of expertise. Please do not hesitate to contact me if I can answer any questions or furnish any additional information.

Sincerely yours,

George Papcun, Ph.D.

epithets recorded on the Holliday video. They asked for a copy of the tape they could send to a voice expert. I checked with Lerman, who was happy to accommodate them.

On May 15th, 1991 I received a fax from KCET-TV, containing a letter from voice expert George Papcun, Ph.D., an audiologist with the University of New Mexico. Papcun wrote, "Existing at A.M. 00:53:04, a male voice is heard to say, 'Nigger, put your hands behind your back.' "

During the third week in May, 1991, KCET aired the video with Dr. Papcun's enhanced audio. Ted Briseno's unmistakable command was racial, making it an important element of a hate crime. The one question not yet answered was, when would the evidence of racial epithets be used in the prosecution of the officers?

■

Each time I watched the Holliday video, I saw something I hadn't noticed before. During one of my first viewings, I saw a gray Ford Probe drive across the screen from left to right. The car had apparently been caught in the traffic jam that followed the termination of the pursuit and had to stop because traffic was blocked from both directions by police activity in the middle of the street. As the car moves to the right, it passes within twenty feet of the beating scene. For days, I pondered how I could locate the Ford Probe and talk to the driver.

On March 12, 1991 a call came into Lerman's office from someone identifying himself only as Hector. He told Lerman's secretary that he had watched Holliday's video on television and believed the Ford Probe was his. The quick-thinking secretary put Hector on hold and called my pager. I immediately called her back. She explained who was on the other line and then conferenced me to Hector.

He wouldn't give me his last name or his address except to say he lived in the Arleta section of the San Fernando Valley. He'd seen his car on TV and would like to talk to me, but was afraid of police and the media. I attempted to reassure him but he hung up before I could get his address.

As near as I could tell, he was the closest civilian to the beating and must have important information. I decided to go out to Arleta and try to find the damn car somewhere. For the next several weeks, whenever I had the chance, I drove the streets of Arleta during normal commuting hours, morning or evening. I had noted there was a distinctive decal on the post of the passenger door and could eliminate cars without the decal. I couldn't define the type of decal but the fact that it was there was significant enough. I must've seen a thousand gray Ford Probes during those weeks, some blue/gray, some light gray, but none the correct gray color, with a decal on the right door post.

Then, just as I was about to give up the search, I got lucky. At a shopping center, I saw a dark gray Probe drive into the parking lot. I waited for the driver to get out of the car and go into the supermarket, then I walked to the passenger side. There, on the door post was a white Local Motion decal at the same location as the one in the Holliday video. Home run! I took down the license number of the car and called it in to my offices for a DMV run of the plate. By the next morning, I had the address of the Probe's owner. I used the address to cross reference his name and phone number. That afternoon, I called and asked to speak with Martin Leon. The woman who answered told me Martin was at work but would be home after 7:00. At 7:05 I called again and *Hector* Leon picked up the phone.

He confirmed he was the same Hector I had spoken to and wondered how in hell I'd gotten his name and number. I told him I couldn't divulge trade secrets and assured him I would keep his identity confidential if he would grant me an interview. This time he agreed and the appointment was set for the following night. He went on to say other family members had been with him in the car the night of March 3, and he would try to get them to talk to me also. He said his brother, Martin, was driving and Martin's wife, Martha, was in the rear seat with two children. I remember thinking, my God, a bonanza of uninvolved witnesses who have no connection to this case, untainted by threats of notoriety from the police or D.A.

The following night, I kept my appointment with the Leon family. Martin had left for work. I was told that Martha, his wife, didn't speak English and I hadn't brought an interpreter with me, but I did interview Hector. Before entering the house, I had walked to the rear parking lot and photographed the family's gray Ford Probe with the Local Motion decal on the passenger door post.

In his recorded interview, Hector Leon told me, "Me and my brother and his family had been out to San Bernardino to attend a birthday party. We were driving back home and it was about 1:00 A.M. My brother Martin was driving and I was in the front passenger seat. Martha was in the back seat with the children. We got off the 210 freeway near the Hansen Dam, then onto Foothill Boulevard. Ahead of us, I saw a bunch of police lights. It looked like they had a car stopped. All the traffic was stopped in both directions. Martin was able to get to within twenty-five feet before he stopped the car completely."

Hector said they were not in a position to see how the beating had started, but when the Probe was stopped, they sat and watched it continue. "I could clearly see the officers hitting and kicking Mr. King. King was clearly in pain as the officers continued to hit him. I heard King screaming from the pain and I heard the officers panting and breathing hard. I was very frightened for myself and family. I feared the officers would start hitting us. After we watched for a couple of minutes, an officer came and told Martin to move the car, to get out. I think they didn't want us to watch anymore. I heard one officer, the tall skinny one with a long nose [Ted Briseno], say something to King about 'black.' "

"The officer shouted 'nigger' and 'black,' " Martha said in broken English, which surprised me because I'd been told she spoke only Spanish.

"Yeah, that's what he said. I just don't like using those words and I don't want the police coming after us," Hector admitted. Later, Hector volunteered, "You know, seeing those cars parked like that, in a kind of circle, and the helicopter overhead with the light on the middle of the circle, the laughing and joking of the cops . . . hitting each other on the back . . . it reminded me of watching a movie showing a meeting of the KKK. I wanted to leave before the officer told us to go. I was really scared."

I went back to the Leon's house a few days later and recorded the statements of Martha and Martin Leon. They echoed Hector's words. Martin Leon was still frightened of the police knowing his identity. He feared retaliation. He was nervous as he hedged on his memories of the night King was beaten. He told me he recalled some language he didn't like, but wouldn't commit to the specific words. I could see the fear on his face as we sat across from each other at his dining table.

The Leons were never called to testify in Simi Valley.

■

All involved LAPD, CHP, and School District personnel filed reports supporting their use of force following the events of March 3, 1991. The LAPD had taught a lesson to a black man and there it would have ended, except for the existence of George Holliday's video tape. Near the end of that video, the camera caught another unsuspecting group of witnesses, a bus with Banda El Rincon painted on the side. People in the bus were in the middle of everything. I had to find them, too.

No one in the area had ever heard of Banda El Rincon. I called just about every Hispanic booking agent in Los Angeles. During the second week of April, I finally hit paydirt. A band by that name was based in San Jose. I located the manager and on April 27, 1991, flew to interview seven musicians who'd seen what had occurred. They had already been contacted by the District Attorney's office and several of the defense attorneys, but were happy to repeat their statements to me.

Of the seventeen people on the bus, ten slept through the incident. The remaining six band members and the bus driver saw everything that occurred from the time the Hyundai stopped until the bus was ordered to leave the scene by one of the officers directing traffic. The story told by these band members is considerably different from the story told by the officers, but fairly consistent with all civilian witnesses I had interviewed.

The driver, a Mr. Martinez, told me he became fearful when he saw the officers begin to beat and kick King. "He appeared to be doing what the officers were telling him to do, and then without a visible reason, the black man was shot with something by one of the officers. Then other officers began to hit the man with their sticks. After a few minutes, I could see other officers standing nearby laugh, like it was funny, what was happening to the man. I thought I should leave before they could get me too, because I was watching what they were doing to the man."

The other band members echoed Martinez's statement with minor differences that could be explained by their angle of view from inside the bus. All were unanimous in their feeling that King was fully compliant with the instructions he was given and were surprised when, "King was assaulted by the officers." By late afternoon, I had their recorded statements in the bag and drove my rented car back to the San Jose Airport, confident that I'd see these men again when the criminal trial began.

Like the Leons, they were never called to testify in Simi Valley.

■

Manipulation by and of the media began almost immediately after the first airing of the video. Events were planned to coincide with local 4:00 P.M. early newscasts. Midday news conferences allowed reporters to get their video footage back to the station and edited in time to air. We noted that the defense attorneys soon became adept at timing their disclosures. On March 28, 1991, I was sitting in Lerman's office for a strategy session when the phone rang. An L.A. *Daily News* reporter asked Lerman for a comment on reports that Rodney King had been identified as the man who robbed a Sylmar pizza store on January 12, 1991 and a Sun Valley video store on February 21, 1991. The female clerk at the video store was shot in the arm. The robbery victims recognized King from photos shown to them by investigating officers from Foothill Division. They had also seen him on television.

I immediately called the watch commander at Foothill, who referred me to the office of Police Chief Daryl Gates, who referred me to the district attorney's office, who referred me to the office of the attorney general. I was becoming adept at phone tag and bureaucratic keep-away. By the end of the day, I knew only that King had been identified as a suspect in both robberies and the investigation was "ongoing." My information came from the media, which were reporting allegations leaked by the LAPD, but the cops weren't telling me anything.

Lerman immediately called King and asked him to account for his whereabouts on the dates in question. This wasn't too difficult, since both robberies occurred while King was at work, remodeling concession stands at Dodger Stadium. By the following day, I had documented that King was indeed at his job site when the robberies occurred and had faxed the documentation to the Department of Corrections. King's time sheets for those days showed he was working, and his coworkers specifically recalled his presence.

Lerman called me at my office. An investigator from the attorney general's office was on another line; Steve wanted to conference the three of us together. The investigator introduced himself as George Shaw (name changed). He had learned we had developed a defense to the robbery allegations and wanted to know names and statement content of the people who said King was working those days and, therefore, couldn't have committed the crimes. The call lasted only minutes. Like the FBI and the D.A., all he wanted to do was suck me dry of information then go out and see if he could crash and burn my witnesses. It was obvious he was under great pressure to send King back to the slammer.

We spoke several times during the next few days. During one of our conversations, he inferred I told King's bosses to doctor his time cards for both incidents. Hell, his allegations were so flimsy, I didn't even go into the field to resolve them. All my follow-up was done by telephone. I talked to King's employers, his coworkers, even the director of personnel at Dodger Stadium, all by phone. Oddly enough, when I tried to talk to the robbery victims and set up appointments to take their statements, both women referred me to their lawyers. They reminded me of vampire victims holding up a crucifix to keep the evil bloodsucker away.

In another conference call with Lerman, Shaw refused to accept that our witnesses were accurate in their recollections. He accused me of "cribbing" the witnesses, meaning he thought I had prompted their testimony solely to clear King. The accusation set me off. "Look, if you think you have a strong case against King, then fucking file it. When we get to court, we'll shove it right up your ass!" Lerman remained silent as I slammed my phone down.

Several minutes later, it rang again. It was Lerman. I was still fuming, but Steve only chuckled. "You really pissed him off," he said. "He asked me not put you on the line ever again. He doesn't want to talk to you anymore. He'll talk to me, but not you, and by the way, you done good."

"Okay, here's what I think we should do," I told Lerman. I was cooling down. "How about if we send a copy of my investigation to the CDC (California Department of Corrections), you know, to Tim Fowler, under a letter of confidentiality, for his eyes only. We'll let the parole authorities know that this whole caper was a set up by the LAPD meant to mitigate King's image, detract from his credibility and integrity, make the four cops look good by making King look bad. That ought to get them thinking. Let them go out and reinterview the witnesses and satisfy themselves that this thing smells. It should take some of the heat off Fowler, and help keep King on the streets."

Several hours later, Lerman called me back with instructions on how to complete the cover letter to the California Department of Corrections and Parole Agent Tim Fowler, while not violating attorney-client privilege, and worded so the attorney general's office couldn't have access to the information.

On April 24, 1991, California Attorney General Dan Lundgren issued a press release confirming King was no longer a suspect.

There was unprecedented public, media, and government interest in the day-to-day activities of everyone involved in the King case. I didn't have to determine whether or not I was being followed, I assumed I was. On one occasion, I drove to the home of my old friend, Jack Jansen, to pick up materials on another police abuse case I felt had value in the King investigation. A medical supply truck parked behind me. I entered the house, counted to ten, then Jack and I burst out and raced toward the truck parked across the street, about one hundred thirty feet away. He was setting up surveillance equipment, but before we could get to him, he started up the truck and hauled ass, not before I'd gotten the name and telephone number painted on the side of the truck. Searches of state and local records revealed no company known as Ultimate Medical Equipment.

Normally, a plumbing repair truck parked outside my office wouldn't be considered unusual, but everything about the King case was unusual. So when I noticed the truck in mid-April, I called the toll-free number painted on its side. No such number existed. I watched as the driver pointed a parabolic microphone, used for eavesdropping on distant conversations, at my window. I ran out to the truck and the driver sped away.

Office of the Attorney General
Daniel E. Lungren

News Release

| Dave Puglia | (916) 324-5500 | — | Christine F. Mullen | (916) 324-5443 | Rad Carsaw (916) 739-5239 |

Dave Puglia
Press Secretary
1515 K Street
Sacramento, CA 95814

(916) 324-5500

Christine F. Mullen
Denise Davis
Information Officers
1515 K Street
Sacramento, CA 95814

(916) 324-5443
(916) 324-5494

Rad Carsaw (916) 739-5239
Information Officer
Division of Law Enforcement
4949 Broadway
Sacramento, CA 95820

LUNGREN RELEASES FINDINGS OF INVESTIGATION INTO
ROBBERIES ALLEGEDLY LINKED TO RODNEY KING

CONTACT: Dave Puglia
Press Secretary
(916) 324-

April 24, 1991
91-29

LOS ANGELES -- Attorney General Dan Lungren today announced the findings of an independent investigation into allegations that Rodney King may have been linked to two separate robberies which occurred in the Los Angeles area during January and February of this year, and made the following statement:

"Based upon a thorough review of this matter, we conclude that the existing evidence is insufficient to support the filing of criminal charges against Mr. King relative to the two robbery incidents.

"After being asked by the Los Angeles Police Department and the Los Angeles County District Attorney to assume responsibility for an independent investigation into these allegations, an exhaustive investigation was conducted by special agents from our Bureau of Investigation. Their reports were then reviewed by the legal staff of our Criminal Law Division. This morning we notified both the LAPD and the district attorney of our findings.

"With respect to the first incident, a January robbery of a Sylmar pizza

-more-

parlor, the single victim-witness was unable to identify Mr. King as the suspect.

"With respect to the second incident, the February 21 robbery of a Sun Valley video store, one victim, who was wounded during the incident, identified a photograph of Mr. King as the robber approximately three weeks after seeing him on the local television stations' coverage surrounding the appalling events of his March 3rd arrest. The other victim-witness involved in the incident was unable to identify Mr. King as the robber.

"Our investigation was unable to produce any further evidence to link Mr. King to the video store robbery. However, our investigators located and interviewed credible witnesses who established that Mr. King was working at a job site located approximately 14 miles from the video store at the time the robbery occurred.

"Additional findings of our investigation support this conclusion. However, due the fact that both robberies remain unsolved, we must refrain from discussing any other details surrounding the critical evidence in order to safeguard future investigations or prosecutions.

"I would like to commend the Bureau of Investigation for their professional conduct throughout this investigation. The high level of attention given to this particular matter can sometimes hamper agents in the course of their work, but our special agents did a commendable job."

# # # # #

■

One of many calls I'd received during the weeks following my assignment came from a man who had a unique story to tell. Mario Gracia was a passenger in a car that was pulled over by Officer Ted Briseno and his partner, Rolando Solano, about two and a half hours after the King beating. Gracia told me Briseno called for a sergeant. Stacey Koon answered. According to Gracia, Briseno said, "You had better be on your best behavior because the sergeant that's coming here has already kicked one nigger's ass tonight and wouldn't think twice about kicking your ass, too." When Sergeant Koon arrived at the scene, he directed Briseno and Solano to take Gracia, on probation for a prior offense, and a juvenile passenger into custody. At Foothill Station, they were handcuffed to a bench in an interior corridor near the watch commander's office. While there, Gracia and his friend looked on in amazement as Foothill Division officers passed by them laughing and joking about the arrest and beating of a black motorist a few hours earlier.

Within a few days of Gracia's contact, I again met with Blue Throat and was given a page from Foothill Watch Commander Lt. Conmay's log which confirmed a different view of Gracia's arrest from that of Gracia, himself. Based on comments in the log, no use of force report was completed by Briseno following Gracia's arrest, a clear violation of the department's administrative policy, nor was there any acknowledged problem with the arrest.

A few days after I'd finished taking statements from the Leon family, Lerman and I had our first meeting with the prosecutorial team. District Attorneys Terry White and Alan Yochelson and two of their investigators came to Lerman's offices in Beverly Hills. The meeting had been requested by White. He wanted to meet us and get a feel for the progress of our investigation. I hoped the meeting would set a cooperative tone between the D.A.'s office and the King team. It didn't happen.

I had my files arranged on the conference room table. Lerman had his office television and VCR brought in and set up. Coffee and rolls were in place. The meeting started with White defining his role in the criminal prosecution. "We've already begun the pretrial discovery process in anticipation of

CONTINUATION

ACTIVITY (Continued):

ONE OF THE SUSPECTS WERE TAKEN INTO
CUSTODY WITHOUT INCIDENT. THE DRIVER
WAS UNDER THE INFLUENCE OF PCP. HE
STARTED FIGHTING WITH OFFICERS AND WAS
TASED BY LIHD SGT ___ WHO WAS AT SCENE
THE TASER DIDN'T PHASE HIM AND HE
WAS ULTIMATELY SUBDUED AFTER SEVERAL
BATON STRIKES. HE WAS MTD AND ULTIMATE.
BOOKED AT LACUSMC DUE TO HIS PCP INTOXICATION
SGT CATELLANO IS COMPLETING THE USE OF FORCE
AND PURSUIT REPORTS. (G-KOON LOG) AM OK
⑥ MET WITH SGT GORDON AND REVIEWED THE
T/A PROJ. - GAVE SOME INSIGHT INTO
COMPLETION OF THIS PROJECT. HOPEFULLY
IT WILL BE WRAPPED UP TONIGHT.
⑦ W/C WORKED ON COVER LETTER ON
MORENO 181.
⑧ BRISENO AND SOLAND MADE A NICE OBS
ARREST OF (4) 211 SUSPECTS. THEY HEARD
A CRIME BROADCAST SAW THE CAR AND
RECOVERED ALL THE VICTIM'S PROPERTY. THEY
INTERVIEWED AND OBTAINED A COP OUT FROM
THE DRIVER. GOOD JOB REPORT WAS STILL
BEING WRITTEN AT EOW.
Commendab

W/C's signature:
LT P J. Conway 17443

the trial being held in the fall. We're moving forward as quickly as possible and we're hoping you can offer assistance with witness identification. Do you have anything we don't have?"

What a question.

Lerman suggested we give the district attorneys all our investigative materials in the spirit of cooperation. This offer quickly led to discussions about implications of the recently passed Proposition 115, California's new anticrime legislation, calling for full pretrial reciprocal discovery. All information we gave to the District Attorney, would in turn be given to the defendants as part of the discovery process. While we would be helping the criminal case, the defense could then use our information against us in our civil case. We found ourselves on the horns of a dilemma. In the end, Lerman decided we would give the D.A. the names and addresses of our witnesses but not their statements. He'd have to do his own leg work. The Holliday video was next on the agenda. As I began playing it, I explained my interpretation of the officers' actions as the frames advanced. At the point where the Ford Probe drives across the screen, I asked if they had interviewed the occupants. I still can't believe the reply.

Yochelson told me they had taken the statement of "the guy" who had been driving the car.

"The guy?" I asked.

"Yeah, we've talked to the guy in the car. Not much there. He says King got out of his car and refused all orders to get down on the ground. When the officers finally approached, King went after them and knocked a couple of them down."

Somebody had been blowing heavy smoke up White's ass. I knew there was a whole family in the car who saw King attacked by the officers, not the other way around.

"I know you won't give me names, but was there only one guy or were there several people in the car?" I asked.

"No, just the driver. We got him from the defense as a part of discovery. We've talked to him and he'll hurt our case so we probably won't call him."

"How about the passengers in the rear seat?" I asked.

"What passengers?" Yochelson wanted to know.

"Martha and the kids."

"Who's Martha? What kids?" White's investigator, Mike Gillum asked.

Yochelson was catching on. "Do you know anything about the Ford?" he demanded.

"I know there were five people in it, three adults and two young girls. Their name is Leon and I've taken their statements. They were on their way home from a family party in San Bernardino and got caught in the traffic jam when the pursuit stopped. They said King was assaulted by the officers *after* he'd complied with their instructions . . . and your guy's a fake. That's what I know."

I told them about the decal on the car's door post and pointed it out when the car appeared on the video as I played it again. Then, I opened my photo album and showed them the photo I'd taken of the Probe a few days before. Yochelson got the strangest look on his face. I asked him if *his* Probe had a decal on the passenger door post. As if on cue, they all stood up and headed for the door. I cornered Gillum and asked him to explain the differences between his witness's statement and mine.

"Looks like the defense tried to stiff in a witness. We've got some checking to do. We'll get back to you." Right after the meeting, I started getting calls from many investigators involved in the case—the D.A.'s, LAPD's, even the FBI's. The defense didn't call any witnesses from the Probe during their case in Simi Valley, nor did the prosecution.

■

In late May, I was finally getting some sleep. But in Hollywood, at about 11:30 P.M. on May 26th, Rodney King was arrested by LAPD vice officers in what appeared to be a prostitution sweep. When I turned on the news the next morning, the top story was again about my client. King had been taken into custody and was under investigation for Assault with a Deadly Weapon (ADW) on a police officer. According to the news accounts, King had tried to run down two vice cops in a Hollywood alley.

Unshaven and disheveled, I fought the morning traffic, unnerved by what I was hearing on the radio. Steve Lerman called on the car phone to advise me King had been released pending completion of the official investigation. I drove straight to Lerman's house. Within a few minutes, the sleepless King arrived. As the morning sun rose above the foothills, King described his turbulent night.

He had been on his way home and stopped in at a local market for cigarettes and a soda. While there, a woman approached and told him her car had broken down and she needed a ride home. He didn't know it then, but this woman was really a man—a "shim," a drag queen. The shim directed King to an apartment complex where he pulled into a parking space. After a moment, King saw two Hispanic men in his rearview mirror sneaking up behind him. One of them carried something that looked like a gun. King panicked. He told his passenger to get down as he backed up and screeched toward Hollywood Boulevard in search of help. Less than a minute later, King flagged down an LAPD patrol car. His passenger fled on foot. King told Officer Jim Simonechi (an old partner of mine) and his rookie partner of the robbery attempt. Shouting and waving for the officers to follow, he raced back to the parking area. As soon as he pulled in, he was arrested for attempting to run down two vice officers.

LAPD media spokesmen said the vice officers identified themselves to King but as they went to arrest him, he tried to run them over in an attempt to escape. They fed the story to a media voracious for every detail of such a scandalous tale: Rodney King had offered money for sex with a male prostitute dressed as a woman, then tried to run down arresting officers.

I wasn't surprised by the story. The gun King saw was actually a two-way radio in the hand of a vice cop. The shim had beat feet and was long gone. Immediately following King's arrest, Chief Gates asked the D.A.'s office to investigate the circumstances. He felt the LAPD might appear vindictive if they were involved in the investigation. The D.A. then asked the attorney general's office to handle the follow-up, feeling the heat of this hot potato. The attorney general accepted the assignment and began investigative efforts. Once again, George Shaw got a shot at sending King back to the joint, and once again, I beat him out into the field.

It looked like it would be King's word against the LAPD, and this time there was no video. I spent the day talking to residents of the apartment complex where the incident occurred. It turned out to be a day full of surprises.

Bernice Dunn and Daisy Patton had lived for many years in

apartments above the alley. It was a warm night and their windows were open, but neither woman heard the police shout their identity. Neither woman heard anybody shout anything.

When I walked around the scene, I noticed something the cops and camera crews had missed, a man sleeping under a stairway. I could see that the man had a perfect view of the scene. Slowly, I began pacing distances and writing figures on a yellow pad, waiting for the sleeping man to awaken. When the alley sleeper stirred, I continued my routine, carefully ignoring him. After a few minutes, he called me over.

In his youth, the man we'll call Joey Gilles had been a dancer on Broadway. Now he lived in this Hollywood alley under a stairway. I hoped curiosity would get the best of him so I let him make the first move. He said simply, "I saw something."

"It was too dark," I said without looking at him.

Gilles was offended. "No, no, it was light enough. I saw the two guys, it was like they were playing a game." I knew he was telling the truth. I knew King had told me the truth.

"I saw them setting up the location a couple hours before King got here. I watched the police park near the corners and wait with their lights off. I knew it was a whore sweep but I didn't know who they'd get. They nearly always get somebody."

KNBC-TV reporter Patrick Healey showed up and had his camera man start to video my interview with Gilles. When the alley sleeper saw the camera, he looked at Healey and said, "I'm not going to talk with that thing on. Cops see me talking to you on TV, they'll be back here and I'll disappear for a few months. I don't need some humbug bullshit hung on me when I'm not even involved." Once Healey and his camerman left, Gilles went on with his story. "I know it was a setup. I saw it and so did some of the other people in the neighborhood. Talk to them, they'll tell you. What they did to Mr. King was dirty . . . then and now." Joey Gilles—Broadway dancer, Hollywood alley resident, frightened material witness.

In a nearby parking lot, I met a Hispanic named Castaneda. He too had watched the confrontation between King and the officers. And like Bernice Dunn, Daisy Patton, and Gilles, his story differed from that of the vice cops. Castaneda told me he was less than one hundred feet away. There was no conversation

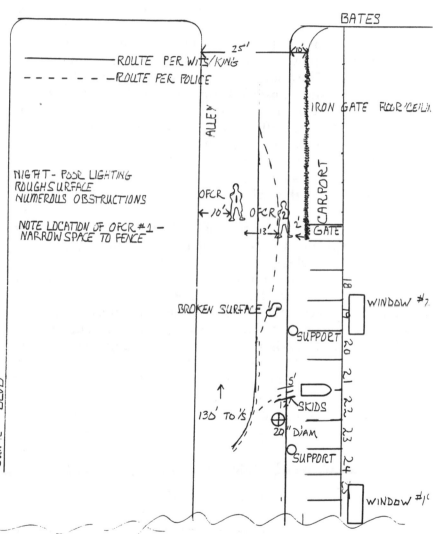

N

|||| STAIR-SLEEPER

BATES

ROUTE PER WITS/KING

25'

ROUTE PER POLICE

10'

ALLEY

IRON GATE FLOOR/CEILING

CARPORT

NIGHT- POOR LIGHTING
ROUGH SURFACE
NUMEROUS OBSTRUCTIONS

NOTE LOCATION OF OFCR #1 —
NARROW SPACE TO FENCE

OFCR

10'

OFCR

2'

13'

GATE

18

WINDOW #2

19

BROKEN SURFACE

SUPPORT

20

21

5'

22

17'

SKIDS

23

130' TO ½'

20" DIAM

SUPPORT

24

WINDOW #1

SUNSET BLVD

and no warning by the officers as they jumped out at the car. Only laughter.

Castaneda stood and watched as the car started up, backed out of the stall and accelerated straight down the alley, away from the two intruders. Contrary to allegations made by the arresting officers, Castaneda claimed King didn't veer in either direction, but drove straight ahead. "Neither guy said anything to the driver, they just jumped towards him and when he started the car, they stopped where they were. I didn't know who they were. They never said they were cops. I watched the car drive out onto Sunset." King saw a police car that was coming in his direction and stopped in the middle of the street. "I saw him talk to the officers but I couldn't hear what he was saying. I saw him wave his arm like, you know, follow me. He made a U-turn and came back to the alley.

"After they arrested him, they didn't want to talk to me. They saw me, but they didn't come over and talk or ask me anything."

I was convinced the arrest of Rodney King was a staged event. My suspicions were confirmed within minutes, as Castaneda pointed out where the shim was staying.

The rundown motel, on the east end of Hollywood's Sunset Boulevard was exactly what I had expected it to be, the kind of place that made you itch and scratch by just entering. With its exterior pink facade faded from years of California sun and the black trim paint graying with age, it had long since lost its appeal to the tourist trade and had become a pit stop in the nightly parade of hookers and pimps—twenty dollars for twenty minutes and no clean sheets.

Hector, the shim, is known on Sunset Boulevard as Diana—illegal alien, transvestite, snitch. In her interview with me, Diana was quick to say that picking up King was a payback to the vice cops for not booking her two weeks prior following a prostitution arrest in the northeast area of the city. The arrest of King canceled her debt; she had paid in full.

After a day of fun in the sun, and one revelation after another, I pointed my car towards home. I faxed my report to Steve Lerman just after midnight. Lerman had already retired for the night but I wanted him to have it when he awakened.

While I sat drinking my morning coffee, the phone rang. It was Lerman. "Read your report. Great work. I got a call late yesterday from Tim Fowler, Glen's parole agent. He's mad as hell, talking about violating Glen's parole and sending him back to the joint for a few months. He's got top brass from the attorney general's office on his ass. It's serious this time. A lot of political pressure seems to be coming from the LAPD to send King back to the slammer."

"No shit," I grumbled. Lerman and I had discussed the possibility of a parole hold or violation before I began my field investigation of the ADW arrest. "Is there anything that might take some of the pressure off Fowler?" I asked.

"Yeah, if they accept what you found to be factual."

I thought that was only a small part of the answer. I remembered the last time we had talked to the attorney general's office on the phone a few days after the pizzeria and video store robbery allegations. Because of perceived potential political pressure in the city, some viewed the charges as harassment by the LAPD. Now, they were faced with another possible harassment allegation stemming from King's arrest in Hollywood. Because of the heat, neither the LAPD nor the D.A.'s office wanted to do that investigation either.

During our phone conversation, Lerman again suggested we keep the parole authorities fully informed of what I found out in Hollywood. I agreed and drove to the Pasadena parole office to meet with Agent Fowler and his supervisor. My investigation report was delivered to the California Department of Corrections less than forty-eight hours after King's arrest in Hollywood.

It was reported in the media the following day that King would not have his parole status revoked. The California Department of Corrections then provided their own twist. In their press release, parole authorities criticized the LAPD, District Attorney's, and the attorney general's offices for their poor judgment in the way the arrest was handled. Three weeks later, the attorney general's office released their findings. Rodney King would not be prosecuted for attempting to run over the two vice cops. It was the first time in my experience that a case in which officers alleging an assault against them by a known suspect, resulting in an arrest, was not prosecuted.

"Good," I thought. "Shaw, you pompous ass, eat shit and die!"

For months, network talk shows from the midwest and New

York kept calling Lerman, hoping to get an exclusive interview with King. Each request was met with the same answer: No. Initially, King's injuries prohibited his appearance. Then, while his injuries were healing, King chose not to appear. In every conversation where television exposure was discussed, he would say he wasn't interested and would tell his story only to a jury. Steve Lerman became known as the guy who was holding King back from the media. The truth is, it was King himself who was holding back. There were several times when we felt it was imperative that King should speak out, the most memorable was immediately following his arrest in Hollywood. King's public image suffered tremendous damage when it was alleged that he had been caught in the company of a transvestite. I believed King could have regained some respect by agreeing to talk, since I had found in my investigation of the incident that he had been had and was not guilty of the charges by police.

No way would King go before cameras. He was embarrassed and felt soiled by the officers. He worried that he had disappointed the many children who had written him following his hospital stay. Neither Lerman nor I could convince him to go public with his side of the story.

After months, it became clear that Rodney King just wasn't available for interviews and requests dried up, but not before one of the tabloids contacted my associate, Don White, and tried to pay him to provide the address where we had moved King after his release from the hospital following his first surgery. Don reported the contact to me and I sent the tabloid hack to Kingman, Arizona, on a wild goose chase. Get your kicks on Route 66!

HEAD HUNTERS AND CLIMBERS

My schedule finally got so mixed up, I couldn't deal with it all. When I wasn't in the field, I was at King's apartment. On those rare occasions when I did try to spend an evening at home, my phone would ring. It would be Lerman with another problem or a witness he needed interviewed and I'd be out the door, Pat cussing Big Steve as I left. My workdays were averaging twenty hours, seven days a week. Three months into the case and my marriage, my business, and my life were all going to hell at incredible speeds.

Rich Sakaguchi couldn't handle the workload from the King case on top of his other commitments and resigned. George Rhodes and his staff had worked three weeks and gave me a bill for $5,500, so they were gone. They'd done a fine job, but I was out-of-pocket and couldn't afford them. Barb Lavarias, the only female on my staff, accepted a job offer from an investigator in Seattle, and Don White was out with his terminal illness. Harry Johnson was playing catch-up on his insurance fraud files while John Huelsman left to go preach on a fulltime basis. I'd caught one of my secretaries forging a payroll check and had her locked up. Some of my insurance company clients were cutting me off from additional work because I wasn't paying the proper amount of attention to their files. Hell, I wasn't paying the proper amount of attention to anything or anybody. My cellular phone bill tripled, the office long-distance bills doubled, and because of the man-hours needed in the King investigation, my payroll soared. Expenses went up, income declined, my cash reserves rapidly dwindled, and cash-flow became a real problem. Lerman paid as much as he could afford but expenses on the case outdistanced income by miles. I was like a captain on a sinking ship, in the middle of a naval battle, with no lifeboat and enemy planes diving in out of the sun.

Pat and I were arguing more about less, my kids were getting flack from their peers, and I hadn't had a day off in months. I was smoking more and eating less. My old car began breaking down at the most inopportune times, and my home investment was being pissed away in a bad real estate deal that I couldn't do a thing to stop. Every time I turned around, someone new wanted a chunk of my ass or more of my money or both. After all, I thought, they can kill me but they can't eat me.

But Rodney King was still the hottest ticket in town and the King investigation never left my thoughts. I'd stepped over the long-term dime to pick up the short-term nickel and couldn't find a polite way out.

When King couldn't persuade my staff to cut him some slack, he told Lerman he wanted someone else to be his security, which was fine with me because I could grab some time with my family. It took a few days to find the right guy to work with King.

International Full Contact Karate Champion, Ray Wizard, took on the job of keeping King out of harm's way. Slight of build, Wizard was not what one would expect a karate champion to look like. Soft-spoken, mild-mannered and friendly, he knew how difficult his job would be and accepted the challenge happily. As long as Ray was on the job, I knew my client was secure from unwanted intrusions. At times, Wizard was assisted by former IDF (Israeli Defense Forces) people, whose reputations were awesome. I wish I'd had them for all my clients.

■

As the cool days of spring turned to the lazy days of summer, Freddie G was killed in a traffic accident. According to witnesses, the car in which he was riding struck a telephone pole after being run off the road by a phantom vehicle they described as a four-door Chevrolet Caprice Classic with painted wheels. Witnesses told me the car resembled others seen in the neighborhood known to be "narc" cars, cars driven by undercover police officers. I failed to confirm this, though my photos of the crash scene clearly show skid marks running parallel to those of Freddie's death car for 170 feet. With no one to identify the phantom vehicle, I was at a dead end.

The accident occurred in front of a house where a party was in full swing. One of the guests heard the sounds of tires squealing and ran outside with a video camera, just in time to capture the death rattle of Freddie G. The ten minute home video is gory in its images of Freddie as he lies dying in the middle of the street. The driver of the car, a friend, had been drinking. He was arrested and subsequently convicted on two counts of manslaughter. Sentenced to two years in prison, he is already back on the streets after serving only one year.

■

Investigators in the Internal Affairs Division are not well respected by their brothers and sisters in blue. Called "Head Hunters" and "Climbers" by the rank and file, their role within the structure of a police department is essential to the department's effective operations. Losing one's sense of humor seems to be required for acceptance into IAD. In my personal experiences with the Los Angeles Police Department IAD, I never felt they were committed to finding the truth or upholding justice. Surely, there are some within IAD who care about being fair but I never met one.

During the summer of 1991, the first internal report on the King incident was presented to Chief of Police Daryl Gates by the commanding officer of IAD. Within days, it came into my possession. Then, at a news conference in June, Steve Lerman announced we were in communication with someone inside the department. Afterwards, my contacts with Blue Throat became fewer and farther between. There was a rumor that an investigation was underway to identify the traitor and cut off his balls.

Days and weeks passed with little or no contact from Blue Throat. It was during one of our last contacts, that I was given the IAD report on the investigation into the King beating. I was sworn to secrecy; Blue Throat feared another public announcement by Lerman.

I called Steve from the field and told him of my most recent acquisition. I had read several dozen pages before calling, so I could provide him a summary of the contents. "Steve there's a God and he smiles down on *us* from time to time. It's dynamite. Finally, they're all locked into a story. No more bullshit, they're on the record."

IAD may not be highly thought of by street cops but on this investigation they'd done a very good job, considering they were being lied to. The officers involved lied to IAD or to others in the investigative process. Either way, they had committed to a lie and I knew I'd eventually see them crash and burn for it.

The IAD interviewed over forty witnesses during their investigation. Statements from three of the four accused officers were included, as were statements of other key players. Now, for the first time, we could begin to piece through the official version of what happened. There were statements from officers present at the incident, as well as from citizens who were present at the apartment building, on the sidewalk, or in the bus. Many names were familiar to me. We also knew many names were missing from their witness list. On the surface, Lerman and I had done a much more in-depth investigation than the cops.

Officer Briseno had a day off when the IAD initiated field investigations at Foothill Division. When he returned to work, he had obtained a medical evaluation claiming stress, preventing him from being questioned. To this date, he has not been interviewed by IAD.

Sergeant Koon completed his interview over a two-day period, separated by a week. Both Powell and Wind submitted to interviews when requested, with Wind providing a statement before he had talked to a lawyer or a Police Protective League representative.

Rookies present the best place to start an IAD investigation because they're on probation and don't have all the protections of an officer on the job. Termination is much easier without the protections of civil service. IAD investigators routinely capitalize on the fear factor of probationary officers. Under California law, an officer can be ordered to give a statement—even if it's self—incriminating—only for the purpose of the internal administrative and disciplinary hearing processes. Failure to comply can be cause for an additional allegation of insubordination, which can result in termination. But because a statement can be compelled, it cannot be used in any criminal court proceedings which may follow. Under the law, this would violate the officer's rights under the Fifth Amendment. This is clearly defined in California by the Liebarger case which states that any compelled materials collected by internal investigators are precluded from use by a criminal prosecutor.

On March 4, 1991, within hours of the first airing of the video, Tim Wind submitted to an administrative order to provide a statement to IAD. He did not have a defense rep with him. Because he didn't testify at the criminal trial, what follows is the only telling of Wind's version of the incident.

He told Internal Affairs investigators that he was assigned to work with Officer Powell that morning. He had worked with Powell on several other shifts but had been on the A.M. watch for just a few nights. He was instructed to read King's arrest report, prepared the previous night by Powell, and told to circle anything he didn't agree with. He read the report and made many circles.

He disagreed with the arrest report where it said Powell stumbled back. Wind thought "Powell backed away intentionally." Wind could see Koon move in with the taser. He was trying to control the driver's feet and believed that King's size intimidated everyone. Koon fired the taser. King uttered "ugh" and sat straight up with a look of *pain* on his face. Koon fired the taser a second time. "Everyone was yelling but no one was giving orders," Wind said. Briseno warned Wind several times to, "Step back and not get juiced by the taser," which reinforced my hypothesis that Bresino was not trying to stop the beating as he stated in his testimony during the trial, but was simply reminding Powell to be careful of electricity from the taser.

According to Wind, "King was shouting incoherently from the *pain* of the taser." Again, this counters the statement of Powell and Koon, who said King didn't feel any pain during the beating. On page 307 of the report, Wind says he then saw

Powell, "hit the driver a second time on the cheek, this time causing his face to bleed." If this had been known to the jury in Simi Valley, it may well have had a dramatic effect on the verdicts. I assume it was this statement, which went against their best interest, that was responsible for keeping Wind off the stand; if he repeated his comments in court, it would have shown both Powell and Koon misled the jury in their testimony. A year later in Simi Valley, both Powell and Koon admitted that head shots to King under the circumstances existing at the time of the incident would have been excessive force. If blows to King's head were proved to have happened, the reports submitted by Powell and Koon would in fact contain false and misleading information.

Briseno's warning to Wind to avoid the taser wires would have destroyed his defense that he was merely trying to stop the beating. It would have shown him to be an active participant, further evidenced by his stomp to the back of King's head twenty-seven seconds after he is seen on the video pushing Powell away from King. Bresino *was* a full participant if we are to accept Wind's statement. In fact, Wind may have been the officer, of those directly involved in the incident, who showed the most restraint, notwithstanding his kicks to King as he lay on the ground, motionless.

"Powell then hit him several more times around his upper torso but I couldn't see where the strikes were landing because I was moving around King. Powell had already moved to an area near King's head. I was really excited and transfixed in not letting the guy get away," Wind claimed.

Wind concluded his IAD interview by saying nothing happened at the hospital after he had arrived there with King in the ambulance. He omitted statements that later came out in testimony.

Months later in the criminal trial in Simi Valley of the accused officers, there would be some discussion of these Liebarger materials. Defense attorneys took great measures in advance of the Simi Valley criminal trial to keep the compelled IAD materials away from the jury. If the jury had seen these materials, the verdicts might have been different. Most important, in my opinion, was that the IAD had already interviewed many civilian witnesses to the beating and summarily dismissed their testimony as invalid. Other witnesses apparently lied to the investigators and the lies weren't confronted.

For example, in the IAD report, Police Officer Corina Smith, who was accompanied by her attorney and administrative defense rep during the interview, failed to tell the investigators that she had once had a conjugal relationship with Larry Powell. On the surface, this omission appears trivial. But it was Officer Smith to whom Powell made what is referred to as the Gorillas in the Mist MDT transmissions that preceded the King incident by several hours. She told the investigators she had no idea what that comment meant or if it was racially motivated. One can conclude, based on her undisclosed relationship with Powell, that she *did* know him very well and *did* know what he meant by the MDT transmission. The IAD Report identifies Smith as the officer to whom Powell sent the MDT message, "Oops . . . I haven't beaten anybody this bad in a long time." She replied, "Oh no, why for you do that?" She denied any racial animosity and told the investigators that her selection of words was "police jargon."

On page 122 of the report, Sergeant Rick Distefano, assistant watch commander on the night of the incident, said he felt that since Sergeant Koon was already at the termination point of the chase, he needn't leave the station to provide supervision at the scene. He went on to say that when Koon returned to the station and explained the incident to him, Koon was critical of the baton actions by Powell. Koon thought Powell was ineffective and had "agitated" King after he was already down, compliant, and still. During Distefano's testimony at the trial, this information slipped his memory.

Officer Kenneth Phillippe was the observer on board the helicopter orbiting above the Tastee Freeze. It was the helicopter light that illuminated the area so Holliday's camera could tape the beating. Without this light, we might not have seen the incident at all.

Phillippe, who appeared with his administrative defense rep, told IAD he didn't see the beating. He testified he was looking into the park next to the pursuit termination point for additional suspects and wasn't paying attention to what was happening directly below. He knew there were plenty of officers present by the number of cars, and he knew the CHP was at the scene because of their distinctive light bars. He saw that traffic was stopped in both directions and he could see the band bus in the traffic snarl. Throughout his questioning, Phillipe maintained that he didn't see the beating. The Code of Silence strikes again. A close examination of the Holliday video shows the chopper light was kept centered on the incident. That light is operated by the observer while the pilot flies the aircraft. In order for the light to remain centered, the observer *must* be looking at the incident.

In the spring of 1992, Officer Phillippe was found guilty of misconduct by a panel of officers and received a forty-four day suspension for "failing to see," his job being that of observer. He remains one of the few officers present at the scene of the incident to get disciplined for wrongdoing. In a subsequent appeal of his suspension, the sentence was reduced to an admonishment or warning. He received no suspension or days off by chief Gates, who was then in the final days of his administration.

■

On March 6, 1991, Officer Larry Powell, represented by two administrative defense representatives, was interviewed by a pair of investigators from IAD. Powell declined to waive his Miranda rights but consented to the interview as ordered, thereby precluding his statement from being admitted in a criminal trial. In his recorded statement, Powell said he was working with his rookie partner, Tim Wind, at about 12:30 A.M. on March 3, 1991. When he heard the radio broadcast of the CHP pursuit, he drove in that direction and saw a white Hyundai containing three male blacks being chased by a CHP car and a police car from the Los Angeles Unified School District. He took a secondary position to the Singers in the chase, with the school cops then falling into third.

The chase ended and he believes a second LAPD unit containing Briseno and Solano arrived within thirty seconds. Powell said only the CHP officers were giving commands at the time. This is in conflict with what other officers present had said in their official recounting of the incident.

Powell stated, "King finally stepped out of the car, placed his right hand on the roof and his left hand in his left pocket. He started looking around, at the air unit, at us. He had a dazed expression on his face." Powell feared King might be reaching for a gun. King was ordered to get down, on his face. "King had a weird expression on his face. His movements were slow and stiff. He stepped away from his car, fifteen to twenty feet. Finally, King went down. But not all the way. He went into a sort of push up position." Still photos made from the Holliday video clearly show King lying flat on the ground.

More officers approached. Powell heard Koon say, "If this guy starts to fight, just get back out of the way." Powell could see Koon had the taser in his hand and knew what that meant. Powell noted King's size, six-three and 225 pounds. For the record, Powell is six-one and 195. Powell says at this time he, Wind, Briseno, and Solano moved in to handcuff King, but as they closed the distance, King began to rise from his pushup position. As this happened, Powell lost his balance and stumbled back onto his haunches. (He later testified in Simi Valley that he was "knocked back.") Once Powell stumbled, King pushed up off his knees. Koon then used the taser for the first time. The beating had begun.

An examination of the Holliday video shows Powell already standing in his Casey-at-the-bat stance. The photos demonstrate Powell wasn't stumbling or falling. He was standing flat-footed, bending at the knees, getting ready to deliver the first torrent of blows to King's head and upper torso.

Powell told the IAD investigators he did not hit King in the head or face with his baton, accidentally, or intentionally. His strokes were aimed at King's upper torso and arms and legs. He said the first stroke seen on Holliday's video, a baseball-style, round-house, home run swing, hit King in the upper torso as King charged at him. He said King's charge surprised him and his swing was a defensive reaction to it. He said King immediately went down after the swing and his face collided with the pavement. He testified that if King's facial bones were broken, it would have happened at that time.

An examination of the Holliday video clearly shows Powell taking two shuffle steps to cut into King's path as he tries to flee. As King runs, Powell begins the swing. That swing connects with King's face and King falls to his hands and knees. Then the camera blurs and is out of focus for several seconds. although more baton strikes by Powell can be seen unmistakably. In the course of my investigation, I've viewed that video over one thousand times and have consistently counted nineteen attempted strokes. What is unclear is, how many connect with King's torso.

In a recent development, Stanley P. Martin who works with Holliday's former attorney, Jim Jordan, has had the first few seconds of the video stabilized with state-of-the-art equipment. The few seconds in which the images are out of focus are now much clearer. In those stabilized frames one can clearly see nineteen strokes attempted, with all landing on King's torso: fourteen on the upper portion, five on the lower back and arms. Most important, there are clearly two hatchet chops, "two from the sky," delivered by Powell to the back of King's head. Also noteworthy is the fact that King's head clearly does not strike the pavement, but remains above the fender of the police car parked nearest to the Hyundai. This single piece of evidence controverts Powell's testimony that King's injuries were self-inflicted when his face hit the pavement.

The most important part of Powell's statement is his denial of any head shots. As he reviewed the video with IAD, he told the investigators that, because the focus was blurred, he couldn't see any out-of-policy blows to King. His entire statement is a denial of any wrongdoing. He said he was acting under instructions from Koon, and that King's actions were controlling the incident. He had no memory of anyone kicking or stomping King and felt his blows were not inflicting pain, insisting King was drugged and oblivious to pain throughout the entire incident. He claimed King made no sounds except grunts as he tried to get up, yet when one listens to the sound track on the video, King can clearly be heard screaming with pain at each attack by the officers. Once, the sound of a baton blow to King's leg can be heard, as the leg is broken by a blow. Again, King screams in pain. Powell later testified at trial that one of the symptoms of PCP intoxication is imperviousness to pain. King's screams belie his testimony.

At trial, Powell denied there was any racial animus involved in the MDT transmissions. It is interesting that Powell was not asked *one* question related to the transmissions during his IAD statement, while other officers were questioned at length about the MDT materials.

■

Tim and Melanie Singer of the California Highway Patrol were interviewed by the IAD, beginning on March 26, 1991 in the CHP headquarters in Los Angeles. Both Singers were represented by hearing reps and attorneys provided by the CHP. Tim Singer began by denying he'd ever told his dispatcher he was following a vehicle at a high rate of speed on the freeway, though this is clearly audible on the broadcast tape of the chase. Then followed a series of misstatements and contradictions:

Singer said, "While on Paxton Street, the Hyundai reached speeds of eighty miles-per-hour." Then in the next sentence he says that once his partner, Melanie, activated their red lights, "the Hyundai never exceeded sixty-five miles-per-hour." He said when King was shot with the second taser dart, he staggered toward his vehicle when in fact, King was on the ground being pummeled by baton blows when the second taser was fired.

On page 260 of the report, Tim Singer states he didn't recall which end of his flashlight was used to push Freddie Helms's head back to the ground, and after discovering Helms was injured, he didn't notice any bleeding, only the laceration. This contradicts statements by other officers, that neither Helms nor Allen were injured in any way, that both had complied with commands, exited the Hyundai, lay on the ground, and were subsequently released without incident.

During the pursuit there was no indication to Tim Singer that the driver of the Hyundai was under the influence; the car was wanted for excessive speed only. He failed to allege elements of DUI and felony evading. Once the Hyundai had stopped at Foothill and Osborne, the driver and passengers complied with the commands of the officers, and the driver (King) slowly did what he was told. As King lay on the ground, Tim Singer heard an unknown male officer shout, "Get back. Everybody get away." He then heard the popping sounds of the taser. After hearing the second taser round fired, Singer could see King's face convulsing from the shock. He watched as Powell "moved in and swung his baton, striking King on the right side of his head." This testimony confirms both Tim Wind's and numerous citizens' statements that head shots were struck.

Melanie Singer also gave a statement to IAD and like her husband Tim, she, too, had representatives from the CHP with her. By this time, she had already completed two written statements, one for the CHP and one for Robbery Homicide Division of the LAPD. During her statement to IAD, she was allowed to examine her previous reports and make any corrections she deemed necessary.

She said after King had exited his Hyundai, he placed his hands on the roof without being told to do so. He then "grabbed his right buttock with his right hand and shook it" at her. She drew her gun and ordered King to lie on the ground. King complied. As other officers approached King, he began to resist and stood up. She felt frightened. Koon ordered the officers to back away from King and fired the taser. She didn't know where the darts struck King. Then a second round was fired.

Melanie Singer said she watched as Powell's first baton blow struck King on the right side of his face, under the cheekbone. She told the investigators, "At this time in the altercation, there were approximately sixteen or seventeen officers present at the scene." In his book, *Presumed Guilty*, Sergeant Koon states there were only seven officers present, including himself.

Singer then describes the torrent of baton blows by Powell that followed: "Powell struck King on his right cheekbone and across his knuckles with his baton. King had put his hands up in front of his face. The remaining baton strikes were in and around his head."

She admitted that while she suspected King was intoxicated, she didn't think he was on PCP. She told the investigators she had not seen any officer kneeling on King's back while trying to handcuff him. This statement conflicts with Powell's. She didn't see King rise up off the ground and throw off an officer. She was only ten to fifteen feet away, and believes she would have seen this if it had happened. She felt King was incapacitated after Koon's second firing of the taser, and that the beating which followed was completely unnecessary.

She said when King went down to his knees after the second taser, she saw Powell step in and *intentionally strike King on his face with the baton*. "Koon never took control of the situation and no one gave any commands to King after the second use of the taser. The officers around King were told to 'get back.' He didn't throw the officers off him. Koon never gave the order to swarm King." Mrs. Singer was in a position to hear all commands by Koon, and never heard him order his officers to strike

King with their batons. Once again, she counters the statements of Powell and Koon.

This statement by Officer Melanie Singer carries with it the same problems as her husband's. While much may be factual and benefit King, other parts detract from her credibility and the whole statement then suffers. She still maintained that the Hyundai was exceeding 110 MPH.

The IAD Report is 315 pages. Investigators interviewed over three dozen witnesses. Every interview was tape recorded. The report is a masterpiece of information and documentation. Hundreds, perhaps thousands of man-hours went into the completion of the document. To what purpose?

Because all officers interviewed were compelled to provide statements, not one word will ever see the light of a criminal courtroom. Not one page of evidence obtained from these witnesses was allowed in the Federal actions against the officers.

Ten or more officers at the scene have received administrative hearings for various allegations of misconduct associated with the incident. Except for some minor disciplinary actions, not one of the so-called bystander officers has yet received a significant suspension. The system allows for a hearing against these officers by other officers from the same school, the LAPD School. They share that binding association. For the accused officers, the system works well. For the citizens of Los Angeles, the system continues to fail them. Many IAD investigators involved in this undertaking are good thinking, responsible men and women who really care about the people they serve. Despite that, I'm not convinced the investigation was as complete as it could and should have been. Some important questions and answers are obvious by their absence:

1. Why wasn't the helicopter crew asked about the on-board video camera and tape of the incident, rumored to have been ordered destroyed?
2. Why wasn't Powell asked about the MDT transmissions and his personal relationship to Officer Smith?
3. How is it I was able to discover this information and the department let it slide?
4. Why wouldn't the LAPD release the recording of the pursuit tape to the King Team but did release it to the media?

5. Why wasn't the recording of the ambulance call from the LAPD dispatcher to the Fire Department dispatcher used?
6. Why didn't the department locate and interview the real people in the Ford Probe, and why weren't they later called to testify in Simi Valley?
7. Who was the witness alleged by the defense to have been driving the Probe and was the witness interviewed? And if not, why?

The public never heard any of this. On several occasions, the King team attempted to attend administrative disciplinary hearings related to the beating and monitor their results. This proved to be a difficult task; hearings were closed or, in other cases, continued to a later date, with no public announcement of the new date.

Months into the investigation, I still had more questions than answers.

MONKEY SLAPPING TIME

Under California law, before a lawsuit can be filed against the City of Los Angeles, a claim for damages must be filed, demanding a sum of money or other compensation from the city for injuries received or other losses. Such was the case in the King incident. As required by law, Lerman filed a $54 million damage claim with the City of Los Angeles.

Why fifty-four? The media was reporting that the LAPD had counted fifty-four baton strikes administered by the officers during the beating. I'd gone through the video several times with King, hoping to trigger some additional recollections. Each time we reviewed the tape, King's anger and frustration grew at seeing himself beaten and humiliated. During one of our viewings King finally blew. He picked up the phone and called Lerman. "I'm watching the video and those bastards should have to pay a million bucks for each time they hit me," he said, anger in his voice.

"Glen, a $54 million claim might seem unacceptable to some people," Lerman said, "but if that's what you want, then so be it." He knew that if the suit went to trial, King would be awarded damages based on proof, not a specific dollar amount, so why not fifty-four million? In an ironic footnote, it has been estimated that fifty-four people lost their lives in the rioting that followed the Simi Valley verdicts.

As I sat and watched King talk to Lerman on the phone, I could see him respond to Lerman's reassurances. Often, a telephone conversation with King would begin on a down note, but Lerman seemed to have a soothing effect on him. I didn't. Many times, my conversations had just the opposite effect. Initially, my focus was on issues related directly to the incident, while Lerman, who seldom talked about the beating with King, was the voice of reason, common sense, and calm. This unintentional Mutt and Jeff teaming of Lerman and me served King well those first months. I became the stern housemother while Lerman continued to be King's friend and confidant.

■

"Well Tom, it's started," Lerman said when I picked up the phone.

"What's started?"

"The cross complaints. Several were filed in the past two weeks. Looks like they're all going to do it."

I wasn't surprised. We'd expected it right from the beginning. We knew the defendant officers wouldn't sit idly by and let King sue them without responding some way on their own behalf. It made sense. Cross complaints slowed the forward momentum of the civil litigation against the officers; by filing a cross complaint, they could protect their statutory time limitations for claims against the city.

"We also received a notice that King has to give his deposition to Briseno's people within two weeks." Lerman's voice sounded aggravated. [King's deposition was taken in November 1993.]

"They're trying to backdoor discovery in the criminal case by using the civil case to get King's testimony," I said.

"Sure they are, and I don't think the court'll allow it. But it really makes me angry that I have to prepare a response and fight it out in court. It's just going to burn needless time and effort on everyone's part."

"Well Steve, that's what makes a horse race," I said, knowing Lerman would tie up Briseno's defense team with responses to their motions.

Meanwhile, Ted Briseno's medical excuse kept him off duty for reasons of stress, which provided two immediate benefits to him. First, according to LAPD policy, no officer can be compelled to give a statement in an internal investigation while on medical leave. Second, in most cases an officer on medical leave can't be suspended without pay. Briseno continued to draw sick pay long after his codefendants were suspended by Gates without pay following the indictments. Briseno had gotten good advice.

While we'd expected at least one of the officers to cross complain against King, we were surprised that the first to file was Ted Briseno. According to his cross complaint, Briseno accused King of assaulting him. In other words, Briseno participates fully in the beating, kicks King in the head, then sues the victim. The guy's got a great sense of humor.

More gallows laughs: Koon and Powell also filed suits against the City of Los Angeles for improper training and supervision, even naming Chief Gates as a codefendant with the city. *We* were making the same allegations. Rodney King and the defendant officers had become allies in actions against the city. Strange bedfellows.

Once Lerman was served notice of the officers' cross complaints, Briseno's civil attorney, Greg Peterson, notified Lerman of Rodney King's deposition, scheduled within two weeks. This surprised us, considering the civil suit against the officers had been placed on hold by both Judge Kamins of the Superior Court and Judge Davies for the Federal Court. Then began a series of motions and countermotions aimed at getting the deposition of King in anticipation of his testimony in the criminal case.

Finally, Judge Davies agreed that the discovery hold applied to all parties for all purposes and denied Briseno's motion to compel King's deposition, but not before dozens of hours of research and writing time had been expended on fighting the motions. Certainly, it was an effort the defense had to make, just on the chance they might have pulled it off. It would have given them months to determine how to crash King's testimony before his anticipated appearance in Simi Valley.

```
 1  Theodore Briseno
    ████ East Chapman Avenue                              FILED
 2  Orange, California 92666

 3  Pro Se Defendant
                                                  JUL 10   2 43 PM '91
 4
                                                   ·· ·  ···  ·· ·· COURT
 5                                                 ··· · · ·· · CALIF.

 6                    UNITED STATES DISTRICT COURT

 7                    CENTRAL DISTRICT OF CALIFORNIA

 8

 9  RODNEY GLENN KING,              )  CASE NO. 91 2497 JGD (Tx)
                                    )
10       Plaintiff,                 )  DEFENDANT THEODORE BRISENO'S
                                    )  CROSS-COMPLAINT AGAINST CITY
11  vs.                             )  OF LOS ANGELES, POLICE CHIEF
                                    )  DARYL F. GATES, LAPD SERGEANT
12  CITY OF LOS ANGELES, MAYOR TOM  )  STACY KOON, STATE OF CALIFORNIA
    BRADLEY, CHIEF OF POLICE DARYL  )  CHP OFFICERS MELANIE SINGER,
13  F. GATES, LOS ANGELES POLICE    )  TIMOTHY SINGER, RODNEY GLENN
    CAPT. JOHN MUTZ, LAPD           )  KING, and MOES 1 through 50
14  LIEUTENANT P.J. CONMAY, LAPD    )
    SERGEANT STACY KOON, LAPD       )  (Indemnity, Assault,
15  SERGEANT TROUT, LOS ANGELES     )  Negligent Training and
    POLICE OFFICERS LAURENCE M.     )  Supervision)
16  POWELL, TIMOTHY WIND, TED       )
    BRISENO, DAVID O. AVILA, TIM    )
17  E. BLAKE, SUSAN J. CLEMMER,     )
    PAUL EAJDUK, INGRID LARSON,     )
18  DAVID A. LOVE, JOSEPH F.        )
    NAPOLITANO, KENNETH A.          )
19  PHILLIPPE, DANNY SHRY, ROBERT   )
    J. SIMPACH, ROLANDO SOLANO,     )
20  LOUIS M. TURRIAGA, OFFICER      )
    AMOTT, CALIFORNIA HIGHWAY       )
21  PATROL OFFICERS LIEUTENANT      )
    ᵀᴼᴺᵞ KILBASA, CAPT. DENNIS      )
22  TRUMAN, SERGEANT ROMAN          )
    VONDRISKI, TIMOTHY SINGER,      )
23  MELANIE SINGER, GABRIEL AID     )
    and FRANK SCHULTZ LOS ANGELES   )
24  UNIFIED SCHOOL DISTRICT, LOS    )
    ANGELES UNIFIED SCHOOL          )
25  DISTRICT OFFICER PAUL           )
    BEAUREGARD and MARK DIAMOND     )
26  and DOES 1 TO 200,              )
                                    )
27       Defendants.               )
                                    )
28  ─────────────────────────────────

    ‖
```

```
 1│ OFFICERS PAUL BEAUREGARD and MARK)
   │ DIAMOND; and DOES 1 through 200, )
 2│                                   )
   │            Defendants.           )
 3│ ──────────────────────────────────)
   │                                   )
 4│ THEODORE BRISENO,                 )
   │                                   )
 5│             Cross-Complainant,    )
   │                                   )
 6│         vs.                       )
   │                                   )
 7│ CITY OF LOS ANGELES; DARYL F.     )
   │ GATES, SERGEANT STACY KOON,      )
 8│ THE STATE OF CALIFORNIA, CHP      )
   │ OFFICER MELANIE SINGER, CHP      )
 9│ OFFICER TIMOTHY SINGER and MOES   )
   │ 1 through 50, inclusive,         )
10│                                   )
   │            Cross-Defendants.     )
11│ ──────────────────────────────────)
```

12   Defendant, TIMOTHY SINGER, (hereinafter "SINGER") for

13 himself alone and for no other party answers the unverified

14 "Cross-Complaint" of Defendant/Cross-Complainant THEODORE BRISENO

15 (hereinafter "Defendant/Cross-Complainant") as follows:

16

17   **FIRST CROSS-CLAIM FOR RELIEF**

18   (Against the City of Los Angeles for Indemnity)

19   1.   In answer to paragraph 1, SINGER admits the

20 allegations therein.

21   2.   In answer to paragraph 2, SINGER lacks sufficient

22 knowledge or information with which to form a belief as to the

23 truth or veracity of the allegations in paragraph 2, and based

24 thereon, denies, specifically and generally, each and every

25 allegation contained therein.

26 ///

27

28

Like many other major metropolitan areas around the country, Los Angeles has a Mayor-Council form of government. Under this structure, the Mayor appoints the various department managers, ie: Water and Power, Street Maintenance, Traffic, Sewer and Waste Treatment, Fire, and Police. The city council either accepts or rejects the mayor's appointment. Because the City of Los Angeles is a civil service employer, appointed department managers also enjoy civil service protections, or did until the June, 1993, elections, when this condition was thrown out by the voters, a direct reaction to Chief Gates's long refusal to retire.

The Civil Service Commission is the final hiring and firing authority for all covered city employees, including police officers. Once an individual completes probationary status and gains regular employment, should the police department want to remove that person, it must forward a recommendation for removal to the Civil Service Commission who then makes the final decision to terminate or retain. Promotions and demotions must also be approved or declined by the Civil Service Commission. These policies came about as a result of the LAPD political corruption scandals in the thirties and early forties. Since then, the reputation of the Los Angeles Police Department has been above reproach, as far as the public is concerned, except for occasional sensational incidents like the Watts Riots in 1965, the Eulia Love shooting in the late seventies, and now the Rodney King incident.

While Chief Daryl Gates managed the day-to-day operations of the LAPD, the real policymaker is the Los Angeles Police Commission, made up of five individuals from the community, appointed by the mayor. Some have called these mayoral commission appointees political payback positions. In the weeks and months following the King incident, there was a great public outcry, demanding Chief Gates resign or be terminated.

It was widely believed Gates couldn't be fired. Not true; he could have been, but not by the mayor or the city council. Because of his civil service protections, Gates's termination could only have occurred for violations of laws and policies—if requested by the mayor and approved by the Civil Service Commission. As the public clamored for the dismissal of Chief Gates, little attention was paid to the fact that Mayor Bradley, who had not been a Gates supporter for years, *never* found enough fault in Gates's management or personnel practices to comment on his performance evaluations written by the police commission. For years, these reports were merely rubber-stamped by the mayor. During the failed attempts to remove him from office, Gates used the argument, "How can I be rightfully removed for misconduct or ineffective leadership when all previous evaluations failed to disclose a pattern of mismanagement?" Eventually, the public infighting between Chief Gates and Mayor Bradley forced other political repercussions. Attorney Melanie Lomax was causing Chief Gates increasing anguish following her 1990 appointment to the police commission by Mayor Bradley. Eventually, the outspoken African-American woman was forced to resign after "leaking" MDT transmissions containing the "Gorillas in the Mist" and other racially motivated comments to the media. Commissioner Lomax had been in the forefront of those calling for the resignation of Gates after the King beating. She had been critical of the Chief's handling of the incident from the beginning.

Retired Assistant Police Chief Jessie Brewer was appointed by Mayor Bradley to replace her. It was no secret that Chief Brewer was critical of his ex-boss, feeling Gates was slow to make policy decisions and inconsistent in their applications. Bob Vernon had assumed most operational functions of the department, Gates delegated the tough decisions to him and other subordinates. While the Holliday video was still being played on local and network news broadcasts, a pattern of accusation and denial was evident at all levels of city government.

As the investigation continued, time blurred—hours turned into days, weeks into months. The business of preparing King's case went forward with all due caution. I took the Holliday video to Hollywood experts, hoping they could work their magic on it. Cinesound Studios got first shot at clearing up the audio track. I hoped sounds of the helicopter circling overhead could be deleted without reducing the vocal audio. Even with Dr. Papcun's expert opinion, I wanted additional corroboration of racial animus on the tape. Metrolight Studios, which won an Academy Award for visual effects in the movie *Terminator*, tried to clean up the visual tracks of the tape. Their efforts were only marginally successful because of the poor quality of the original video. The out-of-focus portions still remain out-of-focus, though some images are clearer.

•

We were so busy locating and interviewing witnesses, collecting written data, and researching previous cases, we hardly noticed the attention being paid to the panel appointed by Mayor Bradley and Daryl Gates to investigate the King incident. Formally known as the Independent Commission on the Los Angeles Police Department, the Christopher Commission, as it's more widely known, officially began their work on April 1, 1991. The Commission was created to put the Los Angeles Police Department under a microscope and make recommendations for resolving any problems encountered, as well as evaluating the department's operational capabilities in the wake of the beating.

The commission began its life as two separate entities formed by the Mayor and the Chief, which were soon consolidated into the more meaningful Independent Commission, headed by Bradley appointee Warren Christopher, former Deputy Secretary of State under President Jimmy Carter and now the top guy in Bill Clinton's State Department. Retired California Associate Supreme Court Justice, John Arguelles, a Gates appointee, was vice-chairman.

Rounding out the Commission were Roy A. Anderson, former Chairman of the Lockheed Corporation; Willie R. Barnes, former California Corporations Commissioner; Leo F. Estrada, Professor of Urban Development at UCLA; lawyer and Clinton campaign manager Mickey Kantor; former Federal Judge Richard M. Mosk; Andrea Sheridan Ordin, a former Federal prosecutor; President of Occidental College, John Brooks Slaughter; and Robert E. Tranquada, former Dean of the USC School of Medicine. All were well-known and highly respected in their fields. The appointees were assisted by a staff of over one hundred for the three months during which the commission conducted preliminary hearings.

On July 8th, the day before the scheduled release of the commission report, I got a telephone call from a friend in the media, offering to provide me an advance copy. I took him up on it and stopped in at a small Mexican restaurant with the report, eager to see what it said. As I read, I took notes on items I considered to be new news. I quickly discovered that what I thought would be yet another cover-up by yet another bureaucratic panel, was in fact a scathing indictment of the LAPD, its policies, practices, and procedures.

The commission began its report by stating:

> The Rodney King beating stands as the landmark in the recent history of law enforcement, comparable to the Scottsboro case in 1931 and the Serpico case in 1967. Rightly called "sickening" by President Bush, and condemned by all segments of society, the King incident provides an opportunity for evaluation and reform of police procedures.
>
> . . . Our report concentrates on excessive force under color of law. Our commission has conducted an unprecedented inquiry into the use of excessive force by a police department. More than fifty expert witnesses, a hundred and fifty representatives of community organizations and private citizens, have been heard in five public hearings. More than five hundred present and retired Los Angeles police officers have been interviewed.
>
> . . . Police work is dangerous. The right to use force carries with it a heavy responsibility not to abuse it. The Commission found that there is a significant number of officers in the LAPD who repetitively use excessive force against the public and ignore the guidelines of the department regarding force. The Commission also found that the problem of excessive force is aggravated by racism and bias.
>
> . . . The failure to control these officers is a management issue that is at the heart of the problem. The documents and data that we have analyzed have all been available to the department; indeed, most of this information came from that source. The LAPD's failure to analyze and act upon these revealing data evidences a significant breakdown in the management and leadership of the department. The police commission, lacking investigators and other resources, failed in its duty to monitor the department in this sensitive use of force area. The department not only failed to deal with the problem group of officers but it often rewarded them with positive evaluations and promotions.
>
> . . . We urge that the leadership of the LAPD go beyond rhetoric in carrying out its existing policies against excessive force. From the chief of police on down to the sergeants, this means taking a firm stand against the "bad guys" and employ-

ing all the instruments available—training, discipline, assignments, and promotion. We urge a comparable effort to root out the manifestations of racism and bias.

The Commission identified by name forty-four officers with unusually high numbers of excessive force complaints. I looked over the list and recognized some familiar names, officers with whom I'd worked, and whose attitudes toward the public I knew. My own name may well have made the list if I had stayed with the LAPD.

As I continued reading, I was impressed by the frankness of the report. Some not-so-nice things had been uncovered by the Commission and those things—brutality, excessive force, racism and bias—were all well addressed on page after page. Leaning back into the booth's Naugahyde, I set the first of three one-inch thick reports to the side.

I sipped iced tea, munched tortilla chips, and thought back to other days when I was much younger, days when altercations and street language were part of my daily life. No, I thought, the department hadn't changed much after all. I reached for the second volume titled *Executive Session Testimony*.

There, neatly divided into four sections, was the closed door testimony of Chief Gates, Assistant Chief David Dotson, Assistant Chief Bob Vernon, and Retired Assistant Chief Jesse Brewer. I thumbed through statements of the top brass of the department, men I had respected while serving on the LAPD. I read the testimony of Chief Vernon, leader of the so-called God Squad. For years, according to police scuttlebutt, Vernon surrounded himself with officers whom he felt shared his conservative religious and philosophical views. These individuals had cushy assignments selected by Vernon himself. Chief Bob Vernon was probably the department's strongest supporter of Daryl Gates. They were and are the closest personal friends. From my experience in the department, I knew that Vernon was considered the number two man, right below the Chief of Police.

While equal in rank, the other two assistant chiefs were not nearly as powerful as Vernon, and their responsibilities were much less extensive. In the past, such inequities at the top of the power structure caused political problems within the department.

In his testimony to the Christopher Commission, Chief

INDEPENDENT COMMISSIONS LISTING OF TOP 44 OFFENDING OFFICERS

RANKING	NAME	SERIAL NO.
1.	SAVALA, N.	22740
2.	COTA, CONRAD R.	23683
3.	CARMONA, STEPHEN M.	23605
4.	BENNETTE, RAYMOND A.	20067
5.	FRITZ, JERRY D.	17122
6.	MERCHANT, WILLIAM	24936
7.	WYETH, LESLIE C.	17223
8.	MITCHELL, J.	29031
9.	JENKS, DONALD J.	13243
10.	FICITH, THOMAS J.	24402
11.	BARRON, ABIEL	24314
12.	WARREN, BENJAMIN	22594
13.	MORA, LEONARD	22009
14.	MASON, TAROO A.	17481
15.	EDWARDS, JOHN D.	16259
16.	MURPHY, DONALD W.	12907
17.	UGARTE, PEDRO J.	24899
18.	PASTERSCWICZ, JOHN A.	24424
19.	HAGERTY, JAMES C.	24329
20.	LANDRUM, MAURICE L.	24132
21.	HERBST, J.	23553
22.	CARDONA, BERNANDO O.	23473
23.	MCGEE, SEAN B.	20053
24.	CASLY, CRAIG D.	23040
25.	HARKNESS, WILLIAM B.	21470
26.	KOLS, STEVE V.	21030
27.	MADISON, RICHARD C.	17136
28.	TOSTI, MICHAEL S.	25598
29.	WILLIAMS, JOHN D.	25162
	MOMBU, ITUM	24448
31.	WUNDERLICH, ANDREW	24236
32.	FALVO, MICHAEL A.	23987
33.	COUSINE, HENRY (COUSIN)	23979
34.	SIMS, CARL A.	23943
35.	DOHERTY, JOSEPH M.	23540
36.	MOORE, JOE L.	23438
37.	GREENFIELD, JERRY J.	23420
38.	VIDAL, RUOY V.	23398
39.	PROVENCIO, JIMMY V.	23309
40.	SHEPHERD, SCOTT H.	22199
41.	TEAGUE, ANDREW A.	22972
42.	TORRES, JUAN M.	20816
43.	GUTIERREZ, RIGOBERTO	20078
44.	GEON, STEPHEN C.	17859

Vernon stated, "I'm the Director of Operations. That means I'm over about eighty-four percent of the department, including its eighteen precincts. We call them areas. I interact primarily with five deputy chiefs. One of those chiefs is over one of the quadrants of the city that we call bureaus. There are four geographic chiefs and one chief over headquarters bureau."

In response to a question relating to the improper use of the LAPD Mobile Terminal System (MDT), Vernon replied, "I was shocked, not so much because of the content of the transmissions, because the department is made up from the culture of the community, but because we have told them [field officers] it's captured (recorded in the departments' computers). It's on printouts, it can be read. I think that somebody's pretty stupid." It appeared the Chief was more critical of officers *having been caught* using MDTs improperly than he was for the inappropriate use in the first place. In his very next sentence, Chief Vernon so much as said it: ". . . While I don't like it, I know that this kind of talk goes on in the locker room, it's a kind of stress reliever. But to put it in writing!"

Vernon really believed the garbage he was feeding to the commission, I thought. His reputation was that of an officer who never swore, drank, or smiled. I believed Vernon hadn't been inside a station locker room in fifteen years. It wasn't his style. He might just hear a dirty word, smell sweaty socks, or have to talk to a street cop with whom he shared little in common.

Vernon's testimony contained no surprises. Page after page recited morality, ethical considerations, and denial of knowledge of adverse information. Whitewash and bullshit. "My staff didn't . . . my captains usually . . . I wasn't aware . . . I suggested that to my staff but I . . ." Stock answers to the questions commissioners asked covered pages. Good bob-and-weave techniques.

■

Chief David Dotson's comments and answers to questions differed considerably from those of Chief Vernon. He appeared to be much more candid and frank. I visualized the interior of the hearing room where Dotson sat across the table from the commissioners, the paneled walls, high ceilings, massive dark

Los Angeles District Attorney Ira Reiner announces the indictment of the four LAPD officers: Stacey Koon, Laurence Powell, Timothy Wind and Theodore Briseno. *(UPI/Bettmann)*

LAPD officer Theodore Briseno defends his actions in the assault on motorist Rodney King.
(AP/Wide World)

Sergeant Stacey Koon during the Simi Valley trial.　　*(Tom Owens)*

Former Officer Laurence Powell in March 1992 during the Simi Valley trial.　　*(Tom Owens)*

Timothy Wind, one of the four defendants facing civil rights charges for the 1991 beating of Rodney King.
(Reuters/Bettmann)

Chief of Police Daryl Gates awards Tom Owens the Police Medal, the second highest award for valor in the LAPD, in 1979. RIGHT: Pvt. Tom Owens upon completion of Marine Corps basic training in 1965. *(Tom Owens)*

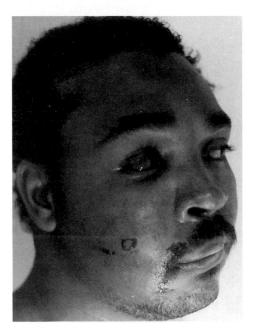
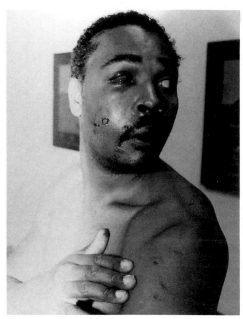

King suffered numerous facial injuries during the beating. The broken blood vessels in his right eye and massive swelling to his right cheek are further evidence of the "head shots" which were denied by the involved officers. RIGHT: Multiple taser strikes on King's left shoulder are visible in this documentary photo.

(Tom Owens)

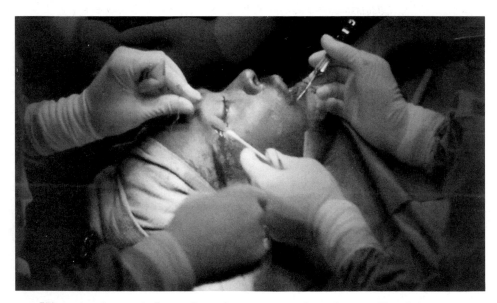

King receives stitches where he was struck with an officer's baton during the beating. *(Tom Owens)*

Rodney King delivers an emotional appeal calling for an end to the rampant violence that has stricken Los Angeles. His lawyer Steve Lerman listens at his left. *(Reuters/Bettmann)*

Author Tom Owens accompanies King to the "Can we all get along" press conference in Beverly Hills. *(Tom Owens)*

Los Angeles burning during the riots   (*Tom Owens*)

Author Tom Owens outside the Federal Courthouse in April 1993.
(Tom Owens)

Rodney King and Tom Owens enjoying a leisurely boat ride.
(Tom Owens)

table in the middle of the room surrounded by leather chairs. I imagined Dotson shifting from side to side in his chair each time a tough question was asked. As Dotson spoke, his career came nearer to its conclusion. He told of the relationships between the assistant chiefs and Gates and Vernon.

Dotson opened his testimony with a bang: "While I hold the Chief of Police in the highest esteem personally, during the past thirteen years, with a few notable exceptions, we have not had, in my opinion, at the top, very effective leadership." I guessed that Dotson's thirty-three year career with the LAPD plunged right into the crapper with those words. I had known Chief Dotson in the early Seventies. He had been captain in charge of the detective unit in which I spent several months while I was on loan to Central Division. Dotson was the Juvenile Detective Captain and even during that time, was an outspoken advocate for street cops. He was well-liked by all those he supervised. It was no surprise to me that he eventually made assistant chief.

Dotson continued, ". . . We have a policy manual full of high-sounding statements of purpose, and how we should treat people, and what it is that we're supposed to be doing, and what our role is in modern society, and all that. But that stays in the policy manual and is not reflected on our day-to-day operation and is not referred to daily or with any degree of regularity. There is no clear statement of mission or purpose. In addition to that, we have no priorities set for our operation. And that's reality in my judgement, where we fail in the top management levels of the department, and a lot of the failure is mine."

Chief Dotson's testimony filled nearly forty pages. He spoke specifically of the King incident and its effect on Foothill Division and on the department as a whole. He spoke of the breakdown in leadership in Foothill Division and the failure of the department to punish prior violators of policy, all the while citing the possible cause of the breakdown as ineffective leadership tied directly to Daryl Gates.

■

Perhaps the most astounding testimony came from retired Assistant Chief Jessie Brewer, former President of the Los Angeles Police Commission. Like Chief Dotson, Brewer was highly critical of Gates as a leader.

> . . . He has done, I'd say, overall, a good job. There are some areas where I find flaws. I would not give him a good grade in his handling of discipline. I'd give him a D. I think I would be generous in giving him a D in discipline, because I felt the way he handled discipline was really not the best for the department, nor for the people of the city.
>
> I thought people should be held more accountable, not only for their own misconduct but also for their subordinates who reported directly to them. I did not see that accountability being held.
>
> After the Rodney King incident. I thought several people should have been moved immediately after that occurred. I thought that the sergeant, of course . . . we all saw where he was *certainly* guilty of misconduct and perhaps certainly he should have been moved right away. I thought the watch commander and his involvement—and I think there was some discussion of him on the tape—he should have been gone right away. I do know that the Captain was not moved . . . I think that for the captain, that was the least that we could have done.
>
> I saw the Chief's responses that he was making to the media. For example, when . . . he was asked about the event when it first happened. His first response was, "Well, we'll look at it," rather than saying, you know, "This was absolutely atrocious and terrible and we are going to do something about it."
>
> Another response he made when someone was talking about apologizing to Rodney King and his family and he [Gates] indicated King was an ex-con . . . and he made some other comments. So I called the Chief up and I said, "I think you and I need to talk, I think you can handle your responses a lot better. I'd like to come down and give you some advice if I could." So he said, "Sure, come on down."
>
> When I walked into the Chief's office he said, "By the way, Jess, [Commissioner] Sam Williams wants to meet with us too and perhaps the three of us can work out a strategy for handling this affair." So we jumped into the Chief's car and drove over to Sam's office. After a few minutes of chitchat Sam said, "Daryl, I want you to step down." I was shocked, and the Chief, I could tell was shocked. I felt embarrassed being present when such an issue was being discussed with the Chief of Police.

I tried to talk Sam out of it. I told him, "Sam, I think your timing is terrible. I think you should wait and see what happens on this thing. I think you ought to give the Chief an opportunity to try to repair some of the damage."

But Sam said, "No, my mind's made up."

The third volume of the report was titled, *Selected Messages from the LAPD Mobile Digital Terminal System.* I began to read through the printout of recorded messages taken from the archives of the department's communications computer.

The commission audited MDTs over a six month period prior to the King incident and selected what it considered "inappropriate messages" for publication in its report. These MDT messages revealed either racial bias, excessive force, or sexism. The following selections are representative.

11/7/89	"Where be u?"
	"In the projects."
	"Good hunting."
11/8/89	"We are going into the jungle with CR[CRASH]64 to take care of business."
11/27/89	"Sounds like monkey slapping time."
1/11/90	"I shot him once and it had no effect. I shot him twice and it had no effect. I shot the motherfucker a third time and it stopped him long enough for me to cuff him.
1/13/90	"Monkeys in the trees, monkeys in the trees, hi-ho-dario, monkeys in the trees . . ."
1/16/90	"Do you have big titties?"
1/20/90	"They found something that does the work of 5 women—one man."

On and on, for seventy-six pages.

Hours had passed since I'd first entered the restaurant. It was getting late, nearly 8:00 P.M., and I still had the long drive back home ahead of me. By seven the next morning, I was standing at my copier, burning copies of the report for Lerman. The media was already airing the commission's findings, its recommendations for the LAPD, and their criticism of Chief Gates.

The Christopher Commission report was far-reaching, including organizational, personnel, administrative, and policy

recommendations. It called for modification of the selection
process for Police Chief and amendments to the City Charter
accommodating these recommendations. Term limits and performance criteria were defined; more control and supervision
by the Police Commission in the daily operations of the department were recommended. The list goes on and on.

In the spring of 1992, Daryl Gates finally retired as the Chief
of Police. In his book Gates recalls,

> The Christopher Commission's recommendations are basi-
> cally aimed at controlling the police. But it has no recommen-
> dations about controlling crime. It is dead-silent about how to
> deal with the crime and violence in Los Angeles today. LAPD
> is portrayed as being too hard-line, too aggressive, too pro-
> active, but the commission is curiously silent about a practical
> alternative.
>
> I could have taken the Christopher Commission report
> apart page by page, but such was the mood of the city, I
> doubted anyone would listen. And so, because a distinguished
> lawyer lent his name to it, the report stands as a kind of
> modern-day bible on big city policing. The commission tagged
> LAPD as a racist organization, composed of back-slapping
> cowboys out for a night of brutality on the town. Then they
> complimented us for our honesty and integrity. Well, maybe
> we read different reports.

Willie Williams, Commissioner of Police in Philadelphia,
was named as the city's first African-American police chief, and
the first chief appointed from outside the department since
World War II.

■

As summer passed into autumn, the defense's pretrial strategies
came into play. Judge Bernard Kamins was selected by the
Supervising Judge for Los Angeles County to try the criminal
case against the officers. Right from the beginning, he ran a
tight ship. California voters had recently passed Proposition
115, calling for revisions in the state's criminal justice system,
including more rapid procedures in the criminal courts. Judge
Kamins seemed hellbent on following the letter of the new law.
Defense motions for change of venue, continuances, discovery,

and all other manner of issues soon bogged the court down again.

I showed up at a pretrial session in Judge Kamins's courtroom to serve a summons on the four defendants for the King lawsuit. It was the first time I would go eyeball to eyeball with each of the four officers. The place was packed with press and spectators. Camera crews lined the hallway. Bright lights heated the air around the entrance to the courtroom, where uniformed deputies searched everyone for hidden weapons.

I identified myself to a bailiff, who said Judge Kamins didn't want the defendants served in his courtroom. So I stood just outside and handed each officer his notice as they passed me on their way out. Three officers accepted the Summons and Complaints almost as if they expected it. Sergeant Koon took his papers, glanced at them while standing next to me, then slowly walked away. As Koon stood reading the papers, I saw pain and frustration in his eyes. I left with the impression Sergeant Koon was feeling the pressures of his ordeal. I later told Lerman that I almost felt sorry for the defendants. Almost.

Months later, I was in Judge Kamins's court on another matter involving a criminal defense case I'd worked after he appointed me to the case at the request of the defendant. During a recess, I approached the judge and asked him to grant me an interview for this book. Initially, Judge Kamins was resistant, "I really don't want to give any interviews about the King case. I've already turned down CBS, and some others; I don't want to create any sense of disrespect to this court."

"But your Honor," I replied, "I'm not Dan Rather or Sam Donaldson. I'm not looking for a thirty-second sound bite. I mean, after all, we went through some of this media crap together. We, better than most, know what went on inside this case. It's those feelings I want to address. Like for instance, I know that you viewed this case as an important and historic issue in the history of Los Angeles. As the first trial judge, what were your thoughts after the verdicts in Simi Valley were announced?"

"Okay, well, I suppose I can comment on that now. I firmly believe that if the trial were held in this courtroom, in this building, the verdicts may well have been different. Meaning that with a different jury pool, more reflective of the area of the occurrence, a different verdict was certainly possible."

As I left the courthouse and stepped out into the warm Southern California air, I thought that at least one person in the system shared my view on moving the trial to Simi Valley.

As the pretrial proceedings continued, my workload on the King case began to decrease somewhat. I was finally having occasional meals with my family and taking in a movie now and then. We lived just a few miles from Anaheim Stadium, and I usually attended a few California Angels baseball games during the summer months. During the summer of 1991, however, I only attended two. I'm sure my absence from the games was felt by the Angels in lost beer and hot dog revenues.

On the downside, I was still neglecting my insurance company clients because I was spending six to eight hours a day with the King investigation. One client after another drifted away and I was powerless to stop their migration to other investigators. The numbers of man-hours generated by my staff remained constant but our efforts were now primarily focused in major police misconduct investigations on behalf of attorneys representing victims. In very short order, Pat's warning about working with attorneys became a prophecy. She was right again, they don't pay worth a damn. By the end of summer 1991, my gross receivables were down by fifty percent. I began fronting my own money to continue work on the King investigation. Paying my staff, office rent, and other monthly expenses out of my own pocket quickly took its toll on my personal life too. At home, our social activities came to a halt with the depletion of funds. Movies and dinners were a thing of the past. All expenses were curtailed. Family outings to Disneyland and other recreation stopped. Too expensive. Groceries and house payments were now my top priorities.

I was in the courtroom the day Judge Kamins found L.A. *Times* reporter Richard Serrano in contempt for failing to identify his source for a story he did on the IAD investigation. Serrano, represented by several attorneys from the *Times*, stood erect in front of the bench and declined to name his source. I saw aggravation on the face of Judge Kamins as Serrano held firm. Serrano was not sent to jail, but the judge fined him $1500 for every day he refused to divulge his source. The IAD document had been ordered sealed by the court weeks before, and I recall sitting in the courtroom secure in my knowledge of its contents. A week later, Judge Kamins rescinded Serrano's fine.

Days later, Judge Kamins was accused of having an improper written communication with the prosecuting attorney, Terry White, giving him assurances that the trial would not be moved out of his courtroom. Defense attorneys discovered this and filed a motion with a higher court to have Kamins removed. Their motion was granted and Judge Kamins was removed from hearing the case. Score a major round for the defense.

The selection of a different trial judge and a change of venue motion further slowed the criminal trial's progress. Much-touted provisions of Prop 115 were blown to hell, and it would be another six months before the jury selection would get under way in Simi Valley.

■

Providing security to Glen was like pissing into the wind. It's difficult to protect the privacy of someone who doesn't want to be protected or private. Glen's encounter with the Hollywood vice cops best illustrates that. When I thought he was home, he was out and, in too many instances, tangled in assorted difficulties.

The defendant officers and their attorneys would have you believe Rodney King was a cold, calculating, hardened, and nefarious criminal. Nothing could be further from the truth. Rodney Glen King is not a highly educated person, and his street savvy is not that of someone brought up in the inner city. With his mother and most other family members devoted to their religion, and because he was raised away from the problems and frustrations of the urban ghetto, Glen doesn't have the street smarts one might expect.

This naivete became apparent in July, 1991, when Steve Lerman and I received almost simultaneous phone calls from Glen. He told us he was in Eagle Rock, a predominantly Hispanic neighborhood of old homes and small businesses in the northeast section of L.A. He said he needed help. I heard a male voice ask him who he was talking to. Glen said, "It's okay, it's only Tom. He's a friend. Gimme the address here and he'll bring me the money you want." Some dude wanted money from Glen, and we believed him to be in danger. Thirty minutes later we found we were right.

I timed my arrival at the house to coincide with Steve's. The house, a small rundown single family dwelling, was nestled on a hillside among a grove of elm trees. The decaying neighborhood was a haven for crack houses. When Steve and I got out of our cars and started walking up the curving concrete driveway, I wished I'd called the cops.

Lerman stood to one side of the door, I stood on the other, my 9mm automatic in my hand. We could hear soft voices speaking inside. The tone of the rap and the slurring of words told me we were on thin ice. "Let me go in first," I told Lerman. "I've got a gun, you don't. If something goes down, get the fuck out as quick as you can and call the cops from your car phone."

"I'll stay with you," Lerman whispered. Steve's a boxing aficionado—actually climbs in the ring and gets punched around—and I figured he was getting the adrenaline rush. At that instant, the front door opened, exposing a scene I'd expected: a crack house, complete with stoned-out druggies lying around in the living room, wasted. I entered, gun in hand, making sure the dude who opened the door saw it. Pushing him aside, Lerman and I entered. I didn't see Glen. Other men, African-American and white, in their late twenties or early thirties, sprawled out in various stages of consciousness. Lerman stood near the door, while I walked into the small dining room, where I found Glen.

Seeing me, he grinned his boyish grin, like a child who knows it's time to go home. Without speaking a word, I took him by the arm and guided him back toward the front door. "Let's go!" Lerman shouted, prodding us outside. His voice was a threat; I'd never seen him like this—before or since.

Glen and Lerman took off while I stayed behind to see if they were followed. After five minutes, I left, satisfied with our efforts. We'd extricated Glen from who-knows-what, without incident, and no one but the dopers ever knew we were there.

Another example of Glen's childlike nature occurred in early August, 1992. Glen was suffering from cabin fever and needed an outing. The battleship, *USS Missouri* was making her last stop in Long Beach before retirement. Glen commented he'd never seen a big ship like the *Missouri*, so I arranged to pick him up the following Saturday and take him to the Long Beach Naval Shipyard to tour Big Mo.

Driving south on the Harbor Freeway, I mentioned to Glen that my old patrol area was just minutes away in Watts. I was astonished when Glen said he'd never been to Watts and didn't know anything about the black inner-city ghetto. I pulled off at Century Boulevard and headed east into Watts. We drove around South Central for an hour, then I entered the Nickerson Gardens housing project at Imperial Highway and Central Avenue. Nickerson Gardens was the flash point of the Watts riots in 1965, the largest incident of civil unrest in the history of Los Angeles and, arguably, the entire nation . . . until the Simi Valley not-guilty verdicts. As I drove my old Chrysler through the project's narrow streets, littered with the signs of urban decay, I watched Glen. Slowly at first, then more rapidly, his facial expression changed from curiosity and anticipation to dejection at the plight of less fortunate brothers and sisters. In those few minutes, Rodney King saw what being black in inner-city Los Angeles really meant.

We passed a group of young children playing basketball in a parking lot and Glen asked me to stop. We got out and I looked around nervously for signs of trouble. After all, I was not African-American and certainly not welcome in this most racially conscious neighborhood. It didn't take long for Glen to be recognized by the kids.

"Hey, look, it's Rodney King over there! Hey, Rodney . . ." A wide grin lit up Glen's face as he limped to where the kids were playing ball. At first they just stood and stared at each other. Glen, who was still walking with his cane, stopped short of the group. Then they began talking, and as the crowd grew, my sense of anxiety and apprehension vanished. "How'd you do in school?" Glen asked each youngster. "Do you know how important an education is?" I saw men and women, parents of the children, take notice of the gathering. In minutes, the crowd had grown to over a hundred people. Then an amazing thing occurred. An ice cream truck happened by. Glen stopped the truck and for the next hour, bought ice cream for the kids and their parents while he spoke about staying away from drugs and finishing school. Actually, it was forty bucks out of my pocket, but I didn't care.

"You know, these guys who sell you drugs don't care about you. They're only interested in the money. Don't have anything to do with them." I could tell Glen was getting tired, but he wouldn't leave. Finally, I reminded him of the time and we walked back to my car. "Where we goin' now?" Glen asked, not recalling our plan to visit the navy yard.

"We're off to see the Wizard," I answered as we reentered the Harbor Freeway. Fifteen minutes later, we stood on the dock next to the giant battleship.

"That's the biggest fucking boat I ever saw," Glen said, showing another example of his lack of worldly experience. No, Rodney King—Glen to his friends and family—is not the hardened criminal many people think he is. Nor is he the saint others may claim. Glen is just a man.

The unplanned meeting in a South Central housing project was not for the benefit of the media and certainly wouldn't help his case in any way. But he stayed there for nearly two hours, talking to kids and parents about important things—drugs, education, and the need for good police-community relations. If I hadn't been there, I wouldn't have believed it myself. I'll never know if any good ever came from that meeting in the streets, but I can hope that one or more of those kids heard and understood Rodney King's message.

■

My son, Steve, related some amusing moments during those first months. He'd report conversations he overheard at work. "Dad, I listen to some of these guys talking, blowing smoke at each other about this fact or that. I laugh at them because I know what they're saying is so wrong. They have no concept of what's really going on here."

"That's because they're only hearing media reports, put out by the city or one of the defendant cops, and they're buying into that load," I chided. "Wait till we get to trial and the real stuff comes out."

"Yeah, I know," Steve said, "but it still tickles me when I hear them talking."

"Have you told anyone your old man's connected to the case?" I asked.

"Nope. It's none of their business. Besides, some of these guys have a real mouth problem. They're sure to say something stupid if they knew, and I'd just have to lay one of 'em out."

"Well, let it slide, don't say anything. The time'll come when we can get our side of the story out there. Then you can tell your friends, I told you so."

Privately, I imagined the expression on some faces when Glen and his wife, Crystal, would show up at Steve's wedding, planned for August in the wedding chapel at Knott's Berry Farm. I'd already alerted Knott's security of King's and Lerman's expected attendance at the wedding. Glen was undergoing extensive medical therapy and Lerman was busier than a one-legged man in an ass-kicking contest. Only a select few of the invited guests knew King and Lerman were invited, and I wanted to keep it that way until the day of the wedding.

I'd invited another close friend, Fernell Chatman, a reporter at KNBC-TV, who I'd known since my early days on the streets as a young cop. He promised to keep Glen's attendance secret. I assured Fernell an opportunity for a one-on-one with King off-camera. At that time, King was still not available to the media. Frankly, I understood the importance of getting at least one person connected to the media to see a side of King different from what was being conveyed by the defense and LAPD media spokespersons.

My son, Steve, and his fiancée, Joanne, were pleased that I'd invited King and Lerman, and didn't consider it inappropriate to allow Fernell and King to meet at the reception. As it turned out King and his wife never showed.

9

SIMI VALLEY—PERCEIVED INJUSTICE

The bright California sun rose over the foothills rimming the San Fernando Valley. Northbound traffic on the 118 freeway leading into Simi Valley was light as Steve Lerman guided his bright red BMW toward the recently constructed Ventura County Criminal Courts Building. I sat beside him small-talking as the miles passed. Judge Stanley Weisburg would start the trial on time. Opening statements were set to begin in thirty minutes. With a television camera in the courtroom, the eyes of the country would be focused on Simi Valley.

"What do you think?" Lerman asked, just a few short miles from where it had all begun a year before.

"Two will walk," I said, hoping Lerman didn't notice my nervousness, "Wind, the unknown rookie and Briseno, the stomper."

"No, I think Wind will get some time," Lerman said. "Maybe not as much as Powell, but I think he'll go down with his partner."

"It all depends on the prosecutors."

"At least the trial stayed in Southern California, but Simi Valley?" Lerman was already sensitive to the trial's location.

Prior to the jury selection, Lerman had moved King to the Residence Inn in Orange, California, less than a mile from my offices. We were still getting occasional threats against King and the hotel location made security a bit easier. From there, we could get him to Simi Valley with little advance notice. So, with Rodney King safely tucked away in his hotel room under the watchful eyes of my assistants, Malcolm Stone and Harry Johnson, the historic trial was finally underway.

In the days preceding the trial's opening, the defendants won a motion barring the jury from considering any lesser offenses; either they were guilty as charged on all counts, or they were not guilty of anything. This stroke of genius by the defense attorneys later proved most critical in the jury's decision.

Rodney King's testimony at the trial was highly anticipated. For the first time he would speak publicly of what happened that cool March morning on the quiet, deserted streets of Lake View Terrace.

Prosecutors assured us we would be given at least two days' prior notice to pepare security for King's appearance in the courtroom. Terry White felt this would be enough time for us to plan and coordinate with local authorities.

I'd already met with Sergeant Dick Southwick, officer in charge of security at the courthouse, and had consulted about security requirements with the sheriffs. I had prepared plans for routes, manpower, and equipment necessary to get King into and out of the facility, while keeping him away from the ever-present media. I provided this information to Sergeant Southwick two weeks before jury selection was scheduled to begin. Lerman, King, and I made a trip to the site as part of King's trial preparation; Lerman felt King would feel more comfortable in familiar surroundings. Moreover, King had expressed concerns about conditions at the courthouse. He wanted to see for himself how security was being implemented. While he trusted us, he still felt uncomfortable trusting officers assigned for his protection; inside the perimeter of the building, security was the problem of court personnel. My plan called for the use of different vehicles every day to transport King. Routes in and out were developed, with alternates prescanned and available. At King's request, a secure room within the courthouse would be provided, with facilities for meals.

During the first week of January 1992, Lerman began his one-on-one sessions with King, to familiarize him with tactics and types of questions he could expect to face from defense attorneys in their cross-examinations. Sessions were also conducted by the prosecutors themselves in the D.A.'s offices, from which Lerman and I were excluded. Our sessions were held in Lerman's Beverly Hills offices. Associate attorneys posed as defense attorneys, Stone, Mounger, Barnett, and DePasquale, trying to emulate their observed habits and personalities.

Noted Los Angeles civil rights lawyer Tom Beck asked difficult questions of King, then evaluated Glen's demeanor and ability to deal with stressful answers. Some prep sessions were also attended by John Burton, Bryant Allen's attorney. Allen failed to participate, saying he had to work. His absence from the sessions was obvious when he later sat in the witness chair in front of the jury.

The most intensive, aggressive and effective trial preparation came from Lerman and Harvey Goldhammer, another member on the King team of lawyers. I brought Goldhammer on board. I had worked with him in a case two years earlier, when he represented a former L.A. gang member who had been shot while riding on a bus in South Central Los Angeles. Despite his client's past gang affiliations, Goldhammer secured a verdict of nearly $800,000 from the district.

After reviewing King's file, Goldhammer went at King with the knowledge and gusto he anticipated King would see from Powell's attorney, Mike Stone. Within minutes, beads of sweat appeared on King's forehead as he sat twisting from side to side in his chair. When Goldhammer paused for a breath, Lerman would take up the questioning. This went on for hours.

When Lerman and his team of lawyers believed King had been thoroughly exposed to the tactics and types of questions he would be facing, the sessions ended. "They won't be that bad will they, man?" King asked, " 'Cause you got me sweating bullets."

"This guy will be a great witness," Goldhammer told Lerman. "The jury'll like him a lot. He comes across as personable, authentic, and like a big teddy bear."

"I think the defense guys'll be all over King on his actions that night," I said. "They'll grill him on how much he'd been drinking, why he didn't stop on the freeway, and his behavior after he got out of the car before the Holliday tape begins."

"I think you're right," Lerman said. "Take Glen out and trace the pursuit route with him to refresh his memory. If he's not sure of the route, the defense'll say he's evading the questions."

My biggest fear, however, was not what King might or might not say in his testimony, but rather the smile that would creep onto his face when he felt pressure or stress. King tired easily. The more tired he became, the broader his grin.

"When he's really stressed out, he gets this puppy dog smile that someone on the jury might incorrectly perceive as smugness," I pointed out to Lerman. "The jury'll see his smile and conclude something that's just not there." I believed nerve damage might also affect King's features during his testimony. I watched his face change expressions when he spoke. Minor muscle convulsions went unnoticed by King, who still suffered facial numbness as a result of baton strikes. Juries watch for the smallest changes in a person's face as a litmus test of truthfulness.

"The tiniest things impact upon a jury, so be aware of your expressions," I warned King. "Don't give them any reason, real or imagined, to disbelieve you. You go into this with a lot of sympathy. Take questions straight on. Don't dodge anything they ask. Listen carefully to the questions and wait for a second before you answer, so the D.A.s can object if they want. And don't say anything beyond the answer. Don't volunteer information. Make them ask the questions." When it was time for the trial to start, Rodney Glen King was ready and looked forward to telling his story to the jury.

Lerman and I knew Terry White would not be calling King until near the end of his presentation to the jury. We believed King would be on the stand for four to five days, most of that time under persistent cross-examination by hostile attorneys for the defense.

Once the trial began in Simi Valley, my days were filled with one distraction after another. When I wasn't actually sitting inside the courtroom, watching the proceedings, I was with King at the hotel watching the trial on television and explaining the activities to him. I was getting up at 4:30 A.M. and wasn't getting to bed most nights until after midnight.

Pat was not a happy camper during those weeks. She resented the time the case demanded because, for the weeks and months I was tied to the trial, I had time for nothing else in my life, including my family and friends. My business was crashing and burning around us, bill collectors were giving her fits wanting their money, and our personal life away from the case had come to a halt. The King case consumed my every waking minute, and often, Lerman would call during the wee hours of the morning to discuss the events of the past day or to plan the following day's events and think out the television sound bites.

I quietly resented Lerman's middle-of-the-night strategy calls, but Pat had no such reticence, especially where Steve Lerman was concerned. "Why don't you tell him to not call after midnight?" she demanded on many occasions after being awakened by the bedside phone's ringing. "He doesn't have a life, so he doesn't want you to have one either. Tell him to get a life."

"You just don't understand," I'd protest weakly, knowing she was irritated but not wanting to face another argument about my confused priorities.

"I don't know why that guy can't wait until we get up in the morning to call. Can't he tell time?"

My standard defense was, "He's too busy during the day to concern himself with planning. Besides, I'm on the clock whenever he feels the need to talk."

"Well, why can't he talk to Glen once in awhile, and give us a night's sleep? I hate the way he uses you. Can't you see what's really going on here?"

I knew what was going on here. What I didn't know was how to stop it.

"He's going to use you any way he can, until he doesn't need you anymore. Then, you'll be history." Pat never held back when she felt she had something to say, or when she felt she was right about an issue we disagreed on.

"All I know is that I'm involved in this case for as long as there is a case, and I'll do whatever needs to be done."

"Don't you realize what this case is doing to you? To this family? What do you expect to have left when it's over?"

I didn't know it then, but once again, Pat would eventually prove much more perceptive than I.

·

I sat in the courtroom and watched as George Holliday and Bryant (Pooh) Allen were thrown to the wolves by D.A. Terry White, who did not make a move to protect his witnesses from venomous questions by attorneys Stone, DePasquale, Mounger, and Barnett. By the end of his testimony, Pooh looked like an idiot and couldn't even find north on a map. At the time of his testimony, Allen was still undergoing therapy for injuries sustained in the incident, but no mention was made that he, like King, had been beaten during the melee following the car chase. I was horrified. Both prosecutors just sat and watched as the four defense attorneys took shots at the credibility of Holliday and Allen. There were a few objections by White and Yochelson, but round one went to the defense. After the hearing ended that first day, I met with Lerman and Pooh's attorney, John Burton, in the parking lot of the courthouse. Burton was beyond angry, he was livid. He said he felt betrayed by the prosecutors. I shared his feelings.

Burton hadn't been present at his client's early morning arrival, so I told him of the scene that had greeted us. Satellite dishes flanked the courthouse. Trailers, tents, even cargo containers were set up as media workshops. Before Steve could park his car, we were set upon by journalists demanding to know where King was, what were Steve's comments on the opening of the trial, etc. We had to fight our way around reporters and cameramen crowding and pushing their way in for a closer shot, shoving microphones in our faces. What about this angle or that? When would King be called? How did we think the verdicts would come out? What did Steve think about the all-white jury?

As we neared the doors, I looked to my left and saw Pooh and his family arriving. Instantly, they too were smothered by media vultures. Some reporters later told me they mistook Pooh for King. Freddie Helms's mother made the trip to Simi Valley with Pooh's family, as did King's Aunt Angela. Their presence excited the newspeople assembled near the doors. Then the stampede. Allen's family was overwhelmed by the onslaught of cameras and microphones. Pooh's mother looked frightened. I said I'd better go help Pooh and his family into the courthouse. Lerman agreed. I had to battle my way through the cameras and crowds to Pooh, who was inundated by people shouting questions at him. He had a look of panic on his face. No one had expected this type of coverage in the parking lot of the building. I recall wondering, where was the security that had been promised by Sergeant Southwick?

As I escorted my charges in, I could see Lerman expounding in front of cameras on the courthouse steps. Later, I learned Judge Weisburg was so angered by what he saw in the parking lot when he arrived, that he ordered media kept away from witnesses. Reporters and technicians were ordered to be on their best behavior or suffer his wrath and lose their privileges. Court TV, a cable channel based in New York, was providing pool video of the entire trial. Locally, independent station, KTTV, would preempt its daytime programming for gavel-to-gavel coverage, a move that improved the station's ratings considerably. Within days, the media mania diminished, but there would still be over one hundred people covering the trial as it neared its end, months later.

■

Initially, defense attorneys were allowed to meet with the press before morning sessions and after the close of daily hearings. I had made friends with a number of media folks and was allowed into the press room to monitor comments of the defense attorneys during their daily briefings. At times only the clicking of computer keyboards could be heard as reporters watched and listened to testimony on closed circuit TV. More often there was a kind of organized confusion; print journalists took notes, radio reporters gave live updates, and TV reporters constantly sought out sound bytes, often interviewing each other when things were slow.

One of these television commentators was Starr Jones, a chunky African-American former New York prosecutor, newly hired by NBC as a legal commentator. Living up to her name, Starr arrived daily in a chauffeur-driven limo and had her own ministage set inside the courthouse. Despite the elaborate trappings, her credibility came into question when she insisted the prosecution would never keep Rodney King off the witness stand.

.

Certainly Mike Stone, Lawrence Powell's attorney, and Darrell Mounger, defending Stacey Koon, were the most vocal of the defense lawyers. Stone made a deliberate effort to learn the first names of reporters. In an effort to personalize his answers to a question, he often responded using the first name of the reporter who asked it, which won him more antagonism than affection, since no radio or television network wants a rival reporter's name mentioned in an answer they want to broadcast on their own air. But the shining star of the defense team, in my opinion, proved to be John Barnett, representing Ted Briseno. Tim Wind's attorney, Paul DePasquale, gave the impression he was merely happy to be there, happy to let the others carry the ball, both in court and at the daily briefings. Before the trial began, I believed DePasquale would turn out to be the main man. I'd thought his pretrial persona—quiet, mild-mannered, even passive—was an act and that once the trial began, DePasquale would be the primary ball-buster. As the trial went on, however, I was more impressed by John Barnett, even though I personally disliked his client more than the others, including Powell. I attribute my dislike of Briseno to my knowledge of his personal history and his relationship—or lack of a relationship—with his older children from his first marriage.

Right from the opening comments by defense counsel, it was clear that not all defendants were thinking alike; there was dissension in their ranks. Koon, Powell, and Wind stood together. Bresino tried to justify his own actions, while claiming charges against the other three were true. Initially, many professionals covering the trial were convinced the four LAPD officers would be convicted. In his book, Sergeant Stacey Koon insists the media did a poor, unbalanced, and provocative job of covering the trial. Most reporters and media managers vehemently disagree. Those assigned to cover the trial were surprised and disappointed by the courtroom performances of prosecutors White and Yochelson. Reporters often discussed among themselves how poorly prepared the prosecutors seemed to be. Steve Lerman quietly fed critical information to the D.A.s to help beef up their case, but they just never seemed to catch fire. The consensus in the press room was the defense outclassed as well as outnumbered the prosecution.

I knew from conversations with Terry White and his investigator, Mike Gillum, that they had been on the right track on several issues. I couldn't figure out why they hadn't followed up on them, unless, as we suspected, the trial was being managed by District Attorney Ira Reiner from long distance in Los Angeles. This prospect bothered me because I knew Reiner had no personal trial experience of this kind, and without being in the courtroom every day he couldn't see the faces of the jurors or feel the tension in the air at critical junctures in testimony.

Reiner's office had lost every other major police misconduct case to go to trial, without exception. Some have pointed out that had the outcome of those cases been different, cops might then perceive him as being too harsh on them and he could lose the support of officers needed in other criminal prosecutions. Five months later, Reiner announced he would not seek reelection because he "didn't want to address the tough issues being raised by the opponent." Clearly, one of those tough issues was his lack of success in police prosecutions.

When it became apparent the prosecution wasn't going to call King to testify, investigators for the defense, most notably Jerry Gozetta, began a series of media interviews designed to make us look like it was our decision. My sources told me the Police Protective League spent many man-hours and went to great expense to serve a subpoena on King on behalf of Tim Wind, dropping the papers off at every residence where Rodney King had ever lived. Gozetta, the defense's top investigator, could be seen huddled up with every reporter at one time or another, leaking information on the progress of the service of a subpoena on King. Had they asked us where he was, we might have told them, but they never did.

Television reporters, hungry for a new slant, made far too much of the subpoena issue during the last two weeks of the trial. They pressured us, demanding to know why Lerman and I were hiding King and wouldn't let him testify. After all, wasn't King the reason we were all there?

A prosecution witness, called by the defense, may be declared a hostile witness. The types and nature of questions asked by defense attorneys are remarkably different in the case of a hostile witness. Leading questions may be asked and answers may be compelled by the court. In theory, the entire nature of King's testimony would then be fair game for the defense without much opportunity for objections by the prosecution, in whom we had little faith anyway. After watching the way White and Yochelson failed to protect Holliday and Allen during their testimony, subjecting King to relentless leading questions by defense attorneys was unacceptable to us, though King desperately wanted to tell his story to the jurors in Simi Valley.

Lerman received a phone call from deputy D.A. Yochelson while we were at the Residence Inn with King. Yochelson said there was intense pressure in the D.A.'s office to allow the defense to call King. Lerman expressed his concerns, then ended the conversation by telling Yochelson that he would call back after speaking with King.

For the next twenty or so minutes, Lerman, King, and I kicked around the possibility of King's appearance as a witness for the defense. Finally we agreed it was a no-win situation and formulated a plan to discourage the scenario.

Yochelson had left his office, so Lerman paged Terry White. Within a few minutes, we heard back from White, who was out to dinner and had not known of Yochelson's call to Lerman, nor had he been informed of the possibility of the defense calling King. Fearing White would be supportive of the proposition, Lerman told him our position on the matter. We had decided that the only way an appearance at court would benefit King in his subsequent suit for damages against the city, was if he gave a wide-ranging press conference outside the court before his testimony—to tell the whole story from his point of view without any possibility of objections from hostile defense attorneys. Doing this would violate the gentleman's agreement between prosecution and defense not to bring racism into the case, a foolish agreement I felt handicapped the prosecution because racism was at the very core of the incident, as evidenced by what happened to truck driver Reginald Denny during the posttrial riots. Denny was a white guy set upon by four blacks as King, a black man, was attacked by four whites. The only difference was, the four whites wore uniforms and did their beating under color of authority, while the four blacks were vengeance-seeking thugs. But racism motivated both confrontations. Had there been no racism in LA, there would have been no beatings, no riots, no fires, no deaths.

At his press conference, King would speak of the taunts of "nigger" during the beating and at the hospital. He would make public for the first time police surveillance of him, the bug discovered on Steve Lerman's phone, the break-in of my office. He would relate the truth behind his arrest in Hollywood with the transvestite male prostitute, an attempt to impugn King's character that backfired. This public disclosure by King would get instant nationwide exposure, regardless of what might later happen to him on the stand.

White knew without being reminded, that the information which would be released would violate their gentleman's agreement and cause additional aggravation to both the prosecution and the defense. Neither side would benefit if the trial turned into a media feeding frenzy on the steps of the courthouse.

White was silent for a long time, then said he would call his office and inform his superiors of Lerman's comments. Lerman hung up and we shared a look of satisfaction; the shit was about to hit the fan in the D.A.'s office.

An hour later, the hotel phone rang. It was Terry White. He told Lerman that Rodney King would not testify. This decision later proved to be a serious miscalculation on the part of the prosecutors.

In October 1992, I phoned Terry White and requested an interview for inclusion in this book. White agreed and instructed me to call him back in mid-November to schedule a time. Per White's instructions, I phoned his office from the second week of November until Christmas. He was always unavailable. Finally, I got the message and gave up.

Following the verdicts, White spoke of his reasons for not calling King to the stand in several magazine and newspaper articles. He told reporters of a telephone conversation he had with King following Melanie Singer's first day on the stand, a conversation in which King was obviously angry. He said King's anger and language caused him concern for how King might react under cross-examination. He felt King might lose it and alienate the jurors.

In making his decision not to call King, White failed to take into account several important considerations, including

King's own desire to testify and that in these situations, the benefit of the doubt generally goes to the victim. Lerman and his staffers had put their client through extensive pretrial prep, anticipating the opposition's aggressive grilling. White didn't consider the persuasiveness of King's anger at Melanie Singer's testimony claiming that his actions at the conclusion of the chase were erratic and that he taunted his assailants. No one knew better than Rodney King that he had complied with their orders. He was also angry at the stipulations made by the prosecutors during the opening arguments that asserted his behavior was bizarre during those first few seconds not seen on the Holliday tape, thereby allowing for higher levels of force to be justified. Damn right, King was angry. So was I.

In retrospect, we should have known when those stipulations were made that the prosecutors would not call any of the civilian witnesses—those in the band bus, the Ford Probe, or the people watching from outside the apartments. Their stories would have conflicted with the Singers' and therefore, with the stipulations.

■

Much has been reported about the "all white Simi Valley jury." In fact, the criminal trial jury in Simi Valley was not all white; one juror was from the Philippines and another was Hispanic. The ten remaining white jurors were from all over Ventura County, not just Simi Valley.

I watched the jury selection as it progressed, from the time initial questionnaires were mailed out to 2,500 prospective jurors, to the final selection of jurors and alternates. The twelve individuals who actually heard the testimony did indeed represent the communities from which they came, and therein lies the root of the jury problem.

From the preselection questionnaires, 500 prospective jurors were called to the courthouse, two groups of 250 each. Of these, six were African-Americans, one percent of the total jury pool. Of the six, three were excused for hardship claims. An additional prospective black juror was excused following an allegation by the defense of possible jury interference by a representative of the Ventura County NAACP, who was seen in a conversation with the juror during a break. Neither of the two remaining African-Americans were seated on the final jury panel.

The following twelve jurors acquitted the defendant officers: Christopher Morgan, juror number one, forty-three years old, from Simi Valley, worked as a technician for a local telephone company. He had a brother who is a retired LAPD sergeant. Astoundingly, Terry White did not excuse him during pretrial questioning.

Virginia Loya, juror number two, the only Hispanic, lived in Saticoy, California. Married, Mrs. Loya worked in the housekeeping department of Ventura Medical Center after leaving her former job as a security officer. Again, no challenge from White. I made eight attempts to interview Mrs. Loya after the trial, but she never returned my calls. Mrs. Loya later appeared on several newscasts where she said she might have voted differently if she had known the two passengers in the Hyundai, Helms and Bryant, were also injured by police during the incident.

Thomas Gorton, juror number three, fifty years old, was employed as a special police officer with the United Water Conservation District. Despite this seeming conflict of interest, White let him stay on the jury. While I wasn't able to interview Gorton, I did speak to a family member of a Thomas Gordon, also a Simi Valley resident, who told me of threats and abuses suffered by her family from callers who mistook her family for that of Mr. Gorton's. She said the threats were so severe that they were forced to move from Simi Valley after the jurors' identities were publicly announced on April 30, 1992, in an article in the *Los Angeles Times*.

Amelia Pigeon, juror number four, was a thirty-nine-year-old Filipino-American. Prior to the trial, she worked at Olive View Hospital in the San Fernando Valley as a nurse. She wouldn't talk to me following the trial and her calls at work were screened. Incidentally, Olive View is a county facility where medical staff and police officers have frequent contacts.

Anna Whitting, juror number five, was a fifty-four-year-old divorcee living in Ventura, California, and employed as a printer. In her jury questionnaire she wrote, "It takes a special kind of person to make a good officer." She made television news appearances in defense of the verdicts, and she too received threats against herself and her family.

Charles A. Sheehan, juror number six, was a retired teacher living in Camarillo, California, with his wife. He, too, had direct ties to law enforcement. While serving in the navy, he was a shore patrol officer. A strong supporter of police sponsored Neighborhood Watch, his belief was that "the LAPD is a fine organization."

Kevin Siminiski, juror number seven, was thirty-eight, married, and living in Thousand Oaks, where he worked as a computer programmer. He wrote in his questionnaire, "Twenty years ago, I was stopped and taken to jail for a robbery I didn't commit." On several occasions during the trial, I watched Deputy Cummins, the bailiff, walk to the jury box and awaken this dozing juror.

Henry King, juror number eight, forty-nine, married, from Santa Paula, California, was employed with the Southern California Edison Company as a cable splicer. He was a member of the National Rifle Association, and "respects the job police officers do."

Gerald R. Miller, juror number nine, fifty-nine, married, from Camarillo, California, was a former air force military police officer, now a retired mental health worker. Miller was another juror who occasionally needed a nudge from the bailiff to keep him from dozing off.

Alice Debord, juror number ten, forty-three, employed by the Ventura County Community College District as a maintenance worker, began the trial as an alternate. Several weeks into the proceedings, an original juror was dismissed for family medical reasons and Debord was seated for the remainder of the hearings.

Dorothy Bailey, juror number eleven, the foreperson, was sixty-five, from Camarillo, a small community north of Simi Valley. Her hobbies included reading and golf. She worked for a company that provides technical manuals to the government for ships and equipment purchased by the navy. Bailey made the talk show circuit after the verdicts, speaking in defense of the jury's verdicts. When I attempted to interview her during my jury poll after the conclusion of the riots, she wouldn't take my calls. She is writing a book, with the jury foreperson from the federal trial of the same four officers, about their experiences on the two cases.

Retta Kossow, juror number twelve, was a sixty-five-year-old retired real estate broker. Married, she and her husband lived in Ojai, California, where her hobbies included quilting and travel. She was also a member of the National Rifle Association.

When the Holliday video was first shown to the jury, their expressions showed their anger over what they were seeing. But as the tape was replayed over and over, sometimes slow motion, sometimes frame-by-frame, shock slowly turned to apathy and the impact of the tape was diminished. This ploy by the defense worked exactly as planned. Following the verdicts, many experts called this process "desensitizing." The more one is exposed to something shocking, the less one is sensitive to what they're seeing. Their eyes began lying to them.

■

Weeks before the trial began, I was able to procure the entire witness list for both the defense and the prosecution. The defense witness list came from a source closely connected to the Police Protective League. Most of the names on both lists were known to the King team, but several were a mystery, like Dr. Carly Ward. Most of the civilian witnesses had already been interviewed by my staff. Police witnesses were off-limits because of the discovery hold placed on the civil case by Judge Kamins and reaffirmed by Judge Weisburg and Federal Judge Davies. When defense attorneys Mike Stone announced Dr. Carly Ward would testify that King's injuries were self-inflicted, I focused my investigation on her area of expertise.

We discovered that Dr. Ward, Ph.D., a biomechanical engineer, had given testimony and depositions in other injury cases in Los Angeles superior courts. Her previous testimony was available through public court records.

I gave D. A. Terry White some of the background information we developed on Dr. Ward, including her previous testimony, her scholastic credentials, and additional information obtained from a professor at the University of California who had taught her in biochemical engineering. Armed with our data, Terry White objected to Dr. Ward until the court could evaluate the nature and applicability of her testimony. The proceedings were held up while Dr. Ward testified out of the presence of the jury.

Dr. Ward said she had conducted tests on cadavers, provided by a local university hospital, to establish the force level necessary to cause King's injuries. She testified that she hit these cadavers with a PR-24 baton and measured the kinetic energy from the blows. Bone breaks and skin abrasions were then examined. She further testified that in some cases, cadaver heads were severed, then dropped from various heights to simulate the force required to cause facial bone fractures. She had a 3-D graphic created from her findings and offered to show it to the jury.

Judge Weisburg worked very hard to keep his composure, occasionally grimacing as Dr. Ward described her experiments. Finally, she demonstrated to the court how she would sit and bang her own head against her desk to gain a sense of the pain associated with head trauma. Judge Weisburg did not allow her to testify before the jury, though her grotesque descriptions of her experiments in Frankenstein research provided a lot of laughs in the press room.

In the end, the Simi Valley jurors simply didn't believe their eyes. Their not guilty verdicts indicated they believed the beating King got was justifiable. But one must ask, what might the verdicts have been if the jury had known as much about the defendants' backgrounds as they knew about Rodney King's past?

CAN WE ALL GET ALONG?

The drama of the trial—and the comedy—belonged to television. Mother Nature, however, showed little respect for the highly styled correspondents. The wind in Simi Valley played havoc with the fancy hair styles, and rain forced them to abandon their designer suits and dresses, especially when torrents transformed the newly graded media parking lot into a mud hole. Many wound up in jeans and boots; some even wore shorts, knowing the camera would only show them above the waist.

When jury deliberations began, reporters, prosecutors, defense attorneys, and court security personnel gathered at a nearby park to relax, eat, talk shop, and prognosticate. They organized a pool to determine what day and hour the verdicts would be reached. The pool, totaling several hundred dollars, was won by a former reporter from KFI radio.

There were also unintended information leaks. While reporting a story, KTTV newsperson Jane Wells, inadvertently disclosed where the defense attorneys were staying, mentioning a nearby hotel. The attorneys were furious, claiming their lives and those of their clients were placed in jeopardy.

The civil unrest that followed the not guilty verdicts began on the steps of the Simi Valley Courthouse. Within minutes, crowds of court watchers were shouting their outrage. The waiting media were quick to turn their microphones over to these emotional, angry people. There had been numerous private discussions among newspeople at the courthouse about the potential for violence after the jury returned their verdicts. But, as with the city, and the LAPD, there was virtually no planning by media managers for coverage of any posttrial rioting. More often than not, the people who call the shots are in control but out of touch. Mostly white upper-middle class, they do not relate to the anger and frustration common on the streets of minority communities.

As television and radio trumpeted the verdicts to an astounded nation, shouts of fury, frustration, and disbelief drowned out praise for the months of work just completed by the jurors. Supporters of the defendants were pleased by the verdicts, but their words were drowned out by cries of injustice.

Minutes after the verdicts, defendants and their attorneys started working their way from the courthouse, across the crowded parking lot, toward their cars. Almost immediately there was pushing and shoving. Voices of anger filled the warm, still April air. Fights broke out. The hostile crowd closed ranks around the defendants as they tried to leave. Obscenities were shouted. Cameras captured the sights and sounds and broadcast them across the community.

In the riots that followed there were numerous casualties among journalists and their crews. Some still photographers were stripped of their cameras and beaten. Several television stations lost video cameras and cellular phones to looters. A television helicopter was hit by gunfire. A number of news vehicles were rammed from behind in hopes of luring their occupants out, a car theft tactic that has grown more popular as car alarms became more sophisticated and has made "carjacking" a new American catch phrase. The situation in South Central became so dangerous that a few media staffers began carrying weapons. Armed private security guards were hired to accompany crews covering stories. Several news organizations even purchased bulletproof vests for reporters assigned to riot areas. Two television stations, KCBS and KCAL, covered over the logos on their vehicles.

Reaction to the verdicts was swift and violent. White cops had beaten a black man, and for the first time their savagery had been captured on videotape. Now, the system had failed to bring those cops to justice. Such was the perception of many people; they saw the video, they saw what had happened in Lake View Terrace that night, and their eyes hadn't lied to them. With the not guilty verdicts, they felt betrayed. At the same time, calmer voices were claiming the system had worked. The officers had their day in court, the system found they had not violated any laws, and now they were free to get on with the rest of their lives.

In fact, only the criminal issues were decided in Simi Valley. There were still other proceedings the officers would have to face. The King case was not over, not by a long shot.

I was at King's Studio City apartment when the verdicts were announced. About an hour later, Steve Lerman arrived. I felt they needed to be left alone, and I went into another room to watch the breaking stories on television. Violence was already erupting all over Los Angeles. I called Pat. She was almost in tears. "Couldn't those people see? Were they blind? Damn it, it just isn't fair," she said.

We talked for a few minutes, then I hung up and looked at the horrors unfold as a news helicopter orbited over the intersection of Florence and Normandie. A white man driving a gravel truck was stopped. Black men dragged him out of the cab and started beating him. I called to Lerman and King. For the next few moments, no one spoke as we watched the attack on Reginald Denny. Rioters were caught in the act of rioting, another merciless beating was captured on videotape, and a bit of history repeated itself. Lerman has since said, "It was like watching a negative film version of King's beating. This time, it was four black men beating a white man."

The infamous beating of Reginald Denny was broadcast live from circling helicopters, but the most graphic images, close up from the ground, were captured on a home video camera by an amateur photographer known as Sandoval. He brought the videotape to NBC-TV first, but somehow could not make a deal to sell it. He then took it to ABC, where he got what he wanted, and his tape was broadcast. Once NBC saw the tape aired by their competition, they contacted Sandoval again. Another round of negotiations produced a deal to Sandoval's liking. Unlike George Holliday, Sandoval understood the value of his footage, so the deals he cut limited use of his tape to only twenty-four hours; every additional day required additional bucks.

Onlookers at Florence and Normandie, who for months had criticized the officers who stood by in Lake View Terrace and watched King getting beaten, were themselves bystanders at Denny's beating. The situation in Los Angeles deteriorated rapidly after that. Rioting and looting broke out. Businesses were torched.

Most local news outlets virtually ignored other even more egregious incidents during the riots, including a triple homicide near Vermont and Vernon, where three people with no direct ties to each other were shot and killed by the same gunman, at the same location, with the same gun.

Gunshots scared the hell out of news crews, who found themselves surrounded by civil disorder, and not a single LAPD officer to be seen. The press corps was preoccupied with arson and just too busy covering events to fully fathom the danger they were in. Firefighters warned reporters to beware of sniper fire, especially in areas where electrical power had been lost. During the first night of rioting, parts of South Central looked like a huge checkerboard after power outages left some city blocks in total darkness.

Mayor Bradley called a news conference, where he questioned the jury's decisions in Simi Valley. "I was speechless when I heard that verdict," Bradley announced.

Where were the police? was the question most asked during those first crucial hours following the verdicts. King sat in front of his television in Studio City and watched the violence escalate, heard cries that these actions were in support of him. Injury reports flooded in from field news crews. Fires blazed in all areas of the city. Police cars were overturned and set afire, all in the name of Rodney King. It made Glen terribly depressed. Lerman called his psychiatrist and asked him to come over.

A peace rally was scheduled for 7:00 P.M. at the First AME (African Methodist Episcopal) Church in South Central Los

Angeles. Many civic leaders and members of the clergy would appear to request that everyone remain calm. Lerman, Glen, and I decided I should go down there and try to make a public appeal in King's name.

With all the news conferences and media appearances I'd made, I felt I'd be known to most of the camera crews and wouldn't have a problem getting the message out. As I left King's apartment, I didn't think about danger I might face in South Central L.A., the eye of the storm, only that I needed to get there with some words we hoped might make a difference.

Parking lots were full around the church, so I parked about a block away and walked back. Others were also headed toward the church, but mine was the only white face. I watched police helicopters pass overhead. The acrid odor of smoke from burning buildings already filled the air.

Hundreds, perhaps as many as a thousand people, had gathered near the church doors, hoping to get in. As I passed through the crowds, I could sense their reaction to the white guy in their midst. They didn't know me, but I could tell they thought I didn't belong there. With some effort, I was finally able to work my way through to a side door. I showed my ID to the door usher and told him I was there at the request of Rodney King, that I had a message to deliver to Reverend Murray on his behalf. The usher told me there was no room left in the church and asked me to remain at the door while he spoke to Reverend Cecil (Chip) Murry.

After a short wait, the usher returned and said I would not be admitted. I don't know if he actually went to Reverend Murry or not, but I was turned away. I headed back to my car. We'd thought a message from King might alter the course of events, and maybe it might have. The fact remains, King's voice was not heard that night and the hostilities continued to escalate.

On my way home, I called Lerman from the car and told him of my failure. "We tried" he said, wanting to make me feel better. "No one can fault us for the effort."

"How's Glen doing?" I asked.

"He's still talking to the doctor. He's taking all this pretty hard. He's blaming himself for the fires and the riots. Hell, they're saying on TV, people are dying in this mess. We've tried to tell him it's not his fault, but he's not dealing with it very well," Lerman said.

"Any chance he might want to face the media himself and ask for a stop to all this?"

"That's what we're discussing right now."

"Let me know what he decides and I'll try to make it happen." I hung up and immediately got a call.

Tom Leykis, a popular talk show host, then on Los Angeles radio station KFI, had been on the air when the verdicts were announced. He changed his format to report the escalation of violence. Many politicians from city and state governments were calling into his show to voice their support or criticism of the verdicts. Leykis's producer was on the phone to me now, asking me to appear at midnight and discuss the riots and verdicts. I accepted the invitation.

When I finally walked into my living room around 8:30, Pat was sitting in front of the TV with tears in her eyes. Live coverage of the looting and burning dominated every channel. I hadn't fully realized how strongly Pat cared about the issues involved in the beating. Glen and his family had been guests in our home a number of times, and Pat's affection for him had grown. For the first time, she told me she regretted her police past. She was ashamed of her former brothers in blue. She had undergone a metamorphosis, much as I had. We were both ashamed of the verdicts.

I slumped in my chair and watched the riots from the safety of my living room. Dozens of fires were burning. Looters were active in South Central. Everywhere a camera pointed it recorded scenes of violence and pain. I watched as the little guard booth in the front parking lot of Parker Center was turned over and set afire.

I remembered the hours and days of my rookie year in the department, when I had sat in that little booth during late evening and early morning hours on station security. In those days, the police were a prime target of terrorism, and an incredible number of manhours were devoted to security of police facilities. As I sat and watched the destruction of the security booth, I felt a strong sense of the separation that had developed between me and the department I had once respected. I wasn't unhappy to see the guard booth go up in flames. I never did like that post anyway. I was experiencing

some of the anger the mobs were displaying. I understood it. I
didn't agree with their methods of showing it, but I understood.
Around 11:30, I headed back for Los Angeles and was on the air
at KFI until 3:00 A.M.

∎

A few hours of fitful sleep and I was up early, swilling coffee
and watching the continuing coverage of the turmoil envelop-
ing L.A. According to media reports, rioting had broken out in
other major cities across the country. People were being arrested in Chicago, Atlanta, and Miami. In many cities, looting
and burning were the order of the day.

In a book titled *Understanding the Riots, Los Angeles Times*
reporters wrote,

> In San Francisco, marauding youths smashed windows, set
> small fires, and raided some of the city's finest boutiques.
> Union Square, the city's beloved shopping district, was littered
> with glass, debris, and an occasional stolen tennis shoe. Guests
> at the elegant St. Francis Hotel watched from the lobby. The
> bell captain at another hotel said unnerved guests had broken
> down and cried.
>
> In downtown Atlanta, hundreds of black youths went on a
> rampage. In Madison, Wisconsin, the windshields of thirty-
> four parked police cars were shattered. "Justice for King," read
> a note at the scene. In New York City, students at a Catholic
> school in Queens walked out of their classes chanting, "Rod-
> ney, Rodney, Rodney." In Providence, Rhode Island, and Seat-
> tle, Washington, city officials and black community leaders
> appealed for calm. In Washington, D.C., all police officers'
> leaves were canceled and units were put on alert in anticipa-
> tion of trouble.

What disturbed me most was the attitude of the looters as
they destroyed the hopes and dreams of local shopowners.
These were not the faces of people angry at the King verdicts.
They were having a good time—partying—in the name of Rodney King. White, brown, and black . . . men, women, and
children . . . looting, burning. In many instances, families were
rioting together, carrying appliances and furniture to their
cars, like it was an early Christmas and they didn't want to

wait for gift wrapping. All laughed and smiled like they were on a TV game show, boldly walking in front of cameras as if to say, "Here we are, do something about it if you can."

As the turmoil continued, Rodney King was safely tucked away in his Studio City apartment with his wife, Crystal; the streets of Los Angeles were not safe to travel. About noon, I received a call from Steve Lerman. He'd been invited to appear on several news shows in Hollywood. Sam Donaldson from ABC was flying in and would interview him later in the day at the ABC studios. Steve wanted me to provide security while he was doing these shows.

"Sure," I answered knowing the riots had spread to Hollywood by midmorning.

"I'll meet you at ABC at 4:00 P.M.," he said, and the phone went silent.

From ABC, we would go to a studio where Lerman would do a live satellite interview with Larry King. One of the jurors would also be on the show, via phone. Some of the jurors were beginning to speak publicly. They were, in my opinion, looking for acceptance of their verdicts or trying to ease their consciences.

I exited the Hollywood Freeway at 3:45 P.M., fifteen minutes before I was to meet Lerman at ABC, and pulled into a small filling station on Vermont Avenue. I stopped my car beside a self-serve pump. As I walked to the cashier's window, I heard the distinctive sounds of an approaching mob. I watched them set fires to some of the buildings they passed. A few had handguns and were firing randomly into the air as they moved along.

The rioters stopped across the street and several began firing in my direction. I don't think they were shooting at me, merely trying to frighten everyone in the area. They were doing a hell of a job. I pulled my 9mm automatic, leaned across the trunk of my car, and sighted in on one of the rioters holding a gun. I'd been lucky during my trip to First AME Church. No problem. But now I was afraid my luck had run out on the streets of Hollywood, before I even got to meet Sam Donaldson.

Several rioters saw my pistol aimed back at them and kept the mob moving north along Vermont. No harm, no foul.

When they were gone, I grabbed my car phone and attempted to call Lerman and warn him away from Vermont

Avenue. Then, I called ABC security and suggested they advise the limo bringing Donaldson from the airport to approach from an alternative direction.

Smoke from hundreds of arson fires stifled the air around ABC studios near Prospect and Vermont. Gunfire echoed from all directions and, like an idiot, I stood outside near the entrance of the studio, waiting for Lerman and Donaldson. Pacing nervously, repeatedly glancing at my watch, I noticed additional security at the studio. As helicopters criss-crossed overhead, I saw retired LAPD and Sheriff's officers, dressed in jeans and raid jackets, positioned at key points around the perimeter. I felt a sense of "been there, done that." But this time, it was an American city, instead of a Vietnamese village.

Lerman arrived at the ABC studios twenty minutes later, and we waited outside for Donaldson's arrival. To the southwest, the sky glowed orange from a fire raging at the famous Frederick's of Hollywood store on Hollywood Boulevard. I looked at the armed men gathered around us, smelled the smoke, listened to the distant gunfire and watched the fire-bright sky. Just like Nam, except here the jungle was concrete.

■

After Lerman completed his round of news shows, we went to dinner. He told me King had decided to go on the air himself and make a plea for an end to the violence. "Glen saw footage of a dead security officer lying in the street and wept," Lerman said, his head bent forward from stress. "He's feeling like he started it all." In his own simple way, Glen thought he might be able to save a life, or keep a business from being torched.

We decided Rodney King should face the media the following day, May 1, 1992, at a press conference in the small courtyard behind Lerman's Beverly Hills offices. We'd used this location in the past. It was small and provided the security I felt we needed. Only blocks away, windows of world-famous stores on Rodeo Drive were being shot out from cars driving by.

Early on the morning of May 1, I was on the phone to the watch commander at the Beverly Hills Police Department, to advise him of our intent. I requested that, if possible, several officers be dispatched to act as backup security to my staff—

just in case. The watch commander sounded suspicious and expressed concern about what King might say. Would it be a call for peace or a call to arms? I assured him King's comments would be one hundred percent positive.

Next, we notified the city news service that Rodney King would give a statement at 3:15 P.M. Fox-TV News was designated as pool camera; we knew from previous experiences King was camera-shy and tended to freeze when multiple lenses were aimed at him. By designating a pool camera, we hoped other video crews would respect our wishes to keep their cameras away from King. He would not take questions, only read a prepared text. Lerman requested I be available to assist with questions from the media. King would have his say, then be escorted back to Steve's offices during the Q&A session.

Shortly before the press conference, *LA Times* reporter, Richard Serrano, was able to get into Steve's offices. As King walked out the door, he saw Serrano and went to speak with him.

During the course of pretrial processing on the King criminal case, Serrano was the one journalist in Los Angeles to stay with the story. He was usually the first to report important issues in the case. I had asked him on any number of occasions to give me some of his sources, but he just laughed. He was aggressive and persistent in his efforts and was, in my opinion, closer to the truth of the case than the D.A.'s office. Like Chris Harris at Fox-TV, Serrano cut through to the real issues more times than even he realized.

Before bringing King out into the press conference area, I wanted to ensure my staff was positioned. I'd placed two men on the seventh-floor roof of the tinker toylike parking structure east of the site. Another man was watching from the roof of Lerman's office building, fifteen floors above the area, while other security staffers were placed in and around the crowd. Four uniformed officers from the Beverly Hills Police Department stood at various locations, under the supervision of the Beverly Hills P.D. lieutenant in charge. I'd arranged for Lerman's internal staffers to stand behind King at the microphone, with orders to grab him and knock him to the ground if a problem erupted.

On that afternoon of May 1, 1992, Rodney King broke his own rule and met with the media for the first time since his release from custody fourteen months earlier. The simple yet thoughtful words and style were purely his. Lerman had prepared a text, but Glen never looked at it, choosing instead to speak his own words from his heart:

> Can we all get along? Can we stop making it horrible for the older people and the kids? We've got enough smog here in Los Angeles, let alone to deal with the setting of these fires and things. It's just not right. It's not right, and it's not going to change anything. We'll get our justice. They've won the battle, but they haven't won the war. We will have our day in court, and that's all we want. I'm neutral. I love everybody. I love people of color. I'm not like they're . . . making me out to be.
>
> We've got to quit. I can understand the first upset for the first two hours after the verdict, but to go on, to keep going on like this, and to see the security guard shot on the ground, it's just not right. It's just not right because those people will never go home to their families again. And I mean, please we can all get along here. We can all get along. We've just got to. Just got to. We're all stuck here for awhile. Let's try to work it out. Let's try to work it out.

As I look at video tape of that moment, I'm both moved and amused by King's words and actions as he faced the cameras. His stiffness and nervousness were genuine. Standing at his left shoulder, I whispered in his ear, "Relax, take a couple of deep breaths, and smile." The sounds of a helicopter overhead almost covered his plea to Los Angeles and the nation. Several weeks later, a black rap singer criticized King for selling out the blacks in America by calling for an end to the violence. Headline grabbing.

Hostilities appeared to be winding down when King spoke. A strict curfew had been in place since the second night of the riots. The California National Guard and U.S. Marines were patrolling the streets, arresting rioters and looters, over 2500 of them. Peace was being restored in Los Angeles and other cities across the country. It appeared the worst was over. That night fewer fires were set. Maybe it's just my own wishful thinking, but I believe Rodney King's words played some small part in halting the unrest. After his moment in the media limelight, King went back into seclusion.

VIOLATING THE CODE

Shortly after the riots ended, the Los Angeles Police Commission formed a panel of advisors to investigate the issues involved in the unrest. Former FBI and CIA director William Webster was named as its head, with Hubert Williams of the Police Foundation second in command. Chief Williams was a friend and strong supporter of Daryl Gates. Regardless, in its report issued October 21, 1992, the panel names Chief Gates as a primary contributor to the escalation of the unrest which followed the verdicts, and calls into question the LAPD's state of readiness. It also cites the media as contributing to the growing violence in the city following the verdicts.

The Commission's report and its backup documentation calls the beating of Rodney King "a racially charged event from the moment of its occurrence, taking place against a backdrop of racial and ethnic tension in the city." It provides a chronology of events leading up to the riots, and the actions—or in too many instances, lack of actions—taken by city agencies in response to those events. Within hours of the report's release, Daryl Gates held a news conference in the studios of his KFI radio talk show (he had taken the place of Tom Leykis, whose contract had not been renewed.) Gates told the assembled press that he had not yet fully read the report but found "some of the conclusions reached by the panel were justified but both William Webster and Hubert Williams are liars." To this day, Gates still continues to voice such comments, even after leaving office, a sad case of trying to justify the unjustifiable.

.

Early on, a few LAPD officers began speaking publicly, calling for changes in the department, including the retirement of Chief of Police Daryl Gates.

I had the opportunity to meet with some very dedicated young officers who had watched the Holliday video on television and wanted us to know that not all cops were like those depicted in the tape. Camera crews recorded these officers, dressed in their blue uniforms, coming out of roll calls around the city, asking for Chief Gates to step aside. I vividly recall the story of Garland Hardeman, an African-American training officer assigned out of the Southwest Division, a predominantly black neighborhood around the University of Southern California, the Coliseum, and the Sports Arena.

On an afternoon newscast, Officer Hardeman announced he had been the victim of racial abuse within the department. The television news story reported that after Hardeman had gone on-camera calling for the departure of Gates, his locker inside Southwest Station (in an area not accessible to the public) was vandalized. A body outline was chalked on the floor in front of his locker with two X's drawn on the head, indicating bullet wounds. It clearly represented the feelings of some officers, and served as a message to Hardeman to keep his mouth shut.

Since that time, he's received other threats and as a result, is presently on leave from work with a stress-related injury. His problems with the department continue. I've met with Hardeman several times since then. On my most recent visit, he told me that while he would not give in to these threats, he was taking them very seriously. Of course, an investigation was begun to examine the incident. There have been no final findings as to who was responsible. Hardeman serves on the city council for the city of Inglewood, California, and has gotten on with the rest of his life.

Officer Charles Hilton (name changed on request), a young African-American, was picked as one of the rising stars of the department. He received his promotion the same month he passed his probationary period; was assigned to Foothill Division and made a training officer. He too found himself in front of a television camera after a roll-call briefing one afternoon shortly after the King beating.

Like Hardeman, Hilton thought that time had come for the departure of Gates, and he expressed his view openly. Soon, he was assigned to the desk at Foothill Station, an assignment most officers find dull and boring. His next written evaluation from his sergeants stated he was "not performing to the level expected of a training officer" and as a result, he would not be allowed to continue working with rookies. He told me he suspected that his supervisors mistrusted him and were concerned he would impart his ideas and values to younger, less experienced officers.

He complained to the department that he felt he was being penalized because of his beliefs, and that some comments made to him by his superiors were discriminatory. The louder and longer he objected, the more grief came his way. His lieutenant told him he would be demoted back to his prior rank and suffer a reduction in pay because he was no longer training rookies.

The last contact I had with officer Hilton, he said his wife had left him as a result of his problems with the department. He told me she didn't want any more to do with him because she claimed he was buckling to the pressures being applied by his superior officers. He was at his limit and was looking for a lawyer to represent him in an action against the city for punitive pressures arising from his comments related to the departure of Gates. He'd been forced out of his home and was living in a small trailer near Venice Beach. While he couldn't afford a telephone, he did have a pager, his only means of communicating.

■

Officer Maxine Spencer (name changed on request) was on assignment to Foothill when she received a direct warning from other officers at the division. She approached her car parked in an area accessible only to staff, after work one day and noticed a flier on her windshield. In that parking lot, anyone other than police personnel would have been stopped and questioned. The flier turned out to be distributed by the KKK and was racially biased and inflammatory. One would not know from officer Spencer's appearance that she was of African-American heritage. In April, 1991, she and other black officers held a press conference and told of her experiences at the Foothill Station parking lot. Shortly thereafter, she was transferred to the Harbor area, about twenty-five miles away from Foothill, and assigned to the day shift, working a one person car. Normally, patrol cars are manned by two officers.

Shortly after starting her new assignment, she received a radio call—bank robbery in progress. While rolling to the call, she requested additional backup, but other units on her shift were either "busy" or en route to Code-7 (lunch). She was left to handle the robbery call by herself.

Like the other officers, she had violated the Code of Silence. Now, she was paying for that violation. Her safety had been compromised, she believed, because she'd reported the KKK threat to the media. She, like her friends, had called for the departure of Gates in the interest of the citizens of Los Angeles. Within weeks, Officer Spencer sustained an injury on the job and was assigned to her home while recovering. She has since returned to work and most recently, gave birth to her first child. Maxine Spencer has put her days and nights at Foothill Division behind her. They are not her most pleasant memories of police work.

■

All of these incidents are evidence of one of the most serious problems of the department—racism. They are only the tip of the iceberg. Several months after the publication of the Christopher Commission Report, assistant chief David Dotson was demoted to the rank of deputy chief following a dispute with Daryl Gates. In his public reaction to the demotion, Dotson cited retribution by Gates for statements Dotson made to the Christopher Commission during their investigation as the reason. Retaliation and retribution inside the department are not limited to lower-ranking officers, but reach up to the highest levels of power in the LAPD.

Several members of the city council also called for Gates to retire, which led to a confrontation between the Chief of Police and Councilman Michael Woo in council chambers. Councilman Woo demanded greater accountability by the department over issues raised after the incident. After an attempt to suspend Gates, with pay, pending results of the Christopher Commission inquiry, the chief filed a lawsuit against the city, which then backed down, halting efforts to remove him from office. They lifted his suspension and returned him to full duty and authority. Much later, Gates announced he would retire from the department, after over forty years of service, in the spring of 1992.

A list of candidates to replace him was announced. The testing process had narrowed the field to ten finalists. Among these were LAPD Assistant Chief Vernon and Deputy Chief Bernie Parks, an African-American highly respected by city government officials. Parks had the qualifications for the job and was "from the inside," a candidate who had come up through the ranks.

Soon I started to get telephone calls from friends in the community, telling me that there appeared to be an effort inside the department to discredit Chief Parks. I had served under Parks when he was still a captain and I was assigned to Central Division. I didn't much care for him in those days. Many cops in the division called him "Captain Midnight," which I took as a racial slur. I was more polite and referred to him as "Bernie the ball-buster."

Inside gossip alleged that Chief Parks had personally interfered with a murder investigation involving a member of his immediate family. The allegations were later determined to be unfounded, but the damage was done. The job went to outsider, Willie Williams. It made sense. Williams would bring an objective eye to the troubled LAPD. He is also African-American, a big plus in helping to calm our angry streets.

Weeks after Chief Gates announced his retirement, he attempted to promote several high-ranking officers to "fill much needed positions in anticipation of the change in command." The police commission reacted to this by filing a complaint with city council, precipitating a heated exchange between

Gates and Council members. Gates threatened to delay his retirement until after Police Chief–designate Williams's appointment date, making the appointment null and void, retribution aimed at the entire city of Los Angeles.

Intense media attention focused on Gates's whereabouts at the outset of the riots. He was attending a fund-raiser that evening in support of stopping an initiative to implement Christopher Commission recommendations. The fund-raiser had been planned weeks before. Despite the verdicts coming in, Gates attended—while the city exploded. Gates's only explanation was that he couldn't cancel his appearance. His absence from the command center during this most critical time was inexcusable, and the media wouldn't let the issue go. In what appeared to be an act of desperation, Gates pointed his finger at lieutenant Mike Moulon, 77th Street Division Watch Commander, as the person responsible for the escalation of street violence.

At a news conference, not mentioning Moulon by name, Gates stated that the lieutenant should have called a tactical alert: a small-scale mobilization allowing for the holdover of the division's departing shifts and a redeployment of men and equipment from other areas. Only those inside the department knew who Gates was talking about. For the next several days, charges and countercharges ricocheted between Gates and Moulon, who finally filed a lawsuit against Gates. Moulon has not been back to work since the accusation and is not expected to return.

One of the most memorable post-incident episodes involved Sergeant Fred Nichols, a widely known and highly respected police academy instructor on the use of force. He had provided statements to IAD and the Christopher Commission relating to the department's use of force guidelines, specifically the escalation and deescalation of force applied by the four defendant officers. He voiced strong criticism of their tactics, testifying that they did indeed use excessive force, force beyond the policies defined in the Los Angeles Police Department training manual.

He later told the Judge in Simi Valley that as a result of his testimony to the commission, he was transferred out of his training job at the academy and reassigned to an insignificant staff job away from recruits. He insisted that while he could be ordered to appear at the trial, he would not testify as a witness against the four defendants. He claimed that since his appearance before the commission, he had received pressure from many fellow officers, who had suggested he change his mind about showing his face in court. He even had his doctor write a letter to the judge, requesting he be excused from testifying, explaining that he was suffering from stress, a common cop copout in these trying times. When he finally did respond to the subpoena, he appeared in court with an attorney at his side, claiming he would rather be found in contempt than testify. The court relented and dismissed him as a witness.

These are only a sampling of stories that have come to me over the past months; they are typical of many others resulting from the turmoil inside the department following the beating of Rodney King. There will be more, and the Code of Silence will survive.

■

Being a part of the King team wasn't all hard work and downers. Within days of Holliday's video being aired, letters, cards, and small packages containing video and audio tapes began arriving in bulk at Steve Lerman's offices. All were addressed to Rodney King. Like Christmas mail addressed simply to Santa Claus, North Pole, some letters arrived with no more of an address than, Rodney King, Los Angeles, CA. One letter was addressed to King in care of Mayor Tom Bradley, City Hall, Los Angeles. The mayor's offices forwarded the unopened letter to Lerman, bearing the comment, "We believe this goes to you."

Young and old, rich and poor, black, white, Asian, Hispanic—thousands of people around the world wrote King expressing their feelings about the incident. Many were sympathetic to the officers and blamed King for the trouble, but most were supportive of Glen and condemned the beating.

Some schools participated in assemblies that were videotaped and sent with the support of parent groups and faculty members. Others were individual supporters who wrote a special song or composed a poem and read it on audio cassettes. Frequently, it was my great pleasure to write, or if there was a phone number, call and thank the young person or the class for their correspondence on behalf of Rodney King. Dozens of hours were spent by Lerman, my wife Pat, and myself contacting school children at their homes.

Oakland, Tucson, Dallas, Chicago, New York City, Baltimore, Washington, D.C., Miami, Oslo, London, Paris, Bonn, even Moscow—people from almost every country in the world wrote letters of support, especially in the days and weeks following the riots.

One letter, in particular, was a heartbreaker. It came addressed to Rodney King C/O Lawyer Lerman, Beverly Hills, CA. It began, "I'm sorry I haven't seen you since my brother died. Sometimes, when I think about you and my brother. I cry."

I hadn't recognized the return address on the envelope, but after reading the letter, I knew Freddie G's younger brother, Rodney Crouse had sent it. I called and asked Barbara Crouse, their mother, if I could speak to Rodney.

She asked why, and I told her of her son's letter to Glen. She was moved. She hadn't known that he had sent a letter to the man who had been his big brother's friend. Young Rodney came on the phone and we talked for a long time about his brother and Glen and life in general as seen through the eyes of a small child. Here was a kid who chose to contact Glen without any help from his mother, simply because he missed his big brother, and hadn't seen Glen since Freddy G's death. The boy just wanted to share stories about his brother with someone who shared his feelings of kinship.

When I think back on my involvement as a member of the King team, these are treasured memories.

THE $6,000,000 MAN

The acquittals in Simi Valley and the resulting riots set the tone for the hot summer that followed. In June, *Vanity Fair*, published an article entitled "The Selling of Rodney King" written by Peter J. Boyer. A day or two before the issue hit the stands, sensationalistic comments by Boyer were leaked to the press. Television news broadcasts led off with quotations from the article, none of which were true. My phone began ringing off the hook. The first caller was an angry Steve Lerman.

"Have you seen the *Vanity Fair* article yet," Lerman asked.

"No, Steve. What'd they write that set you off?"

"This guy Boyer wouldn't know the truth if it leaped up and bit him on the ass," Lerman said, his anxiety showing with every word. "I shouldn't have talked to him, but he called me on a weekend, said if I didn't comment, he'd throw trash at Glen. Tom, listen to this!" He read from the article:

> And Rodney King? He was everywhere that day—on the lips of the pols, on the backs of T-shirts—and he was nowhere. He was not in Los Angeles, nor had he been there much lately. He

was shut away in a safe house in (of all places) Ventura County, wrapped in the arms of psychopharmaceuticals, under the twenty-four hour watch of a private-security team led by (of all people) a former LAPD cop . . . Lerman hired Tom Owens, the former LAPD officer, to supervise a security force which ensures that his "operation" is not penetrated, as well as a psychiatrist to monitor King's psyche and administer antidepressants and other medications. . . .

Boyer attempted to tar everyone connected to King with the same broad brush, and while most of the people mentioned in the article thought little of it, I for one was angry. Not so much by what Boyer alleged, because after all, his job was to write articles that sold magazines, but rather by his glaring lack of factual knowledge about King and his handlers, Steve Lerman and me.

If one accepts Boyer's cynical assertions and allegations, one could conclude Rodney King *never* had anyone good and decent even remotely connected to him. Boyer's article is a slap in the face to everyone who cares about Rodney King, either as a person or about the issues represented in the brutal beating. Boyer didn't even spare Rodney's mother when he wrote, "Odessa, is a deeply religious woman whose faith (Jehovah's Witnesses) prevents her from getting involved in matters of this world—a league in which her son's legal case securely fits."

I made several attempts to phone Boyer but none of my calls were returned. Instead, Boyer tried to reach Angela King, Glen's aunt, wanting an interview for a follow-up article. His original article did accomplish its goals; the issue sold out, evidence of the public's persistent hunger to learn all about Rodney Glen King and those around him.

The truth is, we worked very hard to keep King out of the public eye. It seemed to us that every time King was exposed publicly, his reputation suffered. Boyer's article hurt King further. The only truth I could find in his writings was his assertion that King was still being victimized, this time by those who would benefit financially from his case.

∎

On June 27, 1992 Rodney King was arrested by officers from the North Hollywood Division of the LAPD on allegations he'd battered his wife, Crystal Waters King. The allegations stemmed from a dispute between King and Crystal over a cassette tape recorder. The arrest came on the very day Chief Gates departed the LAPD on his retirement. I first became aware of the incident at 3:15 in the afternoon. The press started calling to check if there was any truth to rumors flying around newsrooms that King was arrested. I called King at his home to check in with him and find out what was happening. He answered on the second ring.

"Everything's cool, no problems," he said. Lerman was already there and was talking to police outside the apartment. King hung up the phone. I sensed something bad was about to go down. I called Lerman's pager. A few minutes later, Lerman returned my page.

Yes, the police were at King's apartment. Yes, there had been a dispute between King and Crystal and yes, the police were taking King into custody. I asked how the media had found out about the arrest. Lerman didn't know and was too busy to think about it just then; he was concentrating on the issues at hand.

I cancelled my schedule for the day and began the long Friday afternoon rush-hour commute to North Hollywood, forty miles to the northeast. On the drive up, I listened to the breaking story on the news: "Rodney King arrested again by the LAPD, this time for beating his wife in their San Fernando Valley apartment." It was the lead story on every radio newscast and the topic of every talk show in Los Angeles. This was the third contact between King and the police since the beating.

The arrest, this time, was made by a command officer, Deputy Chief Mark Kroeker. The news reported that at the very instant Gates walked out of his office for the last time, King was handcuffed and taken into custody.

Several things seemed odd from the start. First, King's arrest was made by a chief officer who had not made an arrest in the field for years. Second, it occurred simultaneously with Gates's departure from the department. Third, King was arrested for a crime, when news reports stated that he merely had a dispute with his wife. Something was wrong somewhere.

I arrived at the North Hollywood station about 4:30 P.M. As I parked my car, I saw a horde of media assembled outside the police station's main entrance. Inside, things were calm and quiet. I was told King and Lerman were in a back office talking to investigators. Crystal King was in another part of the building, also talking to detectives. Chief Kroeker was standing in a small office at the end of the hallway, talking on the telephone. I saw Sergeant John Stilo, an old friend. I'd worked for Stilo in the late seventies after he'd been promoted to sergeant and transferred to South Central Los Angeles. Glancing up from his desk, Stilo immediately recognized me. "What the hell're you doing here?" the youthful-looking sergeant asked.

"I thought you'd retired by now, John," I replied, relaxing now that I'd seen a friendly face. "I'm here on the King arrest. Can you tell me what's going on?" Nodding, he invited me to join him for a cup of coffee, away from the lobby. We discussed what had happened to each of us in the passing years. Then came the real business. What were the charges against King? Would he be booked or not? Would they give us a side door away from the media to leave from? How did the media find out about the dispute before the police? Sergeant Stilo would not discuss the facts of the incident with me.

Lerman finally came out to say that King had not been arrested; he was simply being detained for investigation, classic copspeak, meaning they didn't have reason enough to book him.

"Glen and Crystal had been arguing," Lerman said. "She grabbed a cassette recorder from the bedroom dresser and told him to repeat what he'd said into it. King tried to take the recorder away from Crystal and her hand was scratched. She called the police, identifying herself as Crystal Waters. She never mentioned she was Rodney King's wife." I noticed Lerman appeared calm, almost as if he already knew the outcome of the cop's investigation.

I talked to Sergeant Stilo again, who did confirm that Crystal's notification to the police was received at least fifteen minutes after the media had begun calling me at home. Very odd.

Not publicly known at the time was that Steve Lerman was already in negotiations with the City of Los Angeles to settle the King civil suit. California is a community property state. In a majority of circumstances, a husband and wife are entitled to share equally in the products of the marriage. Damages from injuries and monies paid for punitive damages are not normally considered community property if a separation or divorce occurs after those monies are awarded. The facts speak for themselves.

Finally, at about 6:00 P.M., King was released without being charged with any crimes. An assistant to the watch commander was detailed to escort King and Lerman from the station through the back exit and drive them away in an unmarked car, while I announced to the media that King would be coming out the front door any minute. Once again King was kept away from the media eye.

I caught up with Lerman and King at a local restaurant. We decided that King should put some time and distance between himself and Crystal, so after dinner, I was to take King back to his Studio City apartment to gather some belongings, then drive him back to the Residence Inn in Orange, where he'd stay for a few days while the smoke cleared. We arrived at King's apartment shortly before nightfall, to find nine TV camera trucks parked outside the complex.

■

In late April of 1991, final arrangements were concluded and Lerman, Freddie G, Pooh, and Crystal's aunt, Kandyce Barnes, flew to New York for their first guest appearance on a talk show. This occasion was the first time Kandyce tried playing hardball with Steve and me. As we would learn later, Kandyce had already begun to strengthen her influence with Glen through her niece, Crystal.

The Hyundai King had been driving on the night of the beating belonged to Kandyce Barnes. Kandyce, asleep at home, was awakened by the CHP dispatcher, who called to verify the white Hyundai King was driving had not been stolen, and that Glen was in lawful possession of the car. After the CHP call, Kandyce went back to sleep and had not questioned the circumstances of King's arrest until the case broke in the news with the airing of the Holliday video. I had been told of her relationship to Glen and Crystal by Glen's Aunt Angela, the sister of Glen's father. Angela considered herself to be very close to Glen. During the trial in Simi Valley, she was often sought out by the media for comments, and while she was supportive of Glen, she was also vocal in her criticisms of him for his various encounters with the police.

Angela, who was spending many of her evenings at the hospital with Glen, told me, "Be watchful of that woman Kandyce. Keep her as far from Glen as you can." I made a mental note that Kandyce had not made a single trip to the hospital while Glen was recuperating.

Kandyce was a handsome, seemingly intelligent woman. I formed the opinion that while she might be aggressive and dominant, she really cared for Glen and had his best interests at heart. Kandyce's name first came up in a conversation between Glen and me when we were discussing the speed capabilities of the Hyundai. Since it was her car, I felt she might be a valuable witness as to the car and its maximum speed.

One of my primary responsibilities, right from the beginning, was to provide security for King. Often, he would demand that the security be removed, allowing him more freedom. The subsequent encounters between King and several law enforcement agencies occured during those times of suspended security.

After King was released from the hospital, he took up residence at a high-rise building in the mid-Wilshire district. The building itself provided a degree of security, so we decided Glen could live there without twenty-four hour security guards at his door. It was here Kandyce brought another lawyer in to visit with Glen.

Steve hit the ceiling when he found out, but Kandyce denied the visit was an attempt to replace him with the other attorney. The same attorney was to resurface later, once again at the behest of Kandyce. The attorney was none other than Milton Grimes, who would replace Steve Lerman as King's new civil attorney.

Kandyce hadn't finished yet. Several weeks later, she paid another visit to the mid-Wilshire high-rise, this time accompanied by lawyer James Banks, a partner in Triple Seven Entertainment, a little known production company which, at the time, had produced only one video, a guide for parents wishing to get their children into show business. Glen later told me Banks offered to purchase the rights to his life story for a major motion picture focusing on the issues surrounding the beating. Later, Kandyce returned with a contract from Triple Seven and recommended King sign it. He did. It was weeks before he informed Lerman of what he'd done.

In the interim, other Hollywood production companies had been contacting Steve's office with offers for the rights to King's story. Steve began asking around and found the consensus was that the rights were valued in excess of $200,000 at the time. I wasn't involved in any of these negotiations and wasn't informed by either Lerman or King of the amounts being discussed. I merely knew that Lerman was making inquiries. When I learned that Kandyce had taken advantage of the decreased security at the high-rise to get the Triple Seven contract to King, I was mad as hell. The woman had used her family position to gain access to Glen, circumventing the very security plan designed to keep such things from happening.

Steve told me King had signed with Triple Seven for less than half of what larger production companies were offering. I wondered why Glen would sign a contract without the advice of Lerman, especially since he was still heavily medicated after his recent surgery. I was concerned King hadn't understood the legal language in the contract; he had difficulty reading anything. I was smelling a rat.

．

Meantime, negotiations with the city to settle the civil case were concluding. Six weeks of intensive back-and-forths had taken their toll on the King team. Lerman and his associates went nose to nose with city attorney James Hahn and his top staffers, who had initially requested meetings within days of the riots.

Smoke from thousands of arson fires still tainted the air as negotiators sat down to talk in the fifteenth floor offices of City Hall. When the door leading from the reception room finally closed, thirteen people were seated at the room's massive dark oak conference table. James Hahn was the first to speak.

"Mr. Lerman, I've asked you and your staff here today to begin the process which, hopefully, will lead to the successful conclusion of this litigation. We're here at the request of the mayor and the city council to see if we can find a resolution to this situation. I've been granted authority by the city government to work with you but as you know, the final okay rests with the city council. They're the ones who must vote on any agreement." We settled in for the lengthy process.

On the side of the table representing the city were Hahn's two most senior deputies, Deputy City Attorney Tom Hoakenson and Deputy City Attorney (and retired LAPD Captain) Don Vincent, along with senior staffers in the police litigation unit. Lerman asked his associates Irving Osser, Bob Neubauer, and Tom Beck to join him. All were lawyers specializing in police abuse and misconduct. I was also there because of my intimate knowledge of the facts in the case.

Discussions began cordially enough, but very rapidly turned into posturing by both sides. It was apparent from the outset that the city wanted to settle the case. The city attorney focused solely on Lerman. "We know you're asking fifty-four million on behalf of your client. We suspect you know that the city will not agree to a figure anywhere near that amount."

Lerman sat forward in his chair, his hands folded across each other as they rested on the table. Slowly, he took a deep breath and went right for the throat: "And you must know that the entire country has just witnessed the torching of the second largest city in the nation because of a perceived injustice," Lerman responded. "The citizens will soon know the results of these negotiations, and if they believe Mr. King has not been compensated satisfactorily, we may face this danger once again. These same pressures are being felt by us. We must obtain a fair agreement, not only for my client, but to ease the outrage of the entire community." Both negotiators were dancing around on the same dance floor but one was waltzing while the other was doing the twist.

"Look Steve, the facts are, we came to the table with an authorization of two million, however you want it, plus your reasonable fees and expenses. That could total two-point-five million. If you take it, we're done." Hahn, having fired the first shot, sat back and listened while Lerman replied.

"Mr. King has authorized me to accept twenty-five million. If *you* agree, we're done." Both sides had put their propositions on the table. Now, the real work could begin.

No decisions were reached in the first meeting except that the negotiations would go forward under the supervision of a federal judge, to be agreed upon later. It was also decided that the federal trial judge, John Davies, who would hear the civil case, should be notified of the discussions. Hahn assured the group his offices would handle the appropriate notifications and would find a judge acceptable to both sides to mediate proceedings.

The following week, Judge Harry Hupp of the U.S. District Court in Los Angeles, was chosen to oversee and supervise the ongoing negotiations from that point forward. The agreement between the parties also called for the talks to be conducted secretly. Over the next six weeks, the parties met in the chambers of Judge Hupp, who proved to be a stern but fair mediator. Finally, during the second week of June, an agreement was reached, calling for the City of Los Angeles to pay 5.95 million dollars to Rodney King for all damages, costs and fees associated with the case. Nearly two million dollars in up-front cash would go to King for medical, legal, and other fees and the rest would be to purchase an annuity which would pay him $120,000 annually for the rest of his life, with a twenty-year guarantee. These figures were given to King in the presence of Judge Hupp.

As the sun set on that warm June day, there was happiness on the King team. Lerman and Hahn had negotiated well; both were committed to bringing an end to the King incident. Judge Hupp concluded his remarks by reminding the group that final acceptance must come from the city council.

Lerman, King, and I, and others present during the final session, went to the exclusive Four Seasons Hotel in Beverly Hills to celebrate. We occupied a quiet corner of the hotel's restaurant. Waiters and busboys scurried about filling drink orders and laying out snack trays as conversations eventually turned to King's plans. "Have you given any thought about what you plan to do with some of your money?" I asked.

Glen was unusually thoughtful in his reply. "Yeah, well, I want to be able to do something for the people who suffered in the riots. I want to give some money to set up a scholarship for kids to continue their education. You know, not college, but like trade schools and like that. Something that they can use in a job."

Steve suggested the three of us should go to Catalina Island for a few days. The pressures of the final negotiations had worn him to a nub; he wanted to get away and unwind.

The trip over to Catalina on Steve's boat was relaxing. The

atmosphere on board suggested that something good and important had been accomplished and that we were setting out on a new phase of our relationship.

During the four-hour boat ride to Avalon, my thoughts were on my responsibilities to safeguard King from those who would try to get at his bank account. I had long since identified potential friends and family members who were waiting like coiled snakes for their chance to strike. In our first meeting, Glen requested I watch for leeches and shield him against their efforts until he could hire a financial advisor. I knew once the city council approved the settlement, the money would follow within weeks. I hoped this would give King ample time to find someone he could trust.

James Hahn had anticipated it would take two to three weeks for the city council to vote on the terms of the agreement. If approved by the council, it would then take an additional two weeks for the funds to be generated. Not much time, considering the amount of money King was to receive. In the weeks between the settlement and the city council vote, several things happened politically that would have an impact on the agreement.

Most important, Tom Bradley announced he would not seek another term as the city's mayor. Longtime county supervisor Kenneth Hahn (father of the city attorney) announced he too would retire. Thus started a flurry of activity as local politicians announced, or publicly anticipated announcing, their candidacies for those offices.

L.A. city councilman Zev Yaroslavsky was thought by many to have the inside track for the mayor's job. Currently, he was chairman of the finance committee, first to vote on the appropriation for King. A political moderate, Yaroslavsky represented the conservative West Los Angeles area. His influence on the council was formidable. Lerman had been told by James Hahn that he came to the table with the authority of city council, needing only their approval, which was controlled by Yaroslavsky.

The settlement agreement finally went before the finance committee for vote in September 1992. Behind closed doors, it was voted down by the committee, by a vote of six to three, at the urging of Yaroslavsky. The media, who had assembled at City Hall, reported that three members of the committee walked out on the vote in angry disagreement. The rejection gained Yaroslavsky support from the more conservative members of the community and would probably help him win votes in the upcoming election for mayor or county supervisor or whichever office he might seek.

The finance committee, through the city attorney, issued a statutory offer of two hundred fifty thousand dollars cash to King, from which he would pay his medical bills, already exceeding one hundred-fifty thousand bucks, and other fees, including mine of nearly twenty thousand dollars. In addition King would receive seventy-five hundred dollars a month for twenty years, based on the purchase of an annuity for one million dollars. Under this offer, Lerman would not benefit from the funds, but would have to go before Judge Davies to argue for his outstanding fees and costs. This new offer totaled $250,000 up front and a payout of $1.75 million throughout King's life, roughly a third of our agreement with City Attorney Hahn.

An important consideration of the offer was that the city retain the ability to recover those monies from the other defendants. With over forty named defendants, the city had a good chance to recover much of the payout. Many of the individual officers named as defendants owned homes, and their homeowners insurance policies became subject to claim by the city within the meaning of the settlement. In the end, the taxpayers of Los Angeles would not suffer the entire loss caused by the actions of the defendant officers. While I found the city's actions to be politically motivated and a double cross, I understood their brilliance.

In the weeks that followed, I got several telephone calls from friends close to the city council, who told me the turndown of the settlement and the minimal offer was specifically designed to create misgivings in King about his team, hoping he might change attorneys. A new attorney would be less knowledgeable of the case, and a change of counsel could slow the civil litigation process. Very prescient of them, as things turned out.

■

Once the riots ended and calm was restored to L.A., then-president Bush ordered the U.S. Justice Department to restart their investigation originally begun on March 10, 1991. Under U.S. Code Title 18, Sections 241 and 242, the acquitted officers could be tried again, this time for criminally violating King's civil rights under color of authority. These little-known and seldom used sections of federal law were enacted after the turn of the century, to bring to justice those persons who, under their state authority, escape justice in local courts. For example, when officers accused of crimes involving civil rights are acquitted in local courts, the alleged violators can be prosecuted in Federal Court without a double jeopardy defense application. Federal authorities boast a seventy-five percent conviction rate in these prosecutions.

Thus, with the acquittals in Simi Valley, the U.S. Justice Department, aided by the FBI, began anew its investigation of the defendant officers. The full weight and assets of the U.S. government were brought to bear. Following the May 1 plea for peace by King, the Feds were in contact with my offices and, once again, I was contributing to the criminal investigation efforts of others.

Now, all we had to do was sit back, wait, and try to keep Rodney King out of trouble with the police, which was becoming a full-time job.

As we went into settlement negotiations with the city, my staff's investigative efforts on behalf of King slowed considerably. It appeared the case would soon settle and further efforts of collecting information and data could prove unnecessary. As a result, most of my personal efforts were devoted to King's security.

With the slowdown in field investigation. I began laying off some of my staff. My insurance case work had already dwindled down to nearly nothing, my savings were gone, and my efforts to collect outstanding fees were meeting stiff resistance from too damn many attorneys. Pat's early warning about working for lawyers had become a prophecy. To her credit, Pat has never said, "I told you so," though the very thing she warned me about was coming to pass.

Within my offices, a sense of impending doom filled the air. My staff, once thought to be the cream of the crop, were finding other jobs or opening their own investigation companies providing services to my former insurance company clients. Jack White, John Huelsman, and Steve Chunchick, all former assistant investigators on the King case, opened an investigation company serving my client list. They had been the field grunts working those cases while on my staff, and the insurance companies already knew of their work. I lost the accounts through neglect. Why shouldn't they get the business?

Jack and John are still in the insurance investigation business but Steve is now back selling cars, having given up as an investigator. Bill Anderson, once my senior assistant, has moved to the Seattle area and is working for an investigation company there. Harry Johnson moved to Bend, Oregon, where he opened his own business. I still talk to Johnson, who calls me once in awhile, just to check in and see how things are progressing. Malcolm Stone is working as a fraud investigator for another company, but has expressed interest in coming back to work for me, should I ever need him.

By the end of summer, 1992, I was feeling generally rundown. In a rare but appreciated act of concern, Steve Lerman sent me to see his personal doctor, a cardiologist in Beverly Hills. The doctor insisted I give up smoking. I promised him I would try. Ten days later, I needed a nicotine rush and was back on the butts.

CAUGHT WITH THEIR HANDS IN THE COOKIE JAR

July 16, 1992, 1:00 A.M. The 210 freeway, sneaking its way through low grassy hillsides and small rural communities, was nearly deserted. Smog from the previous evening's rush hour had been swept away by night breezes as if to make way for the new dose that would follow with the morning rush hour. Glen and Crystal had begun their evening with a backyard picnic at their home in Altadena. It was late and they were tired. As Crystal drove their gray Chevrolet Blazer back to the Residence Inn, Glen snoozed. It had been a long day.

Traffic remained light as Crystal made the transition from the 210 to the 57 freeway, entering Orange County. The radio played quietly as she drove. They'd had a nice time today; Glen was finally starting to unwind after the violence that followed the verdicts. He took the riots much harder than one might have guessed, certainly more than he let anyone know. He'd reunited with Crystal following their much publicized family dispute a few weeks earlier, but because the media had discovered their Studio City apartment, both were living in Glen's temporary quarters at the Residence Inn.

Glen stirred awake as they arrived at the hotel. Crystal suggested a late night snack before going to bed. Glen agreed and got behind the wheel to drive to a Denny's restaurant just a few yards down the road.

As they entered the parking lot, Glen saw the black and white markings of a California Highway Patrol car parked to the right side of the driveway. He saw two officers, a male and a female, standing next to another car, talking to the driver. His thoughts flashed back to another male and female team of CHP officers he'd had contact with over a year before. He could see the driver of the other car was African-American. Ironic, he thought. He parked, and Crystal went into the restaurant to order takeout. Glen opened the driver's door a few inches and called a friend on his cellular phone. Lerman had given him the car phone after the Hollywood arrest, in case he got into trouble again.

At 2:05 A.M. Rodney Glen King was once again arrested by officers from the California Highway Patrol.

Officers, A. R. Mangan, and her partner, S. L. Ligan, were both in their mid- to late twenties. Officer Mangan was slight of build with short, dark blond hair. Ligan, about six feet tall and of average build, stood with military bearing at the Department of Motor Vehicles hearing several months later. Certainly, neither were a match for King in size.

The two officers got into their car and proceeded slowly in the direction of Rodney King's parked Blazer. As the black and white neared, the passenger officer aimed a spotlight directly into King's windshield. The patrol car stopped a few feet away and the two officers got out, leaving the spotlight pointing at his face.

As with every other encounter between Rodney King and the police since the beating incident, stories of what happened differ, depending on which side is talking.

At 2:20 A.M., I was awakened by a telephone call from Steve Lerman. "Tom, are you awake?" Lerman asked, his voice sounding tired and strained.

"I am now," I replied as I sat up and rubbed my eyes. "What's going on?"

"Crystal just called. Glen's been arrested again! Cops in Orange got him at that Denny's near their hotel. Crystal says they took him for DUI."

"Damn it! Why was he driving in the first place? We've told him a hundred times to let someone else drive."

"I don't know any of the facts yet. I want you in the field as quickly as possible. Find out what happened."

"I'll call you as soon as I know something." I hung up and stumbled out of bed. Pat grumbled and rolled over.

In his initial report, completed immediately following King's arrest, Officer Ligan wrote, "I was standing at the right front of the CHP unit and my partner, Officer Mangan, was walking back towards the CHP vehicle on the left side, when I observed a Chevrolet Blazer begin to back up in a northwesterly direction in a quick and abrupt manner. I then saw the suspect vehicle make three jerky turning movements, then accelerate slightly and brake harshly and skid three to four feet. The vehicle then rolled back and came to an abrupt stop. I advised Officer Mangan of what I had witnessed and asked her to drive over to the suspect vehicle. The CHP vehicle was then parked in front of the suspect vehicle. I then turned on the right spotlight and pointed it in the direction of the suspect vehicle." Officer Ligan wrote in his report that this was when he recognized the driver as Rodney King.

As Ligan neared the driver's door, he smelled "a strong odor of an alcoholic beverage coming from the interior of the suspect vehicle." He advised King of the reason for the stop and asked for a driver's license and registration. Ligan wrote, "The subject (King) fumbled with his wallet, which he recovered from behind the seat. I verified that the subject was Mr. King. I then asked the subject if he had been drinking to which the subject replied, 'No.'" When Ligan told King he could smell the odor of alcohol coming from within the vehicle, King said, "Hey man, you know who I am, right?" Ligan acknowledged he did, and again asked King if he had been drinking. "This time, he responded, 'Well, I had one beer earlier in the day.'"

Ligan noted King's speech was slightly slurred. He told his partner, Officer Mangan, to get another unit rolling for backup. He then ordered King to get out of his car and submit to a sobriety test. "The subject then asked me if I was scared of him. With this, I turned the investigation over to Officer Mangan."

Officer Mangan, in her preliminary report of the incident, wrote that she too smelled alcohol on King from ten to fifteen feet away. "I asked the subject if he had been drinking and he said, 'Yes, one beer.' " She noted his eyes were bloodshot and watery. "As he spoke, his speech was slightly slurred." She explained the field sobriety test to King, and asserted that he was unsteady on his feet and subsequently was unable to perform the tests as demonstrated.

All the objective symptoms of DUI were articulated in the reports completed by the two officers, including bloodshot and watery eyes, unsteady balance or gait, poor coordination, odor of alcohol on breath, the presence of nystagmus (an involuntary fluttering of the eyes), and inability to balance on one foot. Officer Mangan noted that King failed to complete even one test appropriately. As a result, both officers formed the opinion that King was operating a motor vehicle while intoxicated.

While Mangan and Ligan were administering the field sobriety tests, their backup unit, Officers J. Craig and J. D. Gutierrez, arrived. They got out of their car, drew their PR-24 batons, and took up positions behind Ligan and Mangan. They watched as King attempted to complete the remaining field sobriety tests.

Witnesses later reported that the backup officers kept striking their batons into the open palms of their free hands.

In his statement to me, King said, "I watched the other two officers standing there with their batons in their hands. They were hitting the batons against their open hands, kind'a like threatening me, you know, letting me know if I got out of line, they would hit me with the sticks. It scared me pretty bad. I thought about the other time, in March. . . . Yeah, I was really scared."

The officers told King they wanted him to submit to a blood, breath, or urine test and he refused. They warned him that in California, a refusal would result in an automatic suspension of his driver's license. In essence, King projected the attitude, "Fuck you, I didn't do anything." The handcuffs came out.

Once the decision was made to take King into custody, Craig and Gutierrez entered the restaurant to look for Crystal, so they could release the car to her. A waitress directed them to the ladies' room, where they waited until Crystal came out. They informed her that King had been taken into custody for DUI. She was surprised, to say the least. Crystal then called Lerman from the car phone and told him of the arrest. Lerman called me. Ten minutes later I was at the Orange Police Department, ringing the night bell.

A lone civilian female employee was seated at the counter in the dimly lit lobby of the newly constructed police station. She came over and unlocked the door. I told her why I was there, then waited while she went to speak with the watch commander. She returned and told me King had been transported to the CHP Santa Ana office about ten minutes away. I called Lerman from my car and gave him an update. Good, I thought as I pulled up to the CHP facility, no media yet. Maybe they don't know about the arrest.

Like the Orange Police station, the Santa Ana CHP office was closed. The main entrance is located on the south side of the old building and is dimly lit during nonworking hours. Next to the door is a telephone with a direct line to the CHP dispatch center. I heard laughter coming from inside and King's name in the middle of it. I picked up the phone and told the female dispatcher that I wanted to talk to the supervisor in charge of the King arrest. She told me a sergeant would be out shortly. I hung up and listened to the laughter. Several minutes passed before a blond, thirtyish, quiet-spoken CHP sergeant stuck his head out the door and said King had been transported to the Orange County Jail, where he would be booked. He also told me he had already received a few media calls and thought I should know they were onto the story. It's three in the morning, I thought. How could the media already know about the arrest? I thanked the sergeant and headed for the jail. Again, I called Lerman from the car. We agreed he should draft a statement about King's arrest, then begin the long drive out to Orange County from the Valley.

The familiar KNBC-TV camera truck was parked in front of the jail. I walked past it and heard a technician talking on a cellular phone to his assignment desk. "Yeah, he's already here. Been booked for drunk driving . . . didn't give the officers any shit during the arrest. Went nice and quiet. They say they'll be releasing him in a few hours."

I knew the usual media madness would soon follow. I entered the jail lobby and went over to a lone deputy, seated in the glass information booth, talking on the phone. I stood quietly by until he finished his call. "Help you?" he said with a pleasant smile. I identified myself and asked for the jail watch commander. In a few minutes, Lieutenant Wilkerson, the grave-yard shift watch commander appeared. I asked if I could speak with King. Wilkerson's reply was a quick no, though Lerman would be allowed to see King when he arrived. I asked if King would be permitted to exit from a side door, away from the media, when he was released. Again, the answer was no. Lieutenant Wilkerson told me King would be released ". . . just like every other asshole, no different. Front door only. We don't make special arrangements for celebrities." I thought it strange that the watch commander would want to create a media circus outside the jail when he could avoid it. I pleaded my case but the lieutenant held firm. King would exit through the front doors.

During my last conversation with Lerman, I'd arranged to meet him at another Denny's Restaurant in Santa Ana near the jail. While waiting for him, I called Mike Madigan, another associate, and filled him in on the situation. Until that time, Madigan's work in the King investigation was known only to myself and Lerman. Madigan wanted it that way. I asked him to help get King past the waiting media when he was released. I reminded him that his low profile would get a little taller if he lend me a hand. He reluctantly agreed and joined us at Denny's. Madigan would assist with King while I conducted the site investigation.

The three of us felt a sense of urgency; Angel Johnson, public information officer for the CHP in Santa Ana, was already issuing statements describing the officers' version of King's arrest. According to Angel Johnson, a citizen outside the restaurant complained to the officers that King was "driving erratically in the parking lot, screeching tires, and the officers then watched King back into a parking lot light standard while parking the car. The officers investigated the citizen's complaint and King was subsequently taken into custody for DUI." We heard the CHP's press statement as we stood outside the entrance of the jail awaiting King's release. Cameras were grouped slightly away from the main entrance, but in the direct path where King would have to walk as he exited. Our plan was for Lerman to provide a statement to the media while I stood by. Madigan would drive King away from the building. Later, I would meet with Madigan and King at my home, just ten minutes from the jail. From there, we would start the field investigation.

Steve and I waited for King on the second floor landing of

the stairway in the jail's main lobby. We could see the media gathered outside, blocking the door. Shortly before 7:00 A.M. King was released. As we started down the stairs, I whispered to him to keep walking, right through the assembled media, to Madigan's car in front of the building. As we hurried out, power cables leading from the cameras got tangled in King's legs and nearly tripped him.

Pat was waiting with coffee when Madigan and King arrived at my house. She took notes as King told his story to Madigan. I got home about twenty minutes later, after dealing with the press, and picked King up. We drove to the Denny's Restaurant where he was arrested. He pointed out where he was parked when the officers first confronted him. Immediately, I saw something wrong with the cops' story. The closest parking light standard was at the extreme end of the parking lot, nowhere near where King had been parked. And I found no skid marks anywhere on the parking lot. None. I questioned King intensely, keeping in mind Officer Johnson's comments. He reaffirmed his parking place and mentioned that a small red car, "Maybe a little Ford or Chevrolet," was right beside him. We drove the several hundred yards to his hotel where we were met by Crystal, who identified the same parking space as Glen had.

It was not yet 8:00 A.M., almost an hour since King's release from custody. I drove back to Denny's. Camera crews were already arriving. Reporters and cameramen were busily setting up their equipment in the parking lot. I decided to continue my field investigation in spite of the media presence, an important decision, it would later prove.

I was video taped by camera crews as I photographed the arrest scene. I gave a brief statement to some press guys about the discrepancy between the CHP's description of the arrest scene and the site itself—for example, the distant light standard with no evidence of being run into and the absence of skid marks described by officers Ligan and Mangan and reported by officer Johnson.

Shortly before noon, I called the Orange County D.A.'s office and spoke to Senior Assistant District Attorney Mark Kelly. I informed him of the several major inconsistencies I had identified between the CHP news release and what I had found—or not found—at the restaurant. Our conversation was cordial enough, but I realized this arrest wasn't going to just go away. Kelly was taking a hard line.

My son, Sean, returned home from an errand and overheard my final words to Kelly. Sean told me he had been at Denny's with a few friends during the arrest, and had watched a man being taken into custody, without recognizing that it was King because of the distance and angle of sight. I couldn't believe my good fortune. Witnesses . . . untainted by previous statements to the authorities.

Of course, I knew it would look suspicious as hell, that during an arrest of the highest profile plaintiff in the nation, my own son would be a witness. Without any further discussion, I told Sean to sit down at the dining table, and I turned on my tape recorder. I wanted to make sure that there would be no question later about my "prompting" the witness; I still remembered one investigator's accusations following King's previous police encounter in Hollywood.

Sean told me he watched the arrest from inside the restaurant, seventy to eighty feet from where the driver was taking his field sobriety tests. He didn't see anything about the man's actions that caused him to think King had been drinking. The driver's balance and coordination appeared good as he stood talking to the officers. From Sean's point of view, King appeared to be completely normal and cooperative. He was surprised when the officers cuffed the man. He thought the driver had successfully passed the various tests. Sean was almost apologetic about not recognizing King; they had spent many hours together while King was staying at the hotel.

Sean identified the six friends who were with him and where they had been seated. Once I completed taking Sean's statement, I began contacting his friends. It took three days. Almost without exception, their statements were similar to Sean's. All agreed that King didn't display any DUI symptoms. One of the witnesses had left the restaurant during the confrontation and walked within feet of the officers. He described their demeanor as arrogant and stern. He told me it appeared as though the officers were taking pleasure from their confrontation with King.

■

On July 17th, the day after King's arrest, I was in my office when the phone rang. The female caller refused to identify herself until she was sure I represented King. Once satisfied, she told me her name was Connie Brandon. She worked as a part-time hair stylist in an Orange County beauty salon, and sang in local night clubs. She identified herself as the woman in the red car parked next to King's Blazer. She told me she was with a friend at the time, but he had not yet given her permission to identify him to anyone. She said they witnessed the arrest of King.

We arrived in a red Pacer which was parked next to Mr. King's car in the parking lot. We were inside at a table talking when his car drove into the parking lot. I watched him drive over to where the woman got out of the car and came inside. As he drove past us, I commented to my friend that the driver looked like Rodney King. I didn't see anything wrong with his driving from the time I first saw him until he parked the car. I remember saying to my friend, it was unusual that there was another black family in this part of Orange County. There aren't many blacks in this neighborhood. That's why I remember him. Anyway, as I watched him park, I noticed there wasn't much room between his car and my car.

I saw the woman, I guess it was his wife, come into the restaurant and wait at the counter for her order. Then, as I sat and talked to my friend, King just sat in his car with his door ajar. The restaurant was busy and I guess his wife must've waited at the counter for twenty to thirty minutes. During this time, I could see the police car parked near the entrance to the parking lot. It looked like they were writing a ticket to the other driver, but they kept glancing over towards the car that King was in. It was like they knew who he was.

After awhile, the officers got back into their car and drove in the direction of where King was parked. At the same time, we were leaving the restaurant. As we walked outside, I guess that King saw his car was parked too close to our car so he started up his car, pulled forward a few feet with his wheels turned, then backed back into the stall, leaving more room between our two cars. I thought to myself, this was very courteous.

When we neared our car, the officers turned on their spotlight and shined it into King's face while he was sitting in his car. I could then see it was Rodney King. When we got to the car, the officers' car was blocking our car. We got in and sat there for a few minutes. King was just a few feet away from my friend as he began to talk to the officers. I heard him say to the officers, "What'd I do? I'm just sitting here."

His voice sounded fine. His speech was not slurred and he seemed alert and wide awake. His balance and coordination appeared normal. His eyes were neither bloodshot nor watery. The male officer told him to get out of his car and give the officer his license. We continued to sit and watch and listen. King reached into the back seat area and then handed the male officer his license.

At about this time, another police car arrived. This car contained two officers. They parked a little away from where the other patrol car was parked and walked up behind Mr. King. Both officers had their night sticks in their hands. I felt nervous and asked the female officer from the first car if we could leave now, telling her there wasn't much room between the patrol car and our car. She just glared at me and nodded.

My friend started our car and we drove around to the other side of the restaurant and parked again. I went into my motel room and my friend stayed outside. He told me he walked back to a position where he could watch the officers and not be seen by them. You'll have to get the rest of the story from him.

Two witnesses within five feet of King while he was talking to the officers, I thought, and they didn't see any symptoms of DUI either. They smelled no odor of alcohol from that distance and yet, the CHP was announcing that the backup officers stated they could smell alcohol from a distance of ten to fifteen feet.

Like the other witnesses who had watched King drive into the parking lot, Brandon didn't see anything wrong with King's driving. In fact, she specifically recalled the maneuver King made, as she was leaving, to adjust his car's distance from her car to allow more room between them. Courteous, she recalled, certainly not the actions of a drunk driver. Brandon promised she would call her friend and get his permission for an interview. The following day, she called and gave me her friend's name and phone number.

James Stapleton, a musician and music producer, answered the phone. Yes, he had been with Connie Brandon during the King arrest and, yes, he would talk to me. No, he had not yet provided a statement to the authorities, and unless they were to locate him, he would not. He didn't think the arrest of King was justified and he didn't want to talk to the police. Preferring to be called Sha-Sha, his professional name, he told me virtually the same story as I heard from Ms. Brandon, with a few elaborations.

> As I started the car, I noticed another police car, a white one, pull up near some bushes near the driveway, and the driver just sat there. He didn't get out of the car. Then, another CHP car came into the lot and just drove by where the other officers were talking to King. Like they were sightseeing. Connie asked the woman officer if we could leave. We didn't want to get in the way. She didn't say anything, she just gave us a look like we were stupid if we didn't leave. Real snarly, almost hateful. Then she nodded.
>
> I think the whole thing was bogus, man. He didn't do anything, except sit in his car and wait for the woman that was with him.

■

Through my sources, I got my hands on transcriptions of witness statements given to Sergeant Ted Jones, CHP internal affairs, and Tom Stewart, of the Orange County District Attorney's Office. Saundra King, a mental health nurse in her late twenties, examined King prior to his booking. In her statement, the diminutive African-American said, "His speech was not slurred, it was more like a person talks when they're fearful, nervous, anxious. I didn't smell any alcohol on his person or breath, and except for his limp, he walked normally. Not staggering. His gait was fine. . . . I've examined other prebooks, and I didn't notice any of the same symptoms of intoxication on King when he came in." She declined to respond to questions about King's physical and mental condition, citing medical privilege. She expressed surprise at the attempt by the investigators to get information to which they would not normally be entitled.

A second medical staffer at the jail (whose name is withheld at her request) stated essentially the same as Nurse King. She told Investigator Stewart and Sergeant Jones that, like her associate, she too failed to find any symptom of intoxication on King less than twenty minutes after his arrest. She said she specifically examined his eyes during his prebooking medical and found them to be normal: not bloodshot or watery, no nystagmous. His gait was normal, except for the limp he had since his beating. Like Nurse King, she formed the opinion that Rodney King was not intoxicated. She cleared him to book.

Anna McCarthy, a young waitress employed at Denny's, was also interviewed by Sergeant Jones and investigator Stewart. In her statement, McCarthy said she had watched the arrest of King from inside the restaurant. From her point of view, it appeared that King stumbled slightly while performing the field sobriety tests. From this, she formed the opinion the driver was "slightly intoxicated."

I interviewed the waitress after the authorities did. Initially, restaurant management would not permit her to speak to me, claiming they didn't want the restaurant involved. Finally, they relented. My first question to the witness proved to be my last. Slowly and deliberately, I asked Ms. McCarthy, "When you gave a statement to the police, you said that when you saw King try to walk, he stumbled. Did you see a limp as King walked, or did the officers ask you about a limp?"

Anna McCarthy stood in the lobby of the restaurant and fussed at her shirt while she thought about her answer. Then, placing her hands down to her sides, she replied, "Yes, that stumble could have been a limp." With that, the restaurant manager ordered me to leave; no more questions. Smiling, I turned and walked out the door.

There were several statements from jail personnel in the witness report, including that of the watch commander, Lieutenant Wilkerson, that specifically addressed the subject of King's limp. The absence of a limp during King's contact with the officers could be used in his civil trial to show that his alleged injuries were only that, alleged. If King were found to be lying about his limp, then the rest of his testimony could be discounted.

Steve Lerman retained highly respected Orange County defense lawyer Rob Harley to represent King in his criminal trial and the Department of Motor Vehicles hearing regarding his license suspension. Steve felt that an excellent local attorney would be more familiar to both the D.A. and the judges who hear criminal cases. Because of the other issues involved, King needed the best specialist available.

Steve and I met with Harley in a Marina Del Rey restaurant. As I related the findings of my investigation, Harley just sat and shook his head in disbelief. I began by summarizing the statements I took from King and his wife, my son, Sean, then Greg Netherwood, Dave McCracken, Tony Naarang, Sha-Sha Stapleton, Connie Brandon, Jason Kimes, Mary Wood, Andrew Parker, Jamie Creole and the other witnesses who were in the restaurant at the time of the incident.

"I've never had this large a witness list from people who were actually at the scene of a DUI, Harley said. "Especially when the police had not interviewed any of them."

Next, I handed over a diagram of the location, drawn by CHP officer, A. Yamaguchi of the Santa Ana office, along with photographs of the arrest scene I had taken twelve hours after the incident, in the presence of six reporters with their camera crews, as could be documented by their video footage. Once more, the authorities were caught with their hands in the cookie jar.

Finally, I showed the lawyers copies of dispatch cards from the Santa Ana CHP, related to King's arrrest. The cards clearly show that Ligan had run King's license plate and knew his identity fully fifteen minutes before his report indicated he knew it. In fact, backup officers Craig and Gutierrez were nearly at the location before officers Mangan and Ligan made their initial approach to King. The time sequences established that Ligan and Mangan knew exactly who was sitting in the gray Chevy Blazer, long before their initial approach.

Equally important, the dispatch cards identified the supervisor in charge at the time of the King arrest, the officer who referred me to the jail, as Sergeant Roman Vondriska, the officer suspended for thirty days and administratively transferred after the King beating for failing to properly supervise Tim and Melanie Singer. Vondriska, assigned to the Westminster office of the CHP, had no business being involved in the King arrest in Orange.

■

Three weeks after King's arrest at Denny's, the Orange County district attorney's office issued a press release announcing King would not be prosecuted for DUI. The D.A. asserted that while

11-85	AAA	NAC	BRIDGE	HIGHWAYS	11-41 FIRE			10-29	11-28	11-27	10-

*GIVE REASON BELOW | STATE CO. CITY

REQUESTED 10-7/10-97 (10-8 WITH 10-15) | RECEIVED – SERVICE DESK (10-7 WITH 10-15) | RETURNED – SERVICE DESK | 10-8/10-98/RETURNED

16 JUL 92 01 42 σ

| MECH | GAS | ACCIDENT | ARREST | 11-24 | O.R. | RECOVERY | OTHER |

REMARKS/MISC/VEHICLE DESCRIPTION
2BEX 371

NO WANT	NO RECORD	NO WANT NCIC
10-12	NOT ON FILE	WANTED (ATTACH PRINT OUT)
SYS ACTION		

DEPARTMENT OF CALIFORNIA HIGHWAY PATROL
FIELD SERVICE REQUEST
CHP 141 (Rev. 9-90) OPI 047 | RECEIVED BY 99597 | COMPLETED BY 99597 | LOG NUMBER/MAP INFORMATION | OVER

FREEWAY BOX NUMBER/LOCATION
SE College E/O 5 – Denny's Plot | AREA/BEAT/UNIT 80-51

11-85	AAA	NAC	BRIDGE	HIGHWAYS	11-41 FIRE	OTHER CODE 2 w/572	10-29	11-28	11-27	10-7
						CODE 3				

*GIVE REASON BELOW | STATE CO. CITY

REQUESTED/10-7/10-97 (10-8 WITH 10-15) | RECEIVED – SERVICE DESK (10-7 WITH 10-15) | RETURNED – SERVICE DESK | 10-8/10-98/RETURNED

16 JUL 92 01 47 σ

| MECH | GAS | ACCIDENT | ARREST | 11-24 | O.R. | RECOVERY | OTHER |

REMARKS/MISC/VEHICLE DESCRIPTION
1PWD 682
REQ 11-98 w/572

NO WANT	NO RECORD	NO WANT NCIC
10-12	NOT ON FILE	WANTED (ATTACH PRINT OUT)
SYS ACTION		

DEPARTMENT OF CALIFORNIA HIGHWAY PATROL
FIELD SERVICE REQUEST
CHP 141 (Rev. 9-90) OPI 047 | RECEIVED BY 99597 | COMPLETED BY 99597 | LOG NUMBER/MAP INFORMATION | OVER

I hereby certify that the record to which this is
affixed is a true photographic copy of the original
on file in the Department of California Highway Patrol.

7-17-92 By _____
Date   Officer or Employee
                   CSI
                   Title

FREEWAY BOX NUMBER/LOCATION: St. College E/O 5, Denny's plot   AREA/BEAT/UNIT: 86-572

| 11-85 | AAA | NAC | BRIDGE | HIGHWAYS | 11-41 | FIRE | CODE 2 OTHER w/571 | 10-29 | 11-28 | 11-27 | 10-7 |

*GIVE REASON BELOW   STATE CO CITY   CODE 3

REQUESTED   L.C./55 (97)   RECEIVED – SERVICE DESK   RETURNED – SERVICE DESK   APPROX 2:50

16 Jul 92 01:47 a   16 Jul 92 01:55 a

| MECH | GAS | ACCIDENT | ARREST | 11-83 | D.R. | RECOVERY | OTHER |

					NO WANT	NO RECORD	NO WANT NCIC
					10-12	NOT ON FILE	WANTED ATTACH PRINT OUT
					SVS ACTION		

DEPARTMENT OF CALIFORNIA HIGHWAY PATROL
FIELD SERVICE REQUEST
CHP 141 (Rev. 9-90) OPI 047

RECEIVED BY: R0597   COMPLETED BY: R0597   LOG NUMBER/MAP INFORMATION   (OVER)

SUBJECT	CHK APB ATO	PD	SO	MARSHAL OTHER	DOJS NCIC	PIN	DDL	SPECIFY AGENCY		NOT ON FILE	NO WANT	NO RECORD	WANTED (ATTACH PRINT OUT)

NAME/SUSPECT

DOB/AGE	RACE/SEX	HEIGHT	WEIGHT	HAIR	EYES	MISCELLANEOUS
						16 Jun 92 03:09 a

WARRANT INFORMATION-AGENCY/COURT   ADDITIONAL INFORMATION

AMOUNT	JUDGE

VIOLATION	ABSTRACT ☐ YES ☐ NO
WARRANT NUMBER	PICK UP ☐ YES ☐ NO
WARRANT DATE	BAIL ONLY ☐ YES ☐ NO

CA 743 B

St. Collene E/O S. Denny's P lot   86-54

11-85	AAA	NAC	BRIDGE	HIGHWAYS		11-41	FIRE	CODE 2		10-29	11-28	(11-27)	10-7
*GIVE REASON BELOW			STATE	CO.	CITY			CODE 3					

REQUESTED 10-7/10-87
(10-8 WITH 10-15)

RECEIVED-SERVICE DESK
(10-7 WITH 10-15)

RETURNED – SERVICE DESK

10-8/10-88/RETURNED

16 JUL 92   01 49 α

☐ MECH	☐ GAS	☐ ACCIDENT	☐ ARREST	☐ 11-24	☐ O.R.	☐ RECOVERY	☐ OTHER

REMARKS/MISC/VEHICLE DESCRIPTION

RODNEY G. KING 04-22-65

	NO WANT	NO RECORD	NO WANT NCIC
	10-12	NOT ON FILE	WANTED (ATTACH PRINT OUT)
	SVS ACTION		

DEPARTMENT OF CALIFORNIA HIGHWAY PATROL
FIELD SERVICE REQUEST
CHP 141 (Rev. 9-90) OPI 047

RECEIVED BY   93597

COMPLETED BY   93597

LOG NUMBER/MAP INFORMATION   OVER

FREEWAY SIGN MARKER/LOCATION
St. Collene E/O S. Denny's P lot   86-54   AREA/BEAT/UNIT

11-85	AAA	NAC	BRIDGE	HIGHWAYS		11-41	FIRE	OTHER for 57/S10 CODE 2	10-29	11-28	11-27	10-7
*GIVE REASON BELOW			STATE	CO.	CITY			CODE 3				

REQUESTED 10-7/10-87
(10-8 WITH 10-15)

RECEIVED-SERVICE DESK
(10-7 WITH 10-15)

RETURNED – SERVICE DESK

10-8/10-88/RETURNED

16 JUL 92   01 52 p

☐ MECH	☐ GAS	☐ ACCIDENT	☐ ARREST	☐ 11-24	☐ O.R.	☐ RECOVERY	☐ OTHER

REMARKS/MISC/VEHICLE DESCRIPTION

backwards in p-lot
Stopped hard /
braking hard

	NO WANT	NO RECORD	NO WANT NCIC
	10-12	NOT ON FILE	WANTED (ATTACH PRINT OUT)
	SVS ACTION		

DEPARTMENT OF CALIFORNIA HIGHWAY PATROL
FIELD SERVICE REQUEST
CHP 141 (Rev. 9-90) OPI 047

RECEIVED BY   93597

COMPLETED BY   93597

LOG NUMBER/MAP INFORMATION   OVER

11-25	11-26	11-79	11-81	11-82	11-83	23152	APB (OVLR)	OTHER REASON (FOR APB)

RECEIVED	DISPATCHED	10-97	10-98
03			

11-41/11-85, F.D. SENT ON INITIAL REQUEST	INFORMANT Tom Owen	TELEPHONE/FREEWAY-BOX NUMBER

ADDRESS/ADDITIONAL INFORMATION

Assistant for Steve Lehrman at Santa Ana CHP office to speak with Watch Commander regarding Rodney G King. Spoke with

DEPARTMENT OF CALIFORNIA HIGHWAY PATROL	DISPATCHED BY	RECEIVED BY A9040	LOG NUMBER/MAP INFORMATION	3-1-1	OVER

COMPLAINT-DISPATCH-APB
CHP 140 (Rev. 9-90) CPI 047   CA-1173

VEHICLE INFO.	COLOR(S)		YEAR	MAKE		BODY	LICENSE

RACE/SUSPECT

RACE/SEX	DOB/AGE	HEIGHT	WEIGHT	ADDITIONAL INFORMATION
BUILD	SIZE AND STYLE			Westminster Sgt Vondriska
EYES	GLASSES	FACIAL HAIR		Angel Johnson notified at
HAT	COAT			SNA CHP
SHIRT	TROUSERS			
SWEATER	SHOES			
	WEAPON			

ALL POINTS BULLETIN/REMARKS

OFFICE OF THE

DISTRICT ATTORNEY
ORANGE COUNTY, CALIFORNIA
MICHAEL R. CAPIZZI, DISTRICT ATTORNEY

MAURICE L. EVANS
CHIEF ASSISTANT

JOHN D. CONLEY
DIRECTOR
MUNICIPAL COURT

JAN J. NOLAN
DIRECTOR
SUPERIOR COURT

BRENT F. ROMNEY
DIRECTOR
MUNICIPAL COURT

WALLACE J. WADE
DIRECTOR
SPECIAL OPERATIONS

LOREN W. DuCHESNE
CHIEF
BUREAU OF INVESTIGATION

PLEASE REPLY TO

☐ CENTRAL OFFICE
700 CIVIC CENTER DR. W.
P.O. BOX 808
SANTA ANA, CA 92701
(714) 834-3600

☐ WEST OFFICE
8141 13TH STREET
WESTMINSTER, CA 92683
(714) 896-7261

☐ SOUTH OFFICE
30143 CROWN VALLEY PKWY.
LAGUNA NIGUEL, CA 92677
(714) 249-5236

☐ HARBOR OFFICE
4601 JAMBOREE BLVD
NEWPORT BEACH, CA 92660
(714) 476-4650

☐ JUVENILE OFFICE
341 CITY DRIVE SOUTH
ORANGE, CA 92668
(714) 935-7624

☐ MAJOR FRAUD
CONSUMER PROTECTION
405 W. 5TH STREET
SUITE 606
SANTA ANA, CA 92701
(714) 568-1240

MEDIA RELEASE

Contact Person: Marc Kelly   August 12, 1992
Deputy District Attorney
Special Assignments Section
(714) ██████

The Orange County District Attorney's Office announced today that criminal charges against Rodney Glen King, 27, would not be filed in connection with his July 16, 1992 arrest for Driving Under the Influence.

The Orange County District Attorney Bureau of Investigation, in cooperation with the California Highway Patrol, conducted a thorough investigation of the facts surrounding the incident involving Mr. King's arrest and subsequent refusal to take a blood alcohol test. Twenty-four witnesses were interviewed, including some provided by Mr. King's attorney, Robison Harley.

As part of its analysis, the Office of the District Attorney first determined whether there was reasonable cause for officers of the California Highway Patrol to detain and eventually to arrest Mr. King after their attention was drawn to his unusual driving. We have concluded that the officers did have probable cause to believe that Mr. King was driving under the influence. However, the standard of probable cause to arrest is

MORE. . .

substantially less than the prosecution's burden of proving a criminal case to a jury beyond a reasonable doubt. After review and consideration of all the available facts, the District Attorney's Office has determined that it is unlikely that a jury would convict Mr. King of criminal charges in this incident.

The fact that the Office of the District Attorney has declined to file criminal charges against Mr. King does not affect the consequences facing him for his refusal to take a blood alcohol chemical test. Pursuant to California law, Mr. King faces a revocation of his driving privileges for one year.

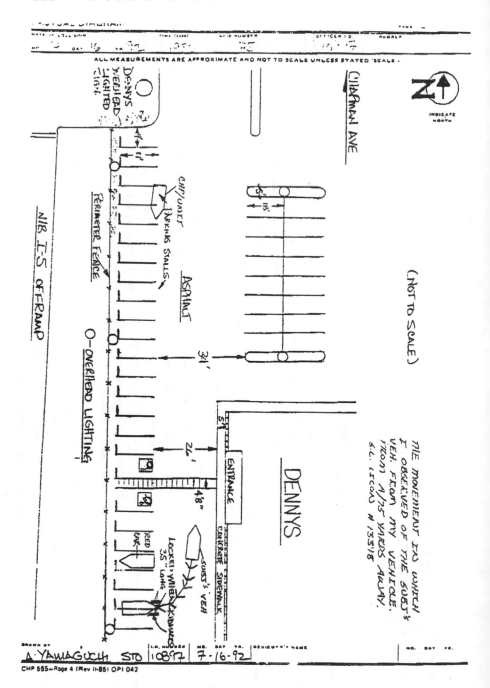

there was more than enough evidence to sustain the arrest of King, "It would be unlikely that the people's burden of proof necessary for a conviction of the charges stemming from his arrest could be met. Therefore, in the interest of justice, King will not stand trial for DUI."

I knew the D.A. was trying to soft-peddle his rejection of the CHP charges. What he failed to report in his press release was the whole truth about what his own investigators had found in their extensive investigation into the circumstances of King's arrest. The D.A.s did not want to take King to trial and subject the arresting officers to cross-examination from King's criminal defense counsel. That left only the DMV hearing about King's automatic license suspension.

Steve Lerman requested that the hearings be closed. The request pleased the DMV, who wanted as little publicity as possible. A DMV official at a preliminary meeting in Santa Ana said to me that they feared we would invite masses of media to the hearings. I assured the official that our only interest was in getting Rodney King the fair and impartial hearing he wanted, which meant no media pressure.

In his May 1, 1992, plea for peace during the riots, King spoke of getting his day in court. On October 19, The DMV hearing provided him his first opportunity. Attorney Harley planned to present evidence I collected, countering allegations made by the arresting officers. That placed the matter of King's driver's license squarely in the hands of the DMV.

Senior DMV hearing officer Kathleen Anderson, an intelligent and attractive woman in her mid-thirties, conducted as fair a hearing as anyone could have hoped for. Working in the Costa Mesa office of the California Department of Motor Vehicles, Anderson heard the testimony of the arresting officers and witnesses for the defense over three days, October 19 and November 2 and 17. The date of the first session was a well-kept secret, resulting in no media presence.

Before the second session, King abruptly changed attorneys from Steve Lerman to Milton Grimes, the African-American attorney from Orange County, who Kandyce Barnes had brought to King's mid-Wilshire apartment. I believe as a result of the change, information related to the DMV hearings was leaked, resulting in the presence of news media at the second and third sessions, which Grimes wanted to establish himself as the new attorney for Rodney King.

On the last day of the hearings, Attorney Rob Harley instructed me to provide information to the media on the results of my field site investigation into the DUI allegations. We hoped the public would finally get an idea about what was really going on in the numerous encounters between King and the law enforcement community. My facts were lead stories on the evening news that night.

Less than a week later, DMV officer, Kathleen Anderson, notified us we'd won. Rodney Glen King could keep his driver's license. The whole thing made me prouder than hell; in four trips to the plate for King, I'd hit four home runs. I was batting a thousand.

With the DMV hearings now successfully behind us, and with the change of lawyers, I felt my formal association with King was at an end. I was happy that I'd been a major player in the case of the century, and that I could now reintroduce myself to my family and what few friends I still had left, and get on with my life.

Over the previous twenty months, I'd lost many friends in law enforcement because of my association with the King case. Other friends I lost simply because I had not contacted them over the months. I was just too busy. Too busy . . .

RODNEY GLEN KING
(HEREINAFTER, "RESPONDENT")

DL#C2184790

860 ALCOHOL REFUSAL FINDINGS OF FACT

I

On July 16, 1992, Officer Licon of the California Highway Patrol did not observe respondent's vehicle driving in an erratic manner.

II

The officer did not have reasonable cause to believe that the respondent was driving a motor vehicle in violation of section 23152 or 23153 of the California vehicle code.

III

Respondent was not lawfully arrested for driving under the influence of an alcoholic beverage, a violation of section 23152 or 23153 of the California vehicle code.

IV

The officer did advise the respondent of the chemical test requirement by reading the admonition verbatim from the back of the DS367 form.

V

Respondent did refuse to submit to a chemical test, when requested to do so by the police officer by stating "no" to the offering of the three chemical tests.

DETERMINATION OF ISSUES

Cause does not exist to suspend the respondents driving privilege pursuant to sections 13353, 13358 and 23157 of the vehicle code as set forth in the findings of fact, in that;

1. The officer did not have reasonable cause to believe that the respondent was driving a motor vehicle in violation of section 23152 or 23153 of the California vehicle code.

2. The respondent was not lawfully arrested.

3. The respondent was told that his privilege to operate a motor vehicle would be suspended or revoked, if he refused to submit to and did not complete a chemical test.

4. The respondent did refuse to submit to a chemical test of his blood, breath or urine after being requested to do so by the peace officer.

K. Anderson

11-10-92, K. Anderson, P.D.I.A.
KA:yb

A ONE-WAY STREET

I was nothing more than a spectator during the four officers' federal civil rights trial in downtown Los Angeles. Pat and I argued every morning when I headed for the federal courthouse. She didn't think I had any business there and was just feeding my ego. My reasoning was that Steve Lerman and I still represented the estate of Freddie Helms, a plaintiff in the civil case against the City of Los Angeles. Testimony from the criminal trial could be significant in any subsequent settlement or civil trial.

"You're not a part of the case anymore," Pat maintained. "You don't work for King. He's crapped on you already, I can't understand why you still feel loyalty to him."

"It's not loyalty to King, it's loyalty to the case. Regardless of how I feel about Glen, I owe it to myself and to Freddie G. to stay in touch with what's going on."

"Look, Tom, Lerman still hasn't paid you for the work you've already done, and Grimes told you to sue him when you asked for your pay for the DUI thing. Neither of those guys gives a damn about you or how you feel about the case. Why can't you get that through your thick skull?" Pat had chosen this time to dig in her heels.

"I believe Freddie's mom deserves some level of representation at that trial," I said almost pleadingly, "Even if it's only me."

"Who's going to pay for your time?" Pat asked.

"I'm not worried about that," I replied. "It's never been primarily about money for me anyway."

"Let it go," she insisted.

"I'll let it go when it's over. Not before." Frankly, I wasn't concerned with what Steve Lerman or Milt Grimes thought about my presence at the trial. By the time jury selection was under way in February, my affection for Steve Lerman wasn't what it once was.

While my investigative efforts for King continued well into November, 1992, Lerman hadn't paid me for any services or expenses since July, a week before King's arrest in Orange County. My bill following the DMV hearings had swelled to over $22,000. I'd been working out of pocket for six months. My savings and operating capital were gone. I had laid off four investigators and was about to pink-slip two others when the DUI arrest happened.

With the replacement of Lerman by Grimes in October 1992, my payments for King's cases became cause for immediate concern. My agreement with Lerman was that I would not carry more than $15,000 against the file at any time. However, as the investigation progressed, costs mounted and I found myself fronting more than I could afford to keep King protected—from himself as well as others. I can fairly say that caring for Rodney King, and keeping him secure, was an expensive proposition. Over 160 man-hours were logged in DUI defense and related investigative efforts, including thirty hours at the DMV hearings. My efforts, which resulted in having DUI charges against King dropped and his driving privileges restored—almost unheard of in Orange County—never got me even a thank you from Glen or a dollar from Lerman or Grimes.

Days after Grimes became King's attorney, I tried calling him. I felt I needed to brief him on the status of the investigation and to offer comments on previous defense strategy. Additionally, I'd hoped Grimes would discuss my bills for work related to the Department of Motor Vehicles driving under the influence charges. I called Grimes's Orange County office nine times in three days. Each time, I left a message informing Grimes of who I was—on the off-chance he didn't know. Not one of my calls was returned.

One day before the second DMV hearing, I finally got through to a Mr. Bryant Callaway, an associate counsel in Grimes's office. I explained that I'd been trying for days to talk to Grimes but he hadn't taken my calls. Callaway defended Grimes's failure to acknowledge my calls by stating, "You can imagine how busy Mr. Grimes has been since subbing in. He just doesn't have time to talk to everyone who calls about Rodney King." I immediately understood what Callaway was saying: in the middle of an important issue closely tied to the civil rights case, I'd become one of "everyone who calls about Rodney King."

"Okay," I said, "What am I supposed to do about the witnesses for tomorrow's hearing? Do I have them there, or is Mr. Grimes going to take care of that himself?"

"Since you know more about what's going on than we do, go ahead and do what Lerman had planned. No changes yet. Milton will talk to you tomorrow, after the hearings." Calloway had me on the speaker phone and I had the feeling Grimes was listening in.

"Alright, I'll have the witnesses there but I do want to talk to Grimes about several things, including my bills." I wanted to get my concern about my outstanding fees on the record with Grimes as quickly as possible. Callaway hung up before I'd finished talking. I felt like I'd just been fucked without getting kissed. The events of the next several days confirmed my feelings.

■

Rob Harley and I were scheduled to meet with Grimes and King an hour before the DMV hearing on November 2, so Grimes could be filled in on the defense plans and King could be briefed on what to expect. Harley said Grimes had assured him—twice—that they would be at the meeting in time to prepare. Instead, Grimes and King showed up with a friend of King's less than ten minutes before the start of the hearings. No time for any briefings, much less discussions. Grimes only wanted to know whether media would be present. I'd driven by the DMV an hour earlier. Camera crews were already setting up. I told Grimes, "What the hell do you think?" I had stopped and spoken with a representative sent down from Sacramento to adminster security at the hearings. Together, we'd devised a plan for getting King in and out of the hearings through a back door without the media knowing he was there.

Grimes cut me off, saying, "My client, Rodney King, doesn't use back doors for anybody!"

Five minutes later, Grimes and King arrived at the Department of Motor Vehicles in Grimes's Mercedes convertible—with the top down. He drove right past the assembled media crews and chose to park at the far end of the parking lot, which gave him an extended opportunity to show off his new client on the way to the hearing offices.

Lerman later described Grimes's actions with King that day: "It was like he was the great hunter who'd shot a big deer and had it laid across the hood of his old truck as he came home from the hunt."

Every time I tried to speak with Grimes that day, he put me off, telling me we'd talk later. Finally, at the end of the day, I took the dapper attorney by the arm and pulled him off to the side. "I want to find out from you what you plan to do about my bill for services here at the DMV," I said flatly, holding onto his arm so he couldn't get away.

"I don't know," he said.

"I've got considerable time and expense tied up in this thing. I just want to know that I'll get paid for my efforts when it's all over."

"Go ahead and finish the job," Grimes said, "We'll settle up after this is finished." Reporters were calling to him, wanting an interview.

"What does settle up mean?" I asked.

"We'll talk about this after the hearings are over. You'll get whatever you've got coming," Grimes said.

"What about my status in the case? You know, I'm on an independent retainer agreement signed by King last year."

Grimes looked surprised. "I've got to go. We'll discuss this later," he said over his shoulder as he walked away.

A week later, we were back for the final hearing session. Once again, I made sure the witnesses were present: Sha-Sha

Stapleton, Connie Brandon, the jail nurse, Mike Madigan, and myself. I was the first witness called to testify. Rob Harley asked questions to establish my expertise in DUI arrests, allowing me to render opinions as I testified. My testimony took nearly an hour and a half.

My moment, the moment I'd dreaded for almost two years, came when Harley asked, "As a result of your investigation, did you form an opinion as to the probable cause of the arresting officers?"

"Yes, I did." My guts were churning inside. I was about to go on the record against my former brothers and sisters in blue for the first time. I felt sweat in the palms of my hands, which shook nervously. "As a result of my investigation, I determined the arresting officers' probable cause was post-incident."

"Can you explain 'post-incident'?" asked the hearing officer.

"Post-incident means the officers fabricated their probable cause after they had King in custody and needed an excuse for the arrest. I formed this opinion after conducting an extensive field investigation, taking statements from fourteen witnesses, and after reviewing the arrest and follow-up reports of the arresting officers and investigators from both the Orange County D.A.'s office and CHP Internal Affairs Division."

I think it's fair to say I'm not a fan of Milton Grimes. I don't know him well enough to like or dislike him as a man. I've spent less than four hours in his presence, but I've heard him speak to the media and I've watched and listened to reports of his personal appearances throughout California since signing King as a client. While Grimes may well be a competent criminal defense lawyer, he has little experience in civil rights cases involving police misconduct or abuse.

After taking over the King case, refusing to take my phone calls, and ignoring my efforts to establish a working rapport with his office for three weeks, Grimes asked me to turn over my files to his investigator. When I raised the issue of my fees, he accused me of holding the files for ransom. It was all I could do to hold my anger. Finally, Grimes agreed to pay me if I worked with his investigator, Dave Sandberg, a big white guy in his late thirties. I spent hours with Sandberg, providing file materials and background information necessary to understand the volumes of materials I'd collected over the previous two years.

Grimes continued to ignore my calls and invoices. Finally, in January 1993, I went to Grimes's office to make one final appeal to get paid. "All I want is what I've earned. Nothing more. You told me during the DMV hearings to continue my efforts and you'd pay me when it was over. Then, you said you'd compensate me for the time needed in explaining my materials to your investigator. Now, you tell me neither you nor Glen owe me money. Just how do you figure that?"

I made a big mistake. I'd allowed Grimes to see my anger and frustration.

"I've spoken to Mr. King about your services and he doesn't recall authorizing you to do any work on his behalf. Therefore, he doesn't feel he owes you anything," Grimes said, sitting back in his overstuffed chair.

"Do you think Glen just woke up one morning, free of all charges, with his driver's license in his hip pocket? I can't believe you're that misinformed or ignorant. If you maintain this position, I'll have no choice but to seek legal remedies. Is that what you want, to see your client's name in the headlines again, this time painted as a deadbeat because you're too cheap to pay for services you authorized?" I was furious. I wanted to reach across his big desk, grab him by his throat, and shake some sense into him. I wanted desperately to see if I could make Grimes a ten on the funky chicken scale.

"The bottom line is, if you don't file your case today, you're wasting time," Grimes said. "I'm not going to pay for anything. Now, if you'll excuse me, I've got an appointment."

"Are you speaking for yourself or are you speaking for Glen too?" I asked, starting to shake from my own anger.

"I speak for Mr. King and for myself," he answered smugly.

"So you're telling me to sue, is that what you're saying."

"You do whatever you feel is right."

I left Grimes's office boiling mad. I'd devoted two years of my life, working day and night to help Rodney King. I couldn't believe he'd condone Grimes's treatment of me. I wanted to believe Grimes was bluffing, challenging me to see if I would take the fee issue any further.

I don't think Grimes knows what King told me in our last meeting during the Department of Motor Vehicles hearings. I'd reminded Glen about my separate retainer and asked him to relieve me from the case. I even tried to resign; I'd already decided I didn't want anything to do with Attorney Grimes. I didn't like the way he'd signed King as a client, and I told Glen that.

"I don't want you to resign. I want to know you're there if I ever need your help," King said. "I want you to still be on the team, just chill out for awhile." He spoke with his head bent forward. He wouldn't look me in the eyes. I feel he knew he was going in the wrong direction, but didn't know how to change course. I was pissed at Kandyce.

■

Grimes was responsible for some serious snafus. He started playing show-and-tell with his famous client, arranging an appearance for King to address students at Santa Monica City College. But before King could open his mouth, Grimes announced that only African-Americans would be allowed to remain in the room; all others were ordered to leave.

Students, faculty, and parents were outraged at this stupid, racist act. The dean of the college published a letter, apologizing to the entire student body for Grimes's thoughtlessness. The media climbed all over the story and it proved to be the last time, to my knowledge, that King spoke to any student group. It can be fairly said that Rodney King's image since hooking up with Milt Grimes is different from what it was before.

■

It became painfully obvious to me that neither Lerman nor Grimes intended to compensate me for work completed. I'd abandoned my business, neglecting other clients to devote myself to the Rodney King case. I'd used all my personal funds and assets in continuing to work on the case for Lerman. Now I was broke. I wasn't surprised when Grimes ignored me and wouldn't take my calls, but when Lerman also became unavailable, it hurt, dammit.

Steve Lerman was devastated by King's defection. "I thought he respected me more than this," Steve said. "Apparently, he's forgotten how close we'd become, or maybe, we were never as close as I thought."

"I can't believe Glen came up with this idea on his own," I tried to reassure him.

"You know," Lerman said, sounding like he wanted to believe what he was about to say, "we'll hear from him again. First time he's in trouble, he'll call, wanting us to help."

"So, if he does, tell him it's all or nothing," I replied, knowing where Lerman was going with his thought. "I for one wouldn't help him cross the street, now that I know how he shows his friendship."

I said it then and I still feel the same way. After nearly two years of constant work, little time off with my family, and the loss of many old friends in law enforcement because of my work on the case, I felt King's switching attorneys was a kick in the face. Like Lerman, I too felt betrayed. I admit a client is entitled to change attorneys when he chooses. After all, the attorney works for the client. But this was not your usual case and ours was not a usual professional relationship. I had put my life and business on hold for this case. For months, it was Tom and Glen and Steve . . . Tom and Glen and Steve. . . .

Glen stopped calling me. In the months since January 1993, I've spoken with Lerman fewer times than I used to speak with him in a week.

■

Between 1976 and 1980, I worked part-time teaching high school and community college students a course entitled Introduction to Criminal Justice, designed to give young adults interested in a career in law enforcement a head start in finding a job with a police department. While researching materials for the class, I came across a document which I used as an example of how the criminal justice system has changed over the past hundred or so years. The following is a sentence pronounced on a man convicted of murder by an Arkansas Federal Judge in the late 1800's. For what it's worth, Judge Davies, who conducted the Federal trial against the previously acquitted officers, strikes me as being similar in disposition. The old Arkansas judge said:

> In a few short weeks it will be spring. The snows of winter will flee away, the ice will vanish, and the air will become soft

and balmy. In short, the annual miracle of the year's awakening will come to pass—but you won't be here. The rivulet will run its purring course to the sea, the timid desert flowers will put forth their shoots, the glorious valleys of this imperial domain will blossom as the rose—still, you won't be here to see.

From every treetop some wild woods songster will carol his mating song, butterflies will sport in the sunshine, the busy bee will hum happily as it pursues its accustomed vocation, the gentle breeze will tease the tassels of the grasses, and all of nature will be glad but you. You won't be here to enjoy it, because I command the sheriff or some other officer or officers of this county to lead you out to some remote spot, swing you by the neck from a nodding bough of some sturdy oak, and let you hang until you are dead.

And then, I command that such officer or officers retire quickly from your dangling corpse, so that the vultures may descend from the heavens upon your filthy body, until nothing shall remain but the bare, bleached bones of a cold-blooded, blood-thirsty, throat-cutting, bile-eating, sheepherding, murdering son-of-a-bitch.

■

The Edward R. Roybal Federal Building, a newly completed brick and glass structure across Temple Street from Parker Center Police Headquarters was the site of the widely publicized Federal criminal trial of the four officers accused of violating Rodney King's civil rights by intentionally using excessive force during his arrest on March 3, 1991. As was the case in Simi Valley, the second trial was covered extensively by world media, only this time, no cameras were allowed in the courtroom.

In the late summer of 1992, nearly four months after the Simi Valley verdicts, federal indictments were returned against Officers Powell, Wind, and Briseno, alleging excessive force, and against Sergeant Koon for aiding and abetting excessive force under color of authority. Under U.S. Code Title 18, sections 241 and 242, the officers would be tried for violating the civil rights of Rodney King without a consideration of double jeopardy. The new allegations were different from those for which the officers had been tried the previous year in Simi Valley.

The preindictment and pretrial investigations completed by

the U.S. Department of Justice and the FBI were much more secretive than those preceding the Simi Valley trial, in which Steve Lerman and I gave considerable input to the prosecution. In the second trial, Steve and I were rarely contacted.

Throughout the first year and a half of my investigation, I maintained very close contact with FBI special agent Dave Harris. We had many conversations, face-to-face and on the telephone, as my investigation progressed. Each significant discovery by my team was handed over to the Feds with a phonecall. Each time I called the Feds with information, they passed it on to the prosecutors. In this way, my team contributed to the discovery efforts against the defendant officers in both trials.

California rules of discovery (disclosure of evidence) mandate that any information developed by prosecutors must be turned over to the defense or that evidence may not be admitted during trial. Under the provisions of Prop 115, reciprocal discovery was mandatory. Because the Feds notified State prosecutors of my information, I assume my information was released to the defense. Ironic, I thought; my own investigative materials could later be used against us in our civil case. Despite this potential, Lerman and I agreed my information was of such importance to successful prosecutions of the officers, that we were willing to run the risk of letting the defense know how strong our case was in advance of our own trial against the city of Los Angeles, which has a less imposing discovery requirement. Unlike the criminal cases, we could have surprises at trial.

I had accumulated in excess of sixty-five thousand pages of information and evidence: statement transcriptions, court records, Simi Valley trial transcripts, police reports, media logs and schedules, background information on the LAPD and the involved officers. Everything was made available to federal investigators and prosecutors. Little was actually requested, and once the Feds went forward at full speed, my contacts with Dave Harris ceased.

When former President Bush ordered the attorney general to resume the investigation, the local U.S. attorney's office became a clearing house of information for the heavy hitters who were then brought in from the justice department's civil rights division in Washington, D.C. The internal structure of the federal effort was divided into two teams. The "dirty team" was responsible for amassing data and information, evaluating and "cleansing" it—editing out that which couldn't be used by the "clean team" in prosecuting the defendants. The compelled statements of other Foothill Division officers, volumes of testimony from Simi Valley, and the IAD investigation, are the most notable examples of known information which would not get into the hands of the clean team and therefore, would not be heard by the jury in the federal case. Under this concept, the likelihood of an appeal in the event of convictions was diminished.

Because not one page of my materials had been obtained through court-initiated or supervised discovery, little of it was useful in a trial, though with it, Lerman and the Feds not only knew what was available as evidence, but who had it and what its significance was as it related to other evidence.

We knew far more about who the witnesses were and what they would say on the witness stand than did the prosecutors in both trials. We'd identified and interviewed witnesses who were unknown to anyone else. Because we represented the victim, Rodney King, many people contacted us instead of the authorities.

Immediately after the riots, Agent Harris and I talked at some length about the status of my investigation. On orders from Lerman, I offered my complete file to the Feds, who showed little interest. They only wanted to know about officers' attitudes and LAPD internal enforcement of policies and procedures. Each time I met with FBI agents or Federal prosecutors, most of their questions were aimed at identifying supervisory and management responsibilities. At that time, they were focused on Koon's actions and his failure to supervise his subordinate officers at the scene.

The FBI attempted to interview dozens of officers assigned to Foothill Station. In every case, those summoned by the FBI said they were forced by the LAPD to submit to the interview, making their statements compelled and therefore inadmissible in a criminal trial. Thus, the FBI decided against taking the compelled statements, knowing that eventually they would be valueless. My investigation disclosed the Police Protective League, under the guidance of Cliff Ruff, had issued memos to the officers instructing them how to disqualify themselves from the interviews according to police policy and law.

Federal prosecution efforts went forward and Judge Davies announced the trial would begin with jury selection in February, 1993. With the passage of time, key prosecution errors were publicized, including the accidental leaking, in November, 1992, of the prosecution's plan, which laid out their strategy and witness assessments. According to reports, the leak occurred when an administrative aide accidentally mailed a copy of the document to defense attorney Mike Stone, representing Officer Powell. Of course, Stone assured Judge Davies that when he saw what the document was, he immediately resealed the envelope without reading its contents and contacted the prosecutors, informing them of the error, like President Clinton who similarly smoked marijuana, but didn't inhale.

I'm sure the Feds know where the leak came from, but they haven't announced it. Many people speculate the Justice Department itself was the culprit, through its Public Integrity Section, a little known unit responsible for informing the media of a case's progress to prevent prosecuting attorneys and investigators from dragging their feet—another example of media manipulation, this time by the government itself.

With the federal trial about to begin, the four defendant officers heightened their media presence. News shows, talk shows, radio, magazine articles, every source was used to air their views in anticipation of jury selection. Soon after the indictments, defense attorneys announced their decision not to request a change of venue as they had previously done, which took the trial to Simi Valley. In fact, the defense engaged in a massive media blitz to make everyone in Southern California aware of defense assertions. At every opportunity, the defense reminded local and national audiences that Rodney King was a despicable person. No item of his history went untold. In an effort to "back-door" information to the public and, indirectly, to potential jurors, the tactic had worked well prior to Simi Valley and there was no reason to believe it wouldn't work at least as well the second time around.

LIARS AND WINOS AND WHORES, OH MY!

In January 1993, jury selection in the matter of The People of the United States of America versus Stacey C. Koon, Laurence Powell, Theodore Briseno, and Timothy Wind began with the mailing of questionnaires to thousands of prospective jurors in the Southern California area. The pool of available jurors, encompassing Los Angeles, Orange, San Bernardino, and Ventura Counties, was immensely larger than in the state case. The four counties accounted for nearly fifteen million people eligible—and probably reluctant—to serve on this particular jury. The preselection questionnaire, formulated by the judge and attorneys for both sides, contained over fifty pages of questions intended to assist in narrowing the field of prospective jurors by eliminating those who could not, would not, or should not serve. Many believed that the selection itself would take one to two months. Surprisingly, jury selection moved rapidly and the trial began right on schedule, March 1, 1993, almost one year to the day after the start of the Simi Valley trial.

Experienced court-watchers and insiders speculated the trial would require six to eight weeks. I thought it might take ten to twelve weeks, given the number of witnesses and document evidence I knew was available to both sides.

I expected an aggressive prosecution followed by a dynamic defense. I felt Tim Wind, once again, would not take the stand in his own defense because of his statement to internal affairs, in which he admitted he saw Powell strike King in the head at least twice, could be very damaging with an effective prosecutor handling cross-examination.

As the trial drew near, the world's media descended upon the Roybal federal courthouse in downtown Los Angeles. Public metered parking was eliminated to make room for the fleets of camera and satellite trucks. Nightly news programs pumped up the hype. February was a ratings sweep month.

While television had quarterbacked the Simi Valley trial with its gavel-to-gavel coverage, this time with the exclusion of cameras from the courtroom, print media would have to carry the ball.

Judge Davies's courtroom was on the eighth floor near the elevators. Additional U.S. marshalls and security personnel were brought in from cities across the country. Metal detectors were arranged outside the courtroom, as well as at the building's entrances. Security, while no better than in Simi Valley, was more visible.

The courtroom itself was much larger than was Judge Weisberg's. Dark marbled walls and indirect lighting made the room seem less crowded than it actually was. The witness stand was thirty feet away from the nearest public seat. The jury box was on the west side of the room, within feet of the witness stand. Jurors would have a clear view of all those called to testify. A sound system was in place so everyone could hear clearly. There was spectator seating for over a hundred people, though most seats were allocated to the press, leaving only twelve for the general public.

I had been given a designated seat for the trial in Simi Valley, but no way this time. Like the rest of the public, Lerman and I—and for that matter, Grimes—would have to stand in line daily for a seat. Even Odessa King, Glen's mother couldn't get an assigned seat. As a result, when Glen was finally called to testify near the end of the prosecution's case, Odessa King could not get a seat in the courtroom and had to sit in a fifth floor waiting area with Steve Lerman, unable to hear or see what was happening.

Like most of King's family, Odessa King doesn't like Milton Grimes. Grimes had offered to drive Odessa to the courthouse for Glen's testimony but she declined, opting instead to have Lerman escort her. Angela King, Glen's Aunt and designated family spokesperson, who had attended the Simi Valley trial every day, couldn't get a seat either. Finally, in desperation, she began arriving at the courthouse at 3:00 A.M. to secure herself one of the twelve public seats. Judge Davies's clerk held firm in his refusal to allow a designated seat to anyone connected to the civil case. As far as he was concerned, we were all just members of the public and could stand in line like everyone else.

The defendants had no such problem. Seats were allocated to each defendant and, by my count on the days I attended, eighteen seats were occupied by various family members and friends.

Unlike D.A.s Terry White and Alan Yochelson in Simi Valley, the Federal prosecutors, Barry Kowolsky and Steve Climer, called a few of the civilian witnesses who'd watched the beating. Dorothy Gibson said the same thing to the jury that she said to me two years earlier. Many jurors were so intent on her words, they stopped taking notes while she spoke. She told the jury a version of the story they hadn't heard before. Elois Camp echoed Ms. Gibson's words as she sat demurely in the witness box in front of the jury.

Chuck Aronburg, an M.D. who had spent the evening with Steve, Glen, and me following the Simi Valley verdicts, also testified. I had supposed he'd focus his testimony on King's psychological injuries, but Mike Stone, attorney for Powell, took him in another direction. Stone was so intent on discrediting Aronberg's testimony that he began to question him about the nature and extent of the facial bone breaks near King's right eye. Before Stone realized what he'd done, he'd qualified Dr. Aronberg to testify in an area of medicine in which he would not normally qualify as an expert. In response to Stone's questions, Aronberg told the jury that in his expert opinion, the bone injuries to King's face could only have come from a baton blow. Stone's momentary loss of direction cost the defense dearly as Aronberg's testimony was allowed by the judge, over the objections of defense council.

Sergeant Mark Conta, a training and self-defense instructor and supervisor at the LAPD academy, was called as the prosecution's use of force expert. I was relieved when I learned Sergeant Conta would be called. I wasn't impressed with Commander Bostic's testimony in Simi Valley. Neither, apparently, was the jury. Some jurors have since said publicly that Commander Bostic, who spent most of his career inside, working his way up the chain of command as a bookworm, lacked the field experience necessary to make him acceptable as a use of force expert.

On the other hand, I knew Conta. He and I were classmates in the police academy. We'd sweated bullets together jogging in the hills around the training facility twenty-three years before. Conta had always been a fair man.

The lines of worry on Conta's face as he entered the courthouse made it clear that he hadn't volunteered to be there. Over the next two days, Conta's testimony was direct and his words well chosen. His testimony was aimed at convincing the jury that the LAPD policy is sound, and the offending officers simply violated policy and used excessive force. He was walking a tightrope, criticizing the cops while absolving the city of any blame, which would affect King's civil suit. The policies are acceptable as written, Conta testified, these were just four rogue cops, acting outside policy, and therefore, the city should have no liability in the civil aspects of the case.

Defense attorneys were quick to air their comments about Conta's testimony. "Whore!" "Buffoon!" "Scum!" were some of the adjectives used to describe Conta before he even reached the parking lot of the Roybal Building. Attorneys Stone and Salzman were the most vocal in their condemnation of Conta's testimony and reputation.

I'm of the opinion the defense's assault against Conta wasn't because he lacked experience or credibility but rather because they felt he, like Sergeant Nichols in Simi Valley, broke the Code of Silence. In a 1991 article for the *Journal of California Law Enforcement*, my friend, Jack Janson, wrote, "Some of the foremost authorities in law enforcement have written about this practice. In 1936, August Vollmer, the former Chief of Police in Berkeley, California, and leading police administration expert wrote, "It's unwritten law in police departments that *police officers must never testify against their brother officers*. This Code of Silence existed long before you were sworn in and has in all probability existed since the first two law enforcement officers started working together. A limited Code of Silence will probably exist forever between police officers who depend on each other for surviving on the streets. After all, police officers are only human. . . ."

Attacking Conta by calling him a whore and scum was really an attack against reasonable people who believe that no police officer is above the law and only through honest interpretation and examination of policies and procedures can flawed practices be resolved. Defense attorney Mike Stone, a twelve-year veteran police officer, knows this as well as anyone.

Because police officers are only human, we can reasonably expect that occasionally, one will make a mistake. In ninety-nine percent of these cases, additional training or counseling can correct the mistake. But once the Code is invoked, we may never know the mistake occurred. The problem compounds itself until a motorist, even one speeding while intoxicated, can be victimized by the police. The defense's angry attack on Sergeant Conta should be cause for serious concern by the public.

Witness after witness, thirty-six in all, told their stories to the jury, but none was as anticipated as Rodney King himself. The trial had been going on more than two weeks when King was called to the stand. On the day King was scheduled to appear, press coverage mushroomed. Reporters from around the world assembled to hear King recount his version of the events of March 3.

His arrival and departure at the courthouse were well-kept secrets. Federal marshalls ushered his car onto a driveway away from the gathered media. Once inside, King cooled his heels in a fifth floor waiting room with his bodyguards and Milt Grimes.

Ironically, as King awaited his turn on the stand, Odessa King, Glen's mother, expressed her displeasure of Grimes by making sure she was seen entering the courthouse on the arm of Steve Lerman. Some old ties are hard to break.

"The prosecution may call their next witness," Judge Davies said from his bench. It was time for the appearance of prosecution witness number twenty-six.

"Your Honor, the People call Rodney Glen King," came the long awaited announcement.

King, sharply dressed in a dark suit, white shirt, and paisley tie, entered the courtroom from the rear, behind the trial watchers. Television reporters began taking notes, anticipating their lead stories, live from the courthouse. It was early in the day. King would be on the stand the entire morning and afternoon sessions. Few believed he would complete his testimony in just one day.

"Please be seated," said the court clerk, "state your name and spell it for the record."

"My name is Rodney Glen King . . ."

For the next day and a half, Glen underwent examination and cross-examination by some of the best trial attorneys in the nation. As I sat in the courtroom watching Glen answer questions, I felt pleased at his demeanor and the manner in which he handled himself on the stand. Our trial preparation sessions with Glen a year earlier were well worth the time. I assume Grimes ran him over the same hurdles.

King sat relaxed, hands folded in front of him, leaning slightly forward. When he wanted to emphasize an answer, he looked directly at the jurors, not backing away from the tough questions. He admitted he'd been drinking and had consumed too much beer before his confrontation with the CHP and police in Lake View Terrace. He admitted he'd smoked a small amount of marijuana earlier that day. He spoke candidly about his criminal conviction, looking directly at defense counsel. He told the jurors he was looking for a well-lighted and populated location to stop because he was frightened of the officers. He said his reason for not stopping was that he feared going back to "the joint," prison. When he couldn't recall requested information, he simply told the jurors he didn't remember. The prosecution's medical experts had set the groundwork for these responses when they told the jurors that King suffered from lapses of memory brought on by head injuries suffered in the beating.

During the morning session on his second day on the stand, King made several statements I didn't understand. He admitted he'd lied to prosecutors in his March, 1991, statement, when he told them he hadn't smoked marijuana or used any drugs the night of the beating. My recollection was that he was only asked, "Did you use PCP before the incident?" a distinctly different question. Everyone knew he'd consumed a small amount of grass based on his blood test taken at USCMC hospital.

My biggest surprise came when King was asked by Mike Stone, "Did Sergeant Koon call you a nigger or did he say "killer," which is it?"

"I'm not sure . . . I can't be sure . . . I don't remember if it was nigger or killer. . . ."

In the entire two years leading up to this question, King had *never once vacillated* on this issue. From the time he'd told me in the hotel, several weeks after the beating, it had always been "nigger." I still can't account for this change. Was he lying to me then, or was he lying now? We know from the statements of Hector Leon, Larry Davis, and King himself, that racial animus was present during the beating and afterwards. And I have the letter from Dr. Papcun, the audio expert who reviewed Holliday's videotape, that the word, "nigger," was used by one of the officers.

Many of the same witnesses we'd seen in Simi Valley were called by the defense in the federal case. Sergeant Charles Duke was again tapped to present his standard line, ". . . It's the policy of the LAPD to beat suspects into submission." I found that statement incredible when he first said it in Simi Valley. Especially since Chief Gates, when asked about Duke's comments, replied, "Well, that is not the policy of the Los Angeles Police Department, and if Sergeant Duke really believes that, I see a need for retraining Sergeant Duke. He's absolutely incorrect."

Also called for an encore performance before the federal jury was Jerry Mulford, another so-called use of force expert. As I watched Mulford and Duke testify, I couldn't help wondering why the prosecution didn't examine the histories of both officers' previous excessive force complaints. I'd worked with Mulford in 77th Division and in Southeast Division during the mid- and late Seventies, and I knew what his violence potential was. Neither Duke nor Mulford were strangers to citizen complaints alleging excessive force or improper tactics. The FBI was sleeping on the job.

As in Simi Valley, the defense called two medical experts to rebut the prosecution's claim that King was clubbed in the face. Dr. Dallas Long, the dentist turned M.D., again testified that King's injuries were "most likely self-inflicted" resulting from his fall to the ground. This time, Dr. Carly Ward, with her Frankensteinian research, was allowed to testify and show the jury her computer generated cartoon showing King's injuries being self-inflicted.

In yet another model designed by Dr. Ward, later used by Stacey Koon in some of his television appearances, King is seen in outline form while a probable "strike zone" accurate to plus or minus six inches, shows King being struck on the right clavicle (collar bone). Where I went to school, approximately six inches (plus or minus) from the clavicle is the right cheek bone.

One of the most damaging witnesses to the defense, oddly enough, was defense witness Melanie Singer. This time around, she was far less verbose about the car chase and what occurred immediately after than she had been in Simi Valley, focusing instead on the actual altercation. "I just couldn't believe what I saw," she said, weeping openly. "I didn't think that much force should've been used, we're not trained that way."

The evening news overlooked Mrs. Singer's testimony, focusing instead on her sobbing appearance in front of the jury. No doubt, her two days on the stand were difficult, especially since her partner would not be called to testify. This time Melanie was on her own.

In a surprising move, the defense rested nearly a week ahead of their anticipated close, without calling Powell, Briseno, or Wind to testify in their own defense, testimony I looked forward to after a comment by Paul DePasquale, attorney for Tim Wind, prior to our appearance on *Good Morning America* following King's testimony. While waiting for the program to start taping, I'd asked DePasquale, "Can we look forward to seeing Wind take the stand in his own defense this time?"

"I believe that's almost a certainty. The prosecutors here are better prepared than those in the last trial," he said, half smiling. I agreed as we entered the small ABC studio in Los Angeles, where two chairs sat side by side, six feet from the camera.

"Yeah, but will he be truthful?" I asked, just as the producer signaled the cut to our local camera from New York. I watched a tape of the show later that morning and was amused by the expression on my face, which failed to hide my satisfaction at getting the question across to DePasquale without an opportunity for a response.

As it finally happened, of the four defendants, only Koon testified, accepting full responsibility for all actions of every officer involved in the beating, while maintaining that, to his knowledge, no officer at the location violated any laws or policies. As a witness, Koon's image didn't change much from the first trial, where he convinced the jury he and his men acted appropriately. It appeared this trial strategy was modeled after Simi Valley. As a team, the defense, led by Mike Stone on behalf of Powell and Ira Salzman on behalf of Koon, decided to rise or fall together on Koon's efforts.

Once the defense rested, federal prosecutors began their rebuttal. Most noteworthy was the plan by the Feds to use the video tape of Briseno testifying in Simi Valley against the other defendants, which raised strong objections by defense attorneys. Judge Davies, in an unexpected ruling, allowed edited portions of Briseno's testimony into evidence, and for two and a half hours the jury sat and watched video monitors as he testified in front of the previous jury that Powell, Wind, and Koon were out of control during the incident on March 3, 1991, and that he had tried to stop the beating by stomping King on the back of his head in order to get King to stay down.

When all was said and done, over fifty witnesses were called to the stand at the federal trial. The pretrial and ongoing media hype had inflated expectations. By comparison, the final impact of each witness's testimony paled. None was able to live up to their pretrial billing, not even prosecution witness number twenty-six, Rodney King.

When one of the jurors became ill after several days of deliberations, concern filled the courthouse. If the juror was unable to resume deliberations, the options were to appoint an alternate juror, or to stay deliberations until the ailing juror could return. Neither option seemed acceptable to anyone involved in the trial, but it gave the media another full night of prime-time contemplation. The issue resolved itself the following day when the juror was able to return to the courthouse and resume the task of reaching a verdict.

During the week the jury deliberated, Los Angeles and the nation sat on pins and needles. Judge Davies had promised

Chief Williams he'd give as much advance notice as possible when verdicts were in, before he announced them. This would enable Chief Williams and other local law enforcement officials to set the final security plan for Los Angeles into motion. When jury deliberations started, the LAPD mobilized, as did the Los Angeles sheriff's department and elements of the California National Guard. Each time an official gave a news interview, the citizens of Los Angeles were reminded of the riots following the first trial, with four days of assaults, arson, and theft, including thousands of handguns and other weapons. Every official, including President Bill Clinton, Governor Pete Wilson, Los Angeles's lame-duck Mayor Tom Bradley, members of the city council, and others, pleaded for the city to remain calm if unpopular verdicts were reached by the jurors.

Barricades were erected around the courthouse and helicopter surveillance was ordered at several key locations around the city. L.A. looked like a camp of armed resisters caught under seige in a Central American coup d'état.

One week after they began considering the fate of the four defendant officers, the jurors finished their assignment. Friday, April 16, 1993, was a beautiful day in Los Angeles, with midday temperatures in the high eighties under a clear blue sky. Even the usual dose of smog and haze seemed to have abated. A sense of anticipation filled the courthouse hallways as the day slowly passed into midafternoon. Then, like an electrical shock wave, word swept over the waiting throng of spectators and media, that at 7:00 A.M. the next day, Saturday, Judge Davies would have an important announcement.

Immediately, rumors of verdicts careened around the waiting masses. All guilty? None guilty? Hung jury? Split decision?

Every television station in Southern California and many others around the country went live to the Federal Courthouse in Los Angeles as speculation mounted. Satellite-truck crews peered at their monitors as reporters with every hair in place sent out the message. Verdicts would be announced within hours. All was ready—all but the peace of mind of the four officers.

On Saturday, April 17, 1993, 7:08 A.M., the jury in the matter of The People of the United States of America versus Sergeant Stacey C. Koon, et al. rendered their verdicts to an anxious city, state, and nation.

"As to Defendant Stacey C. Koon, we the jury, in the above entitled matter find the defendant guilty as charged. . . .

"As to Defendant Laurence M. Powell, we the jury, in the above entitled matter find the defendant guilty as charged. . . .

"As to Defendant Timothy Wind, we the jury, in the above entitled matter find the defendant not guilty. . . .

"As to Defendant Theodore Briseno, we the jury, in the above entitled matter find the defendant not guilty. . . ."

Within hours, the Saturday edition of the *Pasadena Star-News* hit the streets with the headline, KOON AND POWELL GUILTY. Other newspapers would follow with the same news flash. Finally, my eyes weren't lying to me. In interviews I gave to the media following the verdicts, I was asked by every reporter who knew of my connection to the case, "What do you think of the verdicts?" My answer each time was the same. "With only two convictions, I'm half-pleased."

SLAMMER BOUND

July 15, 1993, began unlike most other mid-July days in Southern California. The temperature was cool and the skies overcast and moist, remnants of a tropical storm that had pounded Baja California the previous week. Morning rush hour traffic into downtown Los Angeles was slow as usual, and all seemed well.

On that Thursday morning, months of hard work and exposure to danger by undercover police officers and federal agents were finally about to pay off. Search and arrest warrants were being served in Los Angeles, Orange, and Riverside counties. Eventually, eight members of three white supremist groups, including six adults and two juveniles belonging to the Church of the Creator (COTC), Tom Metzger's White Aryan Resistance (WAR), and the 4th Reich Skinheads, were taken into custody and charged with various weapons violations. These eight urban terrorists can expect to face additional federal charges of conspiracy to commit murder, and construction of homemade bombs, tied to their threats to assassinate Rodney King and

Cecil (Chip) Murray, Pastor of the First AME Church in South Central Los Angeles.

The August 4 sentencing deadline for convicted LAPD officers Larry Powell and Stacey Koon was just over two weeks away, and these Church of the Creator purveyors of hate wanted to capitalize on the nervous mood in Los Angeles. Assassinating Rodney King or machine-gunning a church congregation, would seize the attention of the world's media. Imagine the newspaper headlines: WHITE RACISTS SLAY WORSHIPERS.

The Reginald Denny criminal trial was about to begin jury selection, and tensions within the community were once again at a fever pitch. The Feds decided to terminate their undercover surveillance operation of the hate groups, conducted over eighteen months by a combined law enforcement antiterrorist task force, and announce arrests. Rodney King would now benefit from the efforts of one of the agencies involved in his beating.

Revelations of death threats against Rodney King, and Los Angeles area minority leaders and clergy came as no surprise to me. I can look back with satisfaction at the many conversations I had with Rodney King, during which he expressed his annoyance and discomfort over forced relocations of his residence. On more than one occasion, King hinted I might be overly protective, even paranoid. Moving always caused King some inconvenience. In the early days, the moves were to keep the media and potential cappers away, as well as for King's personal safety. But that soon changed. Within days after the initial airing of George Holliday's home video, cranks, crackpots, and would-be terrorists began to let their presences be known to those most closely involved in the case.

King, Holliday, the defendant officers, even eyewitnesses, began to receive threatening letters and phone calls, to the extent that many of the witnesses, including George Holliday, were forced to move or relocate to escape not only the onslaught of publicity, but the emergence of wackos out for a cheap thrill.

True, King was severely injured during the beating and needed months to recover from his injuries, but the primary reason for keeping him away from public places and events was our concern for his safety, to which even playing keep-away from the intense media interest soon took a back seat. Threats began to arrive at Lerman's offices and at mine, which, we noted, grew more violent and frightening as the weeks and months passed.

I suspected that while many of the letters and anonymous calls were harmless, some were genuine. I met with several African-American LAPD officers who told me stories of internal and external agitation towards them following their public comments about racial prejudice inside the department.

I discussed my concerns with authorities, including the FBI, on a number of occasions. Information from my interviews with officer Maxine Spencer about KKK threats made against her at the Foothill Station following the airing of the Holliday tape, proved useful in locating and identifying individuals as well as the locations of white supremists' mail drops, which were later confirmed by U.S. postal inspectors in Los Angeles and Orange Counties.

The Feds were tight-lipped about their findings, though I eventually got a call from agent Dave Harris, my favorite FBI guy. "I can't give you any details," he said, "but that information you gave me about those Aryan threats and addresses on those cards came back positive. It's the real deal. You just need to know that we've got some things going now and we'll stay on top of it."

Funny how such a small victory can make a person feel good about his work. I'd spent days setting up the interview with Officer Spencer, and a phone call made all the work seem worth the effort. I hung up, walked past my desk, and opened the cabinet containing the volumes of material on the King case. I spotted the brown manila envelope on top of a row of three-ring binders. I opened it and took out the enlarged copy of a card found by Officer Spencer on her car at Foothill. "The Knights of the Ku Klux Klan."

Ironically, as I discussed this issue with friends and colleagues, their reactions, in many instances, were the same as King's. I was paranoid. Indeed, ask Christopher David Fisher and his associates if I was paranoid.

Fisher, a twenty-year-old Long Beach resident and self-proclaimed minister in the Church of the Creator, was booked by federal authorities in Los Angeles County for plotting to bomb the First AME Church, machine-gun the congregation, and assassinate their minister, Reverend Cecil Murray. Assassination plans also targeted John Mack, president of the Los

Angeles Urban League and Danny Bakewell, leader of the Los Angeles Brotherhood Crusade, who with Murray were highly respected voices in the minority community of South Central Los Angeles. Fisher also intended to assassinate Rodney King. Any of those acts, if publicly connected to a white hate group, could have touched off L.A. Riots '93. So I'm paranoid. Paranoids can have enemies, too.

■

King's attorney, Milt Grimes, didn't waste much time in stirring the pot once the convictions against Powell and Koon were handed down. Grimes saw fit to lodge a complaint with the California Bar Association against Steve Lerman, claiming Steve hadn't turned over King's complete file in the weeks following the substitution of attorneys. In his complaint, Grimes further alleged both Lerman and I took unfair advantage of King while he was in our charge by encouraging him to sign the so-called movie and book deal with Jim Banks of Triple Seven Entertainment for a fraction of what the rights were really worth. After reading Grimes's letter to the Bar, it was obvious to me he hadn't done his homework.

Grimes went on to complain that both Lerman and I were giving too many media interviews following the substitution, and requested the bar to order Lerman and me to desist. He claimed we were disclosing confidential materials to the media and the opposition.

Grimes mailed a copy of his complaint to Lerman after he mailed it to the State Bar and, of course, Lerman faxed me a copy for my information. Under California law, my work and all products of my work fall under the control and supervision of Lerman as the former attorney of record on behalf of King. Therefore, any alleged misconduct against me becomes the responsibility of Lerman. In structuring his complaint as he did, Grimes had hoped the California Bar would decide in his favor against both Lerman and me, thus giving Steve a double disciplinary whammy. Grimes's complaint further convinced me that he still wasn't fully familiar with the entire contents of his file. It was all I could do to hold my Irish temper in check as I read Grimes's letter to the bar.

My gut instinct was to cross-complain against Grimes for

interference with my professional contract with King to provide services beyond the investigation, services King wanted
me to continue after the substitution of attorneys that brought
Grimes in on the case. I still haven't forgotten what King said
to me on the balcony outside Grimes's office, that he wanted
me available should he need me.

I wrote Lerman a letter that I encouraged him to forward to
the State Bar as part of his crosscomplaint against Grimes for
interfering with his representation of King. We had documented Grimes's previous efforts to jockey himself into the case
at the behest of Kandyce Barnes, going all the way back to
Grimes's attempt to see King while he was in Westside Hospital
having his face put back together. In my letter to Lerman I
refuted Grimes's allegations.

As the bar complaints were going forward, I took Grimes's
advice and filed a small claims action against him for monies
due me for representing King in the DMV hearings arising from
his July 1992 DUI arrest in Orange County. That case was heard
in Central Orange County Municipal Court on July 26, 1993, by
Judge B. Pam Namoto.

Overall, the case went pretty much as I'd expected. Grimes
offered a weak defense telling the judge, "Your Honor . . . I
simply don't recall telling this man (like he didn't know my
name) to do anything on behalf of Mr. King. If I did, it was
simply because I didn't know what he [Owens] was doing. I
wouldn't have had him on this case at all if it was purely my
decision."

"Your Honor," I responded, "how could Mr. Grimes deny
owing me money for work done if he doesn't even recall giving
me the assignment?" I asked. "At best, his denial signifies his
lack of knowledge of the facts. Does Mr. Grimes believe that
Mr. King simply awakened one morning and had his driver's
license restored and criminal charges dismissed because Mr.
King is a model citizen?

"The case boils down to this basic issue: Did I continue to
provide services to and testify on behalf of King after Grimes
substituted in, and if so, wasn't he the attorney of record in the
superior case? Once the court determines those issues, then the
payment for services rendered rightfully falls to Grimes."

When all testimony had concluded, the judge announced
she would take the case under consideration and advise all

parties of her findings within a week to ten days. Five days later, I received a letter from the small claims court, advising me I'd won. I'd beaten Grimes in his own ballpark. On the last minute of the last day, Grimes filed an appeal to the court's findings.

■

With the convictions of Koon and Powell, their status as police officers is a foregone conclusion. Indeed, Powell and Koon have been fired by a board of rights hearing convened just prior to their incarceration at Club Fed. In an unsurprising move, their attorneys filed an appeal with the federal appeals court in late August 1993 requesting the court allow them to remain out on bail while their appeals go forward. As expected, the appeals court reaffirmed Judge Davies's order that they report for incarceration by late September.

On the very day they reported to the facility at Dublin, a small, minimum security, campuslike setting near Pleasanton, California, U.S. Supreme Court Justice Sandra O'Conner granted a stay to Koon and Powell pending a full hearing before the Supreme Court the following week. Defense attorneys claimed the appeal would take so long the officers would most certainly serve their time before the appeals could be heard. Justice O'Conner ordered both convicted ex-officers remain free until the Supreme Court could hear the stay order.

Within days, the Supreme Court lifted the stay, indicating they would not circumvent the normal appeal process, and ordered Koon and Powell to report the following week to begin serving their thirty-month sentences. About the same time, the U.S. Attorney's office in Los Angeles announced it would file an appeal claiming Judge Davies deviated too far from normal sentencing guidelines in his thirty-month sentence, indicating the prosecutors were unhappy at the light sentences handed out by the trial judge.

■

Just when the King incident seems it will quietly go away, something happens that brings it back to public attention. In mid-August, 1993, King was once again arrested by officers of the LAPD for drinking and driving. I'd been asleep for hours when the ringing of my bedside phone startled me awake at 4:30 A.M.

"Hey shithead, did I wake ya?" I instantly recognized the voice of Blue Throat.

"Yeah, but it's okay, cause I had to get up to answer the phone anyway," I mumbled.

"Your guy's at it again. Can't you fellas put a leash on that jerk and keep him home?" I instantly knew which jerk Blue Throat was referring to.

"What's he done now?" I asked, fully awake and alert.

"Rampart cops popped him a couple hours ago, downtown. DUI. He's at Parker Center jail right now, but he'll be released shortly on his own recognizance."

"How serious is it this time?"

"I hear he blew a point-one-nine on the breath machine, how serious do you think that is?"

"Can you give me any of the details," I asked.

"No, I don't have all the scoop. But I think they have him good this time." Blue Throat sounded miffed. I understood why. Blue Throat had gone the extra mile for King, laying career and income on the line a number of times. Exasperation at King's actions had set in with my friend. I could tell this was the last call I'd get on Rodney King's behalf. The weariness and frustration in his voice said it all.

"Okay, I'll hit the field as soon as I learn the location of arrest. Maybe I'll find something. Talk to you later," I said as we ended our short conversation.

Blue Throat told me the arrest occurred in Rampart Division downtown. That meant King was picked up west of the Harbor freeway, but it was two hours later before I got the exact address of his arrest from an early morning television newscast. The media was, as usual, already on the story. "Rodney King arrested again by LAPD" began the Saturday morning newscast. "Rodney King was arrested by officers outside a downtown nightclub after he crashed his car into a block wall," the female reporter said as she stood in front of the Glam Slam Club, a local hot spot owned by a pop star formerly known as Prince.

"Damn!" I shouted at the tube, "that's the club from my murder investigation." Pat heard me bellowing and came into the front room with a cup of fresh coffee. She too had been awakened by Blue Throat's call. While the sun shot its first smoggy glimpse over the San Bernardino Mountains, I sat down at my computer and pulled up my report to the attorney handling a wrongful death case that occurred a few months earlier at the Glam Slam club.

I started reading, looking for the trigger that would set off my recollection. Two pages later, while recapping the statement of witness Dave Turner, I saw what I was looking for. . . .

> The altercation lasted just two to four minutes. He [Turner] doesn't recall who busted up the fight but he did state that three off-duty officers, whom he identifies as regulars at the Glam Slam, stood just twenty to thirty feet away but failed to take any action until after the fight had stopped. Then, they simply told the crowd to move on. . . .

"I knew it, damn it," I told Pat. "Off-duty cops from LAPD were at the door of the club when King got there."

"You don't suppose they recognized King and dropped a dime on him, do you?"

"Exactly right," I replied "They see him at the door, recognize him, and detain him in conversation long enough to make a call and roll units. When he leaves, they swoop down on him, and snatch him up for DUI. I'm outta here," I said as I walked out the door on my way to the Glam Slam. "Got to find some of those street people and find out what really happened."

Sure enough, the street people were right where I'd expected them to be. The first man I talked to was Dave Turner. "I didn't see anything, I'd already left the club by that time," Turner stated. "I heard this morning that some guy was arrested outside the club, but I didn't know it was King till you told me."

"Do you know who else might've been outside the club at that time," I asked.

"Well, I'm not sure, but I'll go around there and ask. They might talk to me where they might not talk to you," Turner volunteered.

We got in my old Chrysler and drove the two short blocks to the club. As Turner looked for witnesses to King's arrest, I scouted the area for the wall King was alleged to have crashed his car into. That allegation was important because it set up the basis for probable cause needed by officers to make their initial approach to King. After a lengthy search, I failed to locate any evidence of a crash on any wall within one block of the club.

I did find rubber tire marks on a white driveway marker leading out of a parking lot directly across the street from the club. The tire marks resembled those left when a car bumps into a curb or other fixed object, but certainly this wasn't the so-called crash site?

By the time I'd finished my area inspection, Dave Turner had returned with a male African-American in his late forties, who refused to give me his name, telling me he really didn't want to get involved. He feared the police officers who normally worked the area might get word that he'd talked to me and take him to jail on a "hummer" (an invalid charge used simply to get him off the streets for a while, a message to keep his mouth shut), a tactic I'd used many times in the past myself.

"I was standing across the street from the entrance to the club when I saw some police cars arrive on Fourth Street and on Boylston and then stop near the club," the transient said stiffly. "Then, one of the officers told me and my friends to 'move on, something's going down,' and since I ain't stupid, I got out of the area as quick as I could."

"Then what did you see?" I asked.

"Well, we moved down the street about two hundred feet, and because it was so dark, I didn't see much else except when they put the guy in the back seat of the police car. But I couldn't tell if the guy was drinking or not. We was too far away."

My mind was signaling a problem. How could the officers know that something was going down in advance of their initial contact with King? And, if something was to go down, wouldn't it be better for the department and arresting officers if everyone in the world watched it happen?

As I drove back home, I developed a scenario surrounding King's arrest: Officers working off-duty at the club recognized King the instant he arrived, and kept him talking at the door while on-duty officers were summoned by phone. Once the officers arrived outside the club, King was turned away at the door by the off-duty cops, knowing that units awaited his departure. When King rolled across the top of the parking lot marker, he provided them with the necessary probable cause to stop and detain him for investigation of DUI.

If I sound overly skeptical, it may well be because my previous experiences proved officers had arrested King when he was not involved in any criminal activity. In this particular instance, the bottom line is, why was King out that late at night without his security staff, especially after the threats made public against him in the weeks prior? Why was he allowed to drive *any* car at any time, knowing past police efforts to mitigate damages in his civil case by causing confrontational situations between himself and officers from several agencies?

While I'm not professionally or educationally qualified to render an expert opinion, through my close relationship with King in the years since the incident, I've watched him react to various contacts and confrontations with police officers, as well as watching some of his public appearances. Based on both my observations of and my conversations with him, I genuinely believe Glen is self-destructive. He has never wanted media attention, nor does he want to be held up as a role model, hero, or martyr. He appears to rebel against efforts to idealize him. He greatly resents his loss of privacy and on occasion, gets involved in situations where, if he were still a private person, little or no attention would be paid him. He tests the water, so to speak, and often finds it too hot.

17

NO ONE HERE GETS OUT ALIVE

The story of the Rodney King beating is about people—some good, others not so good. It is also a story about issues and values. I believe there was much more involved in Lake View Terrace on that early morning of March 3, 1991, than has ever been revealed by any source or forum. I'm not sure the whole truth will ever get out. In this entire world, only a handful of people really know what happened out there that night. Stacey Koon knows. Larry Powell, Tim Wind, and Ted Briseno know. The Singers, Tim and Melanie, know. And Rodney King knows. The rest of us only know what we were told or what we found out after the incident. Even among the two dozen or so officers who were present, there are many different perceptions of what actually occurred. I believe the years ahead will only serve to convolute the facts we already know.

The King beating and the events which followed have changed the lives of everyone even remotely involved. No one closely connected to this case has escaped the accusations or the adverse reactions that have always been a part of the incident.

It has been said that the only thing consistent in this world, is change. The King incident is no different. What changes have come about for the people? What has happened to those most closely involved?

During the first week of January 1993, George Holliday appeared on a television talk show from New York. He confirmed his wife had returned to Argentina to live with her family because of problems from fallout over the incident. What George didn't tell the national viewers was that he was fighting the U.S. Immigration and Naturalization Service (INS) to remain in the United States. Within weeks of his bolt to stardom as a cameraman, Holliday began to have problems with the INS for having entered the U.S. without papers. The INS wanted to deport Holliday back to South America. Those problems have now been resolved.

Holliday has been working with others, including the man who videotaped the Reginald Denny beating, to form a non-profit organization to provide assistance to rebuild Los Angeles. The group, Rebuild L.A. was formed by Mayor Tom Bradley and Peter Uberroth, after the riots. Monies from the purchase of Holliday's video rights by movie director Spike Lee have been placed into this organization and earmarked in part for Rebuild L.A. Holliday still works with the company he was working for when he filmed the incident. He has testified in the criminal trial in Simi Valley and the federal trial, and will probably testify in every trial yet to come.

Holliday has earned nearly $150,000 from licensing his video, but his wife is not there to share his newfound wealth with him. Most recently, his litigations against many television stations across the country for airing his tape without permission, were dismissed. These suits could have netted him millions of dollars if he had prevailed. Holliday has changed attorneys and is seldom seen away from his new home.

Jim Jordan, Holliday's former attorney, has been contacted by a New York book publisher and is presently working on a manuscript recounting his knowledge of events surrounding the incident, as seen from his perspective.

Judge Bernard Kamins, the original trial judge in the first criminal case against the four officers, remains a Superior Court Judge in Los Angeles County. I've been in Judge Kamins's court several times since his removal from the case and each time our eyes met, I felt his disappointment. I believe he feels cheated in some way.

Judge Weisburg has changed his trial venue to the San Fernando Valley. He remans silent on his feelings about the outcome and aftermath of the Simi Valley verdicts. Ironically, Judge Weisberg's court reporter in the Simi Valley trial, Christine Olsen, seems to have found a new friend in Ted Briseno. I noted with interest, her attendance at the federal trial as an invited guest of Ted and his brother, Mike.

Meanwhile, Judge Weisburg continues to try the most difficult cases in Los Angeles County. At this writing, he is presiding over the infamous Menendez brothers' trial, where two young men face death or life without parole if convicted of murdering their Hollywood producer father and allegedly abusive mother.

Most of the civilian witnesses to the Rodney King beating have moved in the years since they watched the incident. Publicity and threats of physical violence from the full political spectrum are cited as reasons. In my attempts to poll the Simi Valley jury, I found many of them have also relocated, alleging threats as the primary reason for their moves. Those witnesses who have not moved maintain a low public profile and are no longer granting interviews.

Stacey Koon has published his book, *Presumed Guilty*, and looks to the possibility of becoming an educator or a writer, once his ordeal is finished and he's released from prison. He has been on suspension since the weeks following the airing of the Holliday video and now, because of his conviction, knows he will never again be a police officer. He is a defendant in the civil case filed by Steven Lerman on behalf of Rodney King, and if he should lose there, he can expect that King, not he, will benefit from his book sales. He steadfastly maintains that he was the responsible person at the scene of the beating, and for this stance he must be admired.

Sergeant Koon has been called to testify in the case of William Gable versus the City of Los Angeles. The case arises from an incident in which Officer Lance Braun, another Foothill Division patrolman, is alleged to have beaten Gable and a woman companion with his baton. Koon investigated the personnel complaint against Braun, and recommended he be severely disciplined for his assault against Gable and the woman. There are other cases of civil litigation in which Koon was in some way involved, and it is possible he'll be in and out of courtrooms for years after the King case is finally resolved. Within three days of his conviction in the federal trial, Koon reportedly was paid $10,000 to appear on Phil Donahue's television talk show. This followed on the heels of his appearing on the syndicated show, *A Current Affair*. Koon publicly denies being paid for his television appearances.

True to his schedule, Judge Davies announced in early August 1993 that Koon would be sentenced to thirty months in the federal prison system. This light sentence angered many in the community, while others thought Judge Davies was far too harsh. After announcing the sentences, Judge Davies heard pleas from Mike Stone, Powell's criminal defense attorney, and Ira Salzman, representing Stacey Koon, that both be allowed to remain out on bail while their appeals went forward. Judge Davies promptly denied their pleas.

The Board of Rights hearings, or "trial boards," for Koon and Powell were anticlimactic, given their convictions. California law forbids convicted felons from serving as police officers within the state. I would anticipate attorneys representing plaintiffs in the civil case to file motions to protect returned pension monies of both officers, pending the outcome or settlement of the civil litigation. The convictions could spell disaster for the financial future of both Koon and Powell.

Powell had said he looked forward to the federal criminal trial because, he said, in his heart he knew he'd be acquitted. In the wake of his conviction, Powell faces thirty months in federal prison. He and Koon were assigned to a minimum security "Club Fed." On the up side, he and Koon will be able to watch each others' backs, though they will be doing soft time and other soft-time inmates present little threat.

Powell still maintains no excessive force was used on Rodney King, considering the circumstances. He remains highly supportive of the other defendant officers, even Briseno, saying that each defendant officer must do what is right for himself. During the closing months of 1992, Powell seemed to disappear from the public eye. As pretrial preparations continued for his defense in federal court, he was occasionally seen entering and leaving the U.S. District Courthouse in Los Angeles, but he offered few comments to the assembled media. This changed after his conviction. Like his convicted codefendant, Stacey

Koon, Powell negotiated contracts with several television shows, offering him compensation to air his feelings after the verdicts. He hadn't drawn a paycheck for two years.

An interesting development surfaced in December, 1992, when the defense counsels representing Koon and Briseno filed motions with the court requesting Powell's attorney, Mike Stone, be forced to leave the case. His cocounsel alleged a conflict of interest against Stone, based on his involvement in another case they believed was counter to the best interests of Sergeant Koon. On January 14, 1993, federal court Judge John Davies ruled Stone would be allowed to remain as the attorney of record for Laurence Powell.

Little is known about the plight of Tim Wind following his termination from the LAPD. He has continued to maintain a low profile since the beating occurred, and has been the only one of the four primarily involved officers who has chosen to remain silent. Wind appealed his termination from the LAPD in the fall of 1992. The appeal was summarily denied by Chief Williams. Wind and his wife and children are still living in the greater Los Angeles area, but may move back to Kansas after King's civil trial is concluded. Sources indicate Wind is working as a security guard, with occasional odd jobs to supplement his meager income.

Ted Briseno works at various security jobs around Los Angeles. Like his codefendants, he has not returned to the LAPD, and he too has said he fears his law enforcement career is finished, despite having filed a suit to get his job back. Cindy, Ted's former wife, announced she is finally getting some assistance from her local district attorney's office in collecting the $25,000 she says he still owes in back child support. In a September, 1993, telephone interview, Cindy told me that she was able to collect several thousand dollars from Ted following the verdicts. On the day Ted appeared on *Donahue*, he was met at the studio by marshalls with papers from the L.A. County Deadbeat Dads unit, and was served on behalf of Cindy. Within days of his appearance on the show, Cindy received her check.

Briseno, his second wife, and the children from that marriage share a modest home in Sepulveda with his seventy-three year old mother-in-law, from whom he is accepting financial assistance while he undergoes his legal battles and fights to get his job back with the LAPD.

On September 1, 1993, his trial board was convened to determine whether or not to accept Briseno back on the job. After nearly a week of testimony, the hearings were halted due to an evidenciary issue. Like Koon, Powell, and Wind, Briseno has probably seen his last day as an LAPD officer. He's history.

John Barnett, the brilliant defense attorney who represented Briseno in Simi Valley, withdrew from the case for medical reasons following the verdicts there. He was replaced by Harlan Braun, an experienced criminal attorney. Ira Salzman took over Koon's defense. Insiders believe that the two new attorneys did at least as well in the federal trial as their predecessors did in Simi Valley, and are gearing up for the court battles that lay ahead for the defendants in the civil case.

The Los Angeles Police Protective League, who financially supported the defendants through the Simi Valley trial, once again footed the bill for their defense in the federal proceedings. Some estimate the total costs of defending the officers is well over one and a half million dollars of the union's defense fund. It's fair to assume the LAPPL will pay for the appeals of the two convicted officers which have already been filed in federal court. Total defense costs to the LAPPL may well exceed two million dollars once the final bills are tabulated.

Warren Christopher, for whom the independent commission was named, became President Bill Clinton's Secretary of State. One can only hope that in his private conversations with the new President, Christopher will relate his knowledge of the problems facing police departments across the nation.

Daryl Gates retired from the LAPD in the summer of 1992, after forty-three years of service. Shortly before his retirement, his autobiography, *Chief: My Years in the LAPD*, was published.

In October 1992, Gates was hired to replace KFI radio talk show host, Tom Leykis. Gates was given the prestigious 3:00 to 6:00 P.M. drive-time slot. With this change, KFI acknowledged their conservative political leanings. Gates reveled in his opportunity to expound upon his extremely conservative views on the city and the world. One of the lighter moments provided by Daryl Gates in his new role of talk show host occurred in January 1993. Steve Lerman was invited on the show as a guest. The match between Gates and the attorney suing him in several police misconduct cases in one-on-one combat was a delight to hear. Both were cordial and polite during their conversation, and showed themselves to be cautiously respectful of each other. There was even some humor. Gates asked Lerman why King didn't stop on the night of March 3, 1991. Lerman replied, "Well, you know Chief, if King had stopped, we wouldn't be here today, and you'd still be Chief of Police."

Gates's airtime has since been cut to two hours and his program was moved to later evening. Gates still maintains the officers involved in the King incident overreacted and used too much force. He argues that while the officers acted outside of policy, they were treated unfairly when they were tried a second time by the Feds for the same offense for which they had been acquitted in Simi Valley.

Milton C. Grimes still represents Rodney King in his suit against the City of Los Angeles. In the year since his official involvement in the case, however, its focus has shifted. Under Lerman's guidance, the King case concentrated on the violations of a man's civil rights, resulting in injuries and damages. Under Grimes, racism is the primary issue which, in fact, is the truth of the matter. King's injuries and the violation of his rights have taken a back seat. Grimes appears to prefer settlement to trying the case. In the months since he was engaged on behalf of King, Grimes has never contacted either Lerman or myself to inquire about our efforts in the preparation of the case. This conduct will, in the end, cost King many additional thousands of dollars in case preparation. Rather than consult, Grimes hired a new investigator, Dave Sandberg, who has agreed to carry on the investigation where I "left off."

On the Monday following the federal trial's weekend verdicts, I was in the offices of the L.A. County District Attorney on another matter. While waiting in the reception area, I saw Terry White walking in a corridor. I approached him one final time to ask that he give me an interview for this book. He politely but firmly declined. During our conversation, Alan Yochelson happened by. Seizing the opportunity, I asked him to talk to me. Much to my surprise, Yochelson told me to follow him into his office where he responded to every question I asked.

"You know, I'm pretty nervous about this," I told him as we sat down. "I hadn't expected to see you today and didn't expect you'd grant me this interview on the spot." I fumbled through my briefcase for my tape recorder and note pad.

"How do you plan to use the interview?" Yochelson asked.

Distracted by my search for the damn recorder, I replied, "I'm just finishing a book recounting my efforts in the King case. No book on the subject is going to be worth the time to read, without Terry's and your input." Go right for his ego, I thought.

"Quit the bullshit and ask your questions," he said, smiling. "Just make darn sure you quote me correctly."

Yochelson informed me that the Simi Valley trial was not his first major case. I hadn't known it before, but Alan had been coprosecutor in what was popularly called the Night Stalker trial, which resulted in the conviction of Richard Ramirez, a serial killer in Southern California during the late eighties. That case, like the trial of the defendant officers, was high profile and tried in front of the world media. With that in mind, I asked him about his thoughts on having a camera present in the courtroom.

"That's an interesting question. We felt the power of the cameras almost immediately. During the morning break on the first day of opening arguments, trial watchers called into the D.A.'s office, and in a few instances, directly to the court clerk's desk in the courtroom, with suggestions on how we should alter our opening arguments," Yochelson said, appearing relaxed and comfortable.

"I've wanted to ask you for a long time, what ever happened to your witness from the Ford Probe, the one the defense gave you in discovery? I noted with interest that he wasn't called as a part of your case, or the defense's."

"I don't recall that that witness came from the defense. I remember our investigators found a witness living in the apartment complex, near Holliday's apartment, who drove a Ford Probe. I know we interviewed him, but I don't remember why we didn't use him. I think he was too vague in most of his answers to our questions. I don't know if he ever said for a fact that he was the driver of the car we saw in Holliday's video."

"That's not the way I remember it," I replied. "My memory is that Mike Gillum, your investigator, told us during a meeting that the witness was identified by the defense and given to you in discovery. How do you explain that?" I asked, pressing him for an answer.

"Well, your memory is different from mine, that's all," was Yochelson's response.

"How about the civilian witnesses? Why didn't you guys call some of them in Simi Valley?" I pushed on.

"We saw a problem of inconsistencies in their testimonies. Some witnesses saw one thing, while others saw something totally different. No big deal, but we felt we could make better headway in our case with the witnesses we called. We relied on the Singers and thought our case was strong, based on their testimony."

Yochelson sat back in his chair and maintained full eye contact with me. I saw the hint of a smile several times, almost as if he'd anticipated my reaction to his answers. He certainly was no novice. He was sharp and clearly tuned in to my questions.

"Comments made by some of the jurors after the acquittals made me wonder why you didn't even mention that both Freddie G and Pooh were also beaten by officers present that night. How come you didn't try to get that out?"

"Freddie G and Pooh were both irrelevant. There was no evidence that either of them was struck by any of our defendants, and we didn't want to confuse the jurors. Besides, if we'd tried, there would've been objections from every defense attorney. We just didn't want to give them an opportunity to confuse our case. I feel the Simi Valley jury just never believed in our case. I don't think anything would've changed that," Yochelson said matter-of-factly.

"What did you think when the news media aired Wind's admission to IAD that he'd watched Powell strike King in the face at least twice?" I asked.

"I was surprised. We hadn't seen that material until just a couple of weeks ago when the city attorney's office showed it to us. But, even if we'd known it, we couldn't have used it because it was compelled. But it's good knowing we were right in our prosecution." Yochelson glanced at his watch and I knew my time was running out.

"Just to satisfy my own curiosity, why didn't you guys subpoena Gates to testify about his own force policy? Bostic didn't get much respect from the jury."

"We talked to Gates a number of times, but he just wouldn't

testify. He flatly refused. We asked ourselves, how do you compel a chief to testify against his own?"

"By serving him with a subpoena," I said.

"And then one runs the risk of his resenting his appearance
and saying something that hurts your case. No, we decided not
to call Gates. I still think it was the right decision."

"Couldn't you find a better policy expert than Bostic?" I
asked.

"Look, Tom, we talked to any number of other force and
policy experts, who told us the video showed excessive force.
Clearly, there was excessive force on that video, but none of
them would go on the record. They said it would end careers."

Yochelson had put his finger on a critical issue in the case.
The Code of Silence had hurt the prosecution's case, just as I'd
speculated.

"You met him a number of times, what did you think about
Rodney King?" I asked. I recalled White's reply to this question
from his post-verdict talk show appearance.

"Personally, I like the guy. I think he sometimes uses bad
judgment in his drinking, and that gets him into trouble a lot,
but I don't think that makes him a bad person." Yochelson's
answer surprised me. I'd expected him to say he didn't trust
King's answers, that he found him to be questionable at best. I
was pleased.

"Obviously, you've heard the verdicts in the Fed's case.
What're your feelings?"

"Basically, if you closely examine the evidence from both
trials, you'll see that it's essentially the same. I'll say it now,
just like I did after the state verdicts, I think our jury had
enough evidence to convict. They just didn't believe in the case.
The Fed's case didn't differ much from ours, they just had a
more believing jury. They trusted their eyes and what they saw
on that video."

As he finished speaking, Yochelson stood up and extended
his hand. "It's been nice talking to you, but I have to get back
to work. Just be sure you quote me correctly in your book," he
said with a pleasant smile.

■

In March 1993, Steve Lerman successfully negotiated a settlement in yet another major police abuse case against the city of

Los Angeles. This case involved the shooting death of John Daniels, Jr., an unarmed tow truck driver who, while not posing a threat to anyone, was shot and killed by an LAPD motorcycle officer over an expired vehicle registration. The shooting occurred on July 1, 1992, just a few short blocks from Florence and Normandie, the flash point of the riots, and within hours of incoming Chief Willie Williams taking his oath of office.

I conducted the investigation of the incident on behalf of the Daniels family. While the LAPD and the Los Angeles County district attorney's office took their time looking into the shooting, I was in the field and had taken witness statements of fourteen people who had watched the shooting and were horrified by what they'd seen.

In early winter, the LAPD issued an announcement that an internal review board fround the Daniels shooting to have been "out of policy." Steve Lerman and Tom Hoakenson, who'd been on the King case, began settlement negotiations. Because our handling of the Daniels shooting had been so quick and thorough, settlement seemed appropriate by the city, which certainly did not want the case to assume a high media profile on the heels of the King and Reginald Denny trials.

The settlement talks lasted weeks, and concluded when the city council voted to award the Daniels family $1.2 million in the wrongful death of John Daniels. Steve Lerman's efforts on behalf of the Daniels estate netted him a cool $400,000 in contingency fees. I heard about the settlement on a local news program; Lerman had failed to keep me posted on the progress of the negotiations.

I waited two weeks before calling Lerman's office once again to request payment of my outstanding fees. As expected, Lerman claimed he was still broke from his heavy expenditures in the King case, and asked that I wait for the disbursement of funds, which he expected would follow in a few weeks. He told me I'd just have to be patient. Easy for him to say; the wolves were at my door, not his. Then, I remembered what Lerman had told me early in our relationship. "Tom," he said, "sympathy is found in the dictionary between shit and syphilis. I have only those morals and ethics I can afford." I now understood him.

In the end, the Daniels family ensured I was paid for my

investigation of their case. I still have not been compensated for much of the work I did on King's case.

The late summer of 1993 signaled the start of the highly anticipated trial of Damion Williams and Henry Watson, the two primary defendants charged in the beating of Reginald Denny. The beating was televised live from an orbiting news helicopter within hours of the verdicts in Simi Valley. A third defendant, Gary Williams, pled out to lesser charges before the trial and was sentenced to state prison for four years while Antoine Miller, the fourth defendant awaited his trial apart from Damion Williams and Henry Watson. Collectively, they were dubbed The L.A. Four by citizen support groups who maintained from the beginning the Denny beating was a mirror image of the King beating.

Within weeks of the televised incident Damion "Football" Williams and Henry "Kiki" Watson were taken into custody and charged with the beating of Denny and seven other motorists. In an unusual action, Daryl Gates personally supervised Williams's arrest. Initially, these two defendants were charged with thirty-nine crimes including attempted murder, robbery, aggravated mayhem, and torture, all alleged to have been committed at the intersection of Florence and Normandie, during the first hours of the riots.

Once the trial kicked into high gear, media coverage was nearly as extensive as that in Simi Valley. Court-TV carried the trial live to cable subscribers across the country. As expected, Denny's testimony provided the highlight of the prosecution's case although his demeanor and courtroom persona were both forgiving and conciliatory toward his alleged attackers outside the presence of the jury.

As I sat and watched the daily news coverage during Reginald Denny's appearance on the witness stand, I wondered if I could have been as composed as he appeared, given his circumstances. I admired Denny's quiet calm. I recalled thinking in the days following the conclusion of the riots, how appropriate it might have been if I could have introduced Glen to Denny after his discharge from the hospital. King had already agreed to the meet if it could be arranged. He said he felt a kinship to Denny.

After three months of testimony, the case finally went to the jury and Los Angeles geared up for the verdicts. As in King's

Federal case trial, authorities took up a high media profile announcing partial mobilizations of personnel and equipment, should the need for their use arise. Throughout the county, police and sheriff's days-off were cancelled as the city nervously awaited the verdicts. Once again, videotape had played a significant role. Like the accused officers in the King beating, those accused of beating Denny were believed to be caught in the act, live on video.

In yet another parallel circumstance, once the jury began to deliberate, disclosures of possible jury misconduct surfaced, resulting in the removal of one juror immediately. Another juror, a female civilian employee of the LAPD, was accused by her fellow jurors of not deliberating in good faith. The trial judge, John Ouderkirk, quizzed the jury panel following the accusations but didn't find cause to remove the juror.

Finally, after the last alternate juror had been empaneled and fresh deliberations were begun, the jury announced they had reached verdicts against both defendants but some charges were still unresolved and the jury appeared deadlocked.

Judge Ouderkirk scheduled the reading of the verdicts for the afternoon of the following day, giving the jury one last session to fully resolve the verdicts. When this failed, the verdicts were read. Both Williams and Watson were found not guilty on the most serious charges but were convicted on lesser charges including assault and simple mayhem. Media reports later stated the jurors' comments to the media were that they couldn't find the specific intent necessary to convict Williams guilty of attempted murder and that it was likely Williams was simply caught up in the mood of anger, leading to mob actions. Under the law, having served over one and a half years in custody awaiting trial, the verdicts allowed for the instant release of both Williams and Watson from custody.

Several weeks after the verdicts were announced, I contacted Edi Faal, an African-American attorney in his late thirties, who had represented Damion Williams. During our conversation, Mr. Faal told me,

> When I first received this case, it was obvious to me that the District Attorney's office had grossly overcharged my client. They filed nineteen felony counts against Mr. Williams and in

the end, they failed to convict him on any of the original charges.

We tried to present evidence in pretrial relating to this issue but the trial judge wouldn't allow us to. We could only argue the issues. We even called Ira Reiner [the former Los Angeles County District Attorney] as a witness to justify his allegations. We were prepared with two hundred other cases in which more serious crimes were committed but the defendants were not charged in the same manner as my client. . . .

You know Tom, their purpose was not in finding justice in this case, but rather in finding a scapegoat and they found the scapegoat in the persons of Damion Williams and Henry Watson.

Our conversation then turned to the jury and the subsequent problems with this jury, given the allegations of misconduct that surfaced during deliberations.

"What were your feelings about your jury?" I asked.

"Well, our jury was much more diverse than the jury in Simi Valley," he replied almost immediately. "In the case of the first King jury, they were from a far less diverse community. In our case, we drew jurors from within our community." I instantly understood the meaning in his remarks.

"How about the verdicts themselves, were you pleased with the jury's findings?" I asked.

"That's another issue I want to go on the record about. I believe it's important for people to know that the convictions against these defendants were not for crimes charged directly against the defendants. They were for lesser included offenses, based on an instruction by the judge to the jury. These clients were convicted of crimes for which they were not charged, but were included as lesser charges at the time the judge instructed the jury, after the presentation of evidence had concluded. We couldn't offer a direct defense to these charges. I don't feel it was proper."

Within days of the sentencing of Williams and Watson, attorney for Antoine Miller, the fourth defendant, was successful in negotiating a plea bargain calling for Miller to plead guilty to assault charges and was ordered released and placed on twenty-seven months probation, taking into account his time already served in jail awaiting trial. It was apparent the D.A.'s office felt the evidence wouldn't convict Miller on the more serious felony charges once the other verdicts were announced.

■

Christopher Fisher, self-proclaimed minister of the Church of the Creator, arrested by undercover agents in July 1993 for plotting the assassination of Rodney King and others, took a deal offered by the Feds in October 1993. In his plea arrangement, Fisher agreed to a ten-year term for attempting to start a race war, and offered his full cooperation to prosecutors in other cases. Others arrested in that case are still awaiting trial. Federal Judge Matthew Byrne is expected to accept the plea in the Fisher Case, but is not bound by it.

■

I haven't spoken to Rodney King in months. Watching him at the federal trial, I noticed he'd taken off a few pounds and had grown a small beard. He looked good.

In March, 1993, NBC news reported Rodney King has additional legal problems facing him in the months ahead. Child support and paternity suits have been filed or threatened against him. His wife Crystal also faces child support problems. The very things I'd worked so hard to protect him from were now nipping at his backside. He's moved from his small Altadena home, and Crystal recently gave birth to their first child, a little girl.

■

Within days of his release from jail on the most recent DUI arrest, King was ordered into a detoxification center. He had been ordered by the CDC to undergo detox for no less than sixty days, and maybe longer. The CDC may well extend Glen's parole term by yet another year. Maybe, he'll get the message that the CDC isn't just fooling around. In the meantime, King still faces criminal charges arising from the DUI arrest outside the Glam Slam.

■

1	DISTRICT ATTORNEY Child Support Division
2	1950 Sunwest Lane, Suite 200 San Bernardino, California 92415
3	Telephone: (714) 387-8465
4	Attorney for Plaintiff

FILED
SAN BERNARDINO COUNTY

1992 MAR 31 AM 11: 24

Sandra Abarca

DEPUTY COUNTY CLERK

SUPERIOR COURT OF THE STATE OF CALIFORNIA

C047/872

COUNTY OF SAN BERNARDINO

THE COUNTY OF SAN BERNARDINO,	)	CASE NO. **SDA027109**
Plaintiff,	)	
	)	COMPLAINT TO ESTABLISH PATERNITY,
vs.	)	REIMBURSEMENT OF PUBLIC ASSISTANCE
	)	AND CHILD SUPPORT
RODNEY GLEN KING,	)	(Welfare and Institutions Code
	)	Sections 11350 and 11350.1)
Defendant.	)	
	)	**SUMMONS ISSUED**

Plaintiff alleges that:

I

The County of San Bernardino is a political subdivision of the State of California.

II

Plaintiff is informed and believes, and upon such information and belief alleges that RODNEY GLEN KING, Defendant herein, is the father of the following minor child/ren:

CANDICE ROSHAN KING, born 05/23/1982

//

//

//

```
 1    DISTRICT ATTORNEY
 2    Child Support Division
      10565 Civic Center Drive, Ste. 250
 3    Rancho Cucamonga, CA  91730
      Telephone: (714) 945-RODNEY G. KING
 4
 5    Attorney for Plaintiff
 6
 7
 8
 9               SUPERIOR COURT OF THE STATE OF CALIFORNIA
10                    COUNTY OF SAN BERNARDINO
11    THE COUNTY OF SAN BERNARDINO,    )  :  CASE NO. ODA007921
12                                     )
      Plaintiff,                       )
13                                     )     COMPLAINT TO ESTABLISH PATERNITY
                                vs.    )     REIMBURSEMENT OF PUBLIC ASSISTANCE
14                                     )     AND CHILD SUPPORT
      RODNEY G. KING                   )     (Welfare and Institutions Code
15                                     )     Sections 11350 and 11350.1)
      Defendant.                       )
16                                     )     SUMMONS ISSUED
17    Plaintiff alleges that:
18                              I
19    The County of San Bernardino is a political subdivision of the State of
20    California.
21                             II
22    Plaintiff is informed and believes, and upon such information and belief,
23    alleges that RODNEY G. KING, defendant herein, is the father of the following
24    minor child/ren:
25    LORA DENE KING, BORN FEBRUARY 11, 1984
26
```

FILED
SAN BERNARDINO COUNTY

1988 NOV -2 AM 9: 51

WEST DISTRICT
COUNTY CLERK
BY _____ DEPUTY

CD30980

Almost everyone associated with this case is now a former this or ex-that. John Barnett formerly represented former cop, Ted Briseno. Darrell Mounger formerly represented former cop, Stacey Koon. Jim Jordan formerly represented George Holliday. And Steve Lerman formerly represented Rodney Glen King. Tom Owens formerly represented Owens & Associates Investigations. Gone are Mounger, Barnett, Jordan, Lerman. Gone is Owens & Associates. Gone is the excitement and challenges of working this investigation. Gone are the friendships and commitments I thought would last a lifetime. Confusion, dissension, and concern still remain. Maybe some day I'll be able to just let it all go.

And the beat goes on. . . .

Index